Mastering Apache Cassandra
Second Edition

Build, manage, and configure high-performing, reliable
NoSQL database for your application with Cassandra

Nishant Neeraj

[PACKT] PUBLISHING   open source *
community experience distilled

BIRMINGHAM - MUMBAI

Mastering Apache Cassandra

Second Edition

First published: October 2013

Second edition: March 2015

Production reference: 1240315

Published by Packt Publishing Ltd.
Livery Place
35 Livery Street
Birmingham B3 2PB, UK.

ISBN 978-1-78439-261-1

www.packtpub.com

Credits

Author
Nishant Neeraj

Reviewers
Ramachaitanya Kavuluru
Swathi Kurunji
Vaibhav Mohan

Commissioning Editor
Ashwin Nair

Acquisition Editors
Vinay Argekar
Owen Roberts

Content Development Editor
Parita Khedekar

Technical Editor
Ankita Thakur

Copy Editors
Charlotte Carneiro
Shivangi Chaturvedi
Pooja Iyer
Aarti Saldanha

Project Coordinators
Izzat Contractor
Neha Thakur

Proofreaders
Simran Bhogal
Stephen Copestake
Maria Gould

Indexer
Tejal Soni

Graphics
Sheetal Aute
Disha Haria

Production Coordinator
Alwin Roy

Cover Work
Alwin Roy

About the Author

Nishant Neeraj is an independent software developer with experience in developing and planning out architectures for massively scalable data storage and data processing systems. Over the years, he has helped design and implement a wide variety of products and systems for companies ranging from small start-ups to large multinational companies. Currently, he helps drive WealthEngine's core product to the next level by leveraging a variety of big data technologies.

I would like to acknowledge the free and open source software community for this book. I am especially thankful to WealthEngine and my colleagues at WealthEngine for their moral and technical support in writing this book. The encouragement from family and friends kept me going through the many late nights required to complete this book.

The support from the Packt Publishing team for the last six months has been remarkable. I would like to thank the technical reviewers Swathi Kurunji, Ramachaitanya Kavuluru, Vaibhav Mohan, Paul Weinstein, and Jayraj for their valuable feedback. I would also like to thank Kartik Vedam as he was pretty vital in keeping my constantly sliding schedule in check. I appreciate the efforts made by Parita Khedekar and Ankita Thakur to keep me on my toes to finalize this book.

About the Reviewers

Swathi Kurunji is a software engineer at Actian Corporation. She recently received a PhD in computer science from the University of Massachusetts Lowell (UMass Lowell), USA. She has keen interest in database systems. Her PhD research involved query optimization, big data analysis, data warehouses, and cloud computing. Swathi has shown excellence in her field of study through research publications in international conferences and journals. She also received awards and scholarships at UMass Lowell for research and academics.

Swathi has a master of science degree in computer science from UMass Lowell, and a bachelor of engineering degree in information science from KVGCE, India. During her studies at UMass Lowell, Swathi worked as a teaching assistant, helping professors in teaching in classes and labs, designing projects, and grading exams.

Swathi has worked as a software development intern with IT companies such as EMC and SAP. At EMC, she gained experience on Apache Cassandra data modeling and performance analysis. At SAP, she gained experience on infrastructure/cluster management components of the Sybase IQ product. Swathi also worked with Wipro Technologies in India as a project engineer managing application servers.

She has wide experience with database systems, such as Apache Cassandra, Sybase IQ, Oracle, MySQL, and MS Access. Her interests include software design and development, big data analysis, optimization of databases, and cloud computing. Her LinkedIn profile is `https://www.linkedin.com/profile/view?id=171604666&authType=NAME_SEARCH&authToken=hBTf&locale=en_US&trk=tyah&trkInfo=clickedVertical%3Amynetwork%2Cidx%3A1-1-1%2CtarId%3A1427103024189%2Ctas%3Aswathi+kurun`. Swathi has previously reviewed *Cassandra Data Modeling and Analysis, Packt Publishing*.

I would like to thank my husband and my family for all their support.

Ramachaitanya Kavuluru is a graduate from the computer science department of the University of Southern California (USC), Los Angeles, California. He engages his time in building distributed software applications and products.

At NetApp, Inc. in Sunnyvale, California, Ramachaitanya is a software engineer and works with the high-availability and cluster architecture group for NetApp's solid state storage area network solution, FlashRay.

Vaibhav Mohan works as a software engineer at Livingly Media in Silicon Valley, where his work involves dealing with NoSQL databases, MVC frameworks, and cutting-edge web technologies. He completed his master's in computer science from Johns Hopkins University located in Maryland, USA, and his bachelor of technology in information technology from Vellore Institute of Technology, Vellore, India. He has done work in various fields, including computer vision, medical imaging, machine learning, big data, and parallel computing. His research and related work can be found on his website (http://cs.jhu.edu/~vmohan3).

www.PacktPub.com

Support files, eBooks, discount offers, and more

For support files and downloads related to your book, please visit www.PacktPub.com.

Did you know that Packt offers eBook versions of every book published, with PDF and ePub files available? You can upgrade to the eBook version at www.PacktPub.com and as a print book customer, you are entitled to a discount on the eBook copy. Get in touch with us at service@packtpub.com for more details.

At www.PacktPub.com, you can also read a collection of free technical articles, sign up for a range of free newsletters and receive exclusive discounts and offers on Packt books and eBooks.

https://www2.packtpub.com/books/subscription/packtlib

Do you need instant solutions to your IT questions? PacktLib is Packt's online digital book library. Here, you can search, access, and read Packt's entire library of books.

Why subscribe?
- Fully searchable across every book published by Packt
- Copy and paste, print, and bookmark content
- On demand and accessible via a web browser

Free access for Packt account holders

If you have an account with Packt at www.PacktPub.com, you can use this to access PacktLib today and view 9 entirely free books. Simply use your login credentials for immediate access.

I dedicate this book to my parents, Dr. Sushila Devi and Ratan Kumar.

Table of Contents

Preface

Back in 2007, Twitter users would experience "fail whale" captioned with "Too many tweets..." occasionally. On August 03, 2013, Twitter posted a new high-tweet rate record: 143,199 per second, and we rarely saw the fail whale. Many things changed since 2007. People and things connected to the Internet have increased exponentially. Cloud computing and hardware on demand have become cheap and easily available. Distributed computing and the NoSQL paradigm have taken off with a plethora of freely available, robust, proven, and open source projects to store large datasets, process it, and visualize it. "Big Data" has become a cliché. With massive amounts of data that get generated at a very high speed via people or machines, our capability to store and analyze data has increased. Cassandra is one of the most successful data stores that scales linearly, is easy to deploy and manage, and is blazing fast.

This book is about Cassandra and its ecosystem. The aim of this book is to take you from the basics of Apache Cassandra to understand what goes on under the hood. The book has three broad goals. First, to help you take right design decisions and understand the patterns and antipatterns. Second, to enable you to manage infrastructure on a rainy day. Third, to introduce you to some of the tools that work with Cassandra to monitor and manage Cassandra and to analyze the big data that you have inside it.

This book does not take a purist approach, rather a practical one. You will come to know proprietary tools, GitHub projects, shell scripts, third-party monitoring tools, and enough references to go beyond and dive deeper if you want.

What this book covers

Chapter 1, Quick Start, is about getting excited and having the instant gratification of Cassandra. If you have no prior experience with Cassandra, you leave this chapter with enough information to get yourself started on the next big project.

Chapter 2, Cassandra Architecture, covers design decisions and Cassandra's internal plumbing. If you have never worked with a distributed system, this chapter has some gems of distributed design concepts. It will be helpful for the rest of the book when we look at patterns and infrastructure management. This chapter will also help you understand the discussion of the Cassandra mailing list and JIRA. It is a theoretical chapter; you can skip it and come back to it later if you wish.

Chapter 3, Effective CQL, covers CQL, which is the de facto language to communicate with Cassandra. This chapter goes into the details of CQL and various things that you can do using it.

Chapter 4, Deploying a Cluster, is about deploying a cluster right. Once you go through the chapter, you will realize it is not really hard to deploy a cluster. It is probably one of the simplest distributed systems.

Chapter 5, Performance Tuning, deals with getting the maximum out of the hardware the cluster is deployed on. Usually, you will not need to rotate lots of knobs, and the default is just fine.

Chapter 6, Managing a Cluster – Scaling, Node Repair, and Backup, is about the daily DevOps drills. Scaling up a cluster, shrinking it down, replacing a dead node, and balancing the data load across the cluster is covered in this chapter.

Chapter 7, Monitoring, talks about the various tools that can be used to monitor Cassandra. If you already have a monitoring system, you would probably want to plug Cassandra health monitoring to it, or you can choose the dedicated and thorough Cassandra monitoring tools.

Chapter 8, Integration with Hadoop, covers Cassandra, which is about large datasets, fast writes and reads, and terabytes of data. What is the use of data if you can't analyze it? This chapter gives an introduction to get you started with the Cassandra and Hadoop setups.

What you need for this book

If you have any development experience, this book should be easy to follow. A beginner-level knowledge of Unix commands, Python, and some Java is useful to speed up the understanding, but they are not absolute requirements.

In terms of software and hardware, a machine with 1 GB RAM and a dual core processor is the minimum requirement. For all practical purposes, any modern machine (your laptop purchased in 2007 or after) is good. You should have the following software installed: Python, Java development kit 7 (JDK) or newer, Cassandra 2.1.x or newer, and Hadoop 2.6.x or newer. The examples in this book are performed in Ubuntu 14.04 and CentOS 6.3. So, if you have a Linux/Unix/OSX machine, this is ideal. You may need to look for a Windows equivalent if this is your environment.

Who this book is for

This book is for anyone who is curious about Cassandra. A beginner can start from *Chapter 1, Quick Start,* and learn all the way up to advanced topics. If you have an intermediate-level of experience, that is, you have worked on a toy project or better with Cassandra, you can skip to *Chapter 2, Cassandra Architecture.* The motivation is written keeping in mind a user who has a month of experience with Cassandra. *Chapter 1, Quick Start,* is aimed especially at newbies.

A DevOps engineer is probably the best job title for those who need to read the book end to end. If you wear multiple hats during the day (very common in startups) — writing code, managing infrastructure, working on analytics, and evangelizing your product — you may find this book extremely useful.

Conventions

In this book, you will find a number of text styles that distinguish between different kinds of information. Here are some examples of these styles and an explanation of their meaning.

Code words in text, database table names, folder names, filenames, file extensions, pathnames, dummy URLs, user input, and Twitter handles are shown as follows: "Installing Cassandra on your local machine for experimental or development purposes is as easy as downloading and unzipping the tarball (the `.tar` compressed file)."

A block of code is set as follows:

```
cqlsh:weblog> INSERT INTO blogs (id, blog_name, author, email,
password) VALUES ( blobAsUuid(timeuuidAsBlob(now())), 'Random
Ramblings', 'JRR Rowling', 'rowling@yahoo.com', 'someHashed#passwrd');


cqlsh:weblog> SELECT * FROM blogs;


 id             | author      | blog_name         | email             |
password

 ------------+-------------+-------------------+-------------------+---
----------------

 83cec... | JRR Rowling | Random Ramblings | rowling@yahoo.com |
someHashed#passwrd


 (1 rows)
```

When we wish to draw your attention to a particular part of a code block, the relevant lines or items are set in bold:

```
# Cassandra Node IP=Data Center:Rack
# Data-center 1
10.110.6.30=DC1:RAC1
10.110.6.11=DC1:RAC1
10.110.4.30=DC1:RAC2

# Data-center 2
10.120.8.10=DC2:RAC1
10.120.8.11=DC2:RAC1

# Data-center 3
10.130.1.13=DC3:RAC1
10.130.2.10=DC3:RAC2

# default for unknown nodes
default=DC1:RAC0
```

Any command-line input or output is written as follows:

```
# Check if you have Java
$ java -version
java version "1.7.0_21"
Java(TM) SE Runtime Environment (build 1.7.0_21-b11)
Java HotSpot(TM) 64-Bit Server VM (build 23.21-b01, mixed mode)
```

New terms and **important words** are shown in bold. Words that you see on the screen, for example, in menus or dialog boxes, appear in the text like this:

"Choose the **Linux x64-rpm.bin** version to download in order to install it on RHEL-like systems."

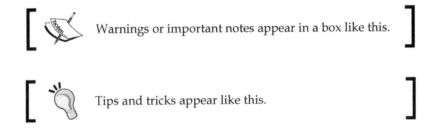

> Warnings or important notes appear in a box like this.

> Tips and tricks appear like this.

Reader feedback

Feedback from our readers is always welcome. Let us know what you think about this book—what you liked or disliked. Reader feedback is important for us as it helps us develop titles that you will really get the most out of.

To send us general feedback, simply e-mail feedback@packtpub.com, and mention the book's title in the subject of your message.

If there is a topic that you have expertise in and you are interested in either writing or contributing to a book, see our author guide at www.packtpub.com/authors.

Customer support

Now that you are the proud owner of a Packt book, we have a number of things to help you to get the most from your purchase.

Downloading the example code

You can download the example code files from your account at http://www.packtpub.com for all the Packt Publishing books you have purchased. If you purchased this book elsewhere, you can visit http://www.packtpub.com/support and register to have the files e-mailed directly to you.

Errata

Although we have taken every care to ensure the accuracy of our content, mistakes do happen. If you find a mistake in one of our books — maybe a mistake in the text or the code — we would be grateful if you could report this to us. By doing so, you can save other readers from frustration and help us improve subsequent versions of this book. If you find any errata, please report them by visiting http://www.packtpub.com/submit-errata, selecting your book, clicking on the **Errata Submission Form** link, and entering the details of your errata. Once your errata are verified, your submission will be accepted and the errata will be uploaded to our website or added to any list of existing errata under the Errata section of that title.

To view the previously submitted errata, go to https://www.packtpub.com/books/content/support and enter the name of the book in the search field. The required information will appear under the **Errata** section.

Piracy

Piracy of copyrighted material on the Internet is an ongoing problem across all media. At Packt, we take the protection of our copyright and licenses very seriously. If you come across any illegal copies of our works in any form on the Internet, please provide us with the location address or website name immediately so that we can pursue a remedy.

Please contact us at copyright@packtpub.com with a link to the suspected pirated material.

We appreciate your help in protecting our authors and our ability to bring you valuable content.

Questions

If you have a problem with any aspect of this book, you can contact us at questions@packtpub.com, and we will do our best to address the problem.

1
Quick Start

Welcome to Cassandra and congratulations on choosing a database that beats most of the NoSQL databases in performance. Cassandra is a powerful database based on solid fundamentals of distributed computing and fail-safe design, and it is well-tested by companies such as Facebook, Twitter, and Netflix. Unlike conventional databases and some of the modern databases that use the master-slave pattern, Cassandra uses the all-nodes-the-same pattern; this makes the system free from a single point of failure. This chapter is an introduction to Cassandra. The aim is to get you through with a proof-of-concept project to set the right state of mind for the rest of the book.

With version 2, Cassandra has evolved into a mature database system. It is now easier to manage, and more developer-friendly compared to the previous versions. With CQL 3 and removal of super columns, it is less likely that a developer can go wrong with Cassandra. In the upcoming sections, we will model, program, and execute a simple blogging application to see Cassandra in action. If you have a beginner-level experience with Cassandra, you may opt to skip this chapter.

Introduction to Cassandra

Quoting from Wikipedia:

> "*Apache Cassandra is an open source distributed database management system designed to handle large amounts of data across many commodity servers, providing high availability with no single point of failure. Cassandra offers robust support for clusters spanning multiple datacenters, with asynchronous masterless replication allowing low latency operations for all clients.*"

Let's try to understand in detail what it means.

A distributed database

In computing, *distributed* means splitting data or tasks across multiple machines. In the context of Cassandra, it means that the data is distributed across multiple machines. It means that no single node (a machine in a cluster is usually called a **node**) holds all the data, but just a chunk of it. It means that you are not limited by the storage and processing capabilities of a single machine. If the data gets larger, add more machines. If you need more parallelism (ability to access data in parallel/concurrently), add more machines. This means that a node going down does not mean that all the data is lost (we will cover this issue soon).

If a distributed mechanism is well designed, it will scale with a number of nodes. Cassandra is one of the best examples of such a system. It scales almost linearly, with regard to performance, when we add new nodes. This means that Cassandra can handle the behemoth of data without wincing.

 Check out an excellent paper on the NoSQL database comparison titled, *Solving Big Data Challenges for Enterprise Application Performance Management* at http://vldb.org/pvldb/vol5/p1724_tilmannrabl_vldb2012.pdf.

High availability

We will discuss availability in the next chapter. For now, assume availability is the probability that we query and the system just works. A high-availability system is one that is ready to serve any request at any time. High availability is usually achieved by adding redundancies. So, if one part fails, the other part of the system can serve the request. To a client, it seems as if everything works fine.

Cassandra is a robust software. Nodes joining and leaving are automatically taken care of. With proper settings, Cassandra can be made failure-resistant. This means that if some of the servers fail, the data loss will be zero. So, you can just deploy Cassandra over cheap commodity hardware or a cloud environment, where hardware or infrastructure failures may occur.

Replication

Continuing from the previous two points, Cassandra has a pretty powerful replication mechanism (we will see more details in the next chapter). Cassandra treats every node in the same manner. Data need not be written on a specific server (master), and you need not wait until the data is written to all the nodes that replicate this data (slaves). So, there is no master or slave in Cassandra, and replication happens asynchronously. This means that the client can be returned with success as a response as soon as the data is written on at least one server. We will see how we can tweak these settings to ensure the number of servers we want to have data written on before the client returns.

From this, we can derive that when there is no master or slave, we can write to any node for any operation. Since we have the ability to choose how many nodes to read from or write to, we can tweak it to achieve very low latency (read or write from one server).

Multiple data centers

Expanding from a single machine to a single data center cluster or multiple data centers is very simple compared to traditional databases where you need to make a plethora of configuration changes and watch replication. If you are planning to shard, it becomes a developer's nightmare. We will see later in this book that we can use this data center setting to make a real-time replicating system across data centers. We can use each data center to perform different tasks without overloading the other data centers. This is a powerful support when you do not have to worry whether users in Japan with a data center in Tokyo and users in the US with a data center in Virginia, are in sync or not.

These are just broad strokes of Cassandra's capabilities. We will explore more in the upcoming chapters. This chapter is about getting excited learning about Cassandra.

A brief introduction to a data model

Cassandra has three containers, one within another. The outermost container is **keyspace**. You can think of keyspace as a database in the RDBMS land. Tables reside under keyspace. A table can be assumed as a relational database table, except it is more flexible. A table is basically a sorted map of sorted maps (refer to the following figure). Each table must have a primary key. This primary key is called **row key** or **partition key**. (We will later see that in a CQL table, the row key is the same as the primary key. If the primary key is made up of more than one column, the first component of this composite key is equivalent to the row key). Each partition is associated with a set of cells. Each cell has a name and a value. These cells may be thought of as columns in the traditional database system. The CQL engine interprets a group of cells with the same cell name prefix as a row. The following figure shows the Cassandra data model:

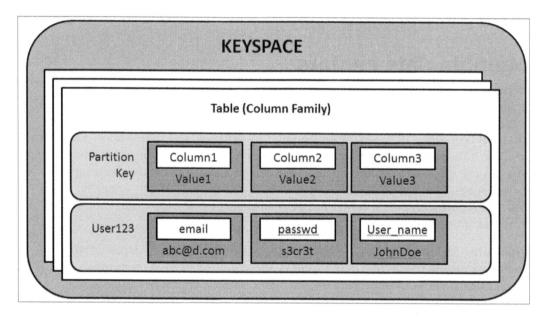

Note that if you come with Cassandra Thrift experience, it might be hard to view how Cassandra 1.2 and newer versions have changed terminology. Before CQL, the tables were called **column families**. A column family holds a group of rows, and rows are a sorted set of columns.

One obvious benefit of having such a flexible data storage mechanism is that you can have arbitrary number of cells with customized names and have a partition key store data as a list of tuples (a tuple is an ordered set; in this case, the tuple is a key-value pair). This comes handy when you have to store things such as time series, for example, if you want to use Cassandra to store your Facebook timeline or your Twitter feed or you want the partition key to be a sensor ID and each cell to represent a tuple with name as the timestamp when the data was created and value as the data sent by the sensor. Also, in a partition, cells are by default naturally ordered by the cell's name. So, in our sensor case, you will get data sorted for free. The other difference is, unlike RDBMS, Cassandra does not have relations. This means relational logic will be needed to be handled at the application level. This also means that we may want to denormalize the database because there is no join and to avoid looking up multiple tables by running multiple queries. Denormalization is a process of adding redundancy in data to achieve high read performance. For more information, visit http://en.wikipedia.org/wiki/Denormalization.

Partitions are distributed across the cluster, creating effective auto-sharding. Each server holds a range(s) of keys. So, if balanced, a cluster with more nodes will have less rows per node. All these concepts will be repeated in detail in the later chapters.

Types of keys

In the context of Cassandra, you may find the concept of keys a bit confusing. There are five terms that you may encounter. Here is what they generally mean:

- **Primary key**: This is the column or a group of columns that uniquely defines a row of the CQL table.
- **Composite key**: This is a type of primary key that is made up of more than one column. Sometimes, the composite key is also referred to as the compound key.
- **Partition key**: Cassandra's internal data representation is large rows with a unique key called row key. It uses these row key values to distribute data across cluster nodes. Since these row keys are used to partition data, they as called partition keys. When you define a table with a simple key, that key is the partition key. If you define a table with a composite key, the first term of that composite key works as the partition key. This means all the CQL rows with the same partition key lives on one machine.

- **Clustering key**: This is the column that tells Cassandra how the data within a partition is ordered (or clustered). This essentially provides presorted retrieval if you know what order you want your data to be retrieve in.
- **Composite partition key**: Optionally, CQL lets you define a composite partition key (the first part of a composite key). This key helps you distribute data across nodes if any part of the composite partition key differs. Let's take a look at the following example:

```
CREATE TABLE customers (
  id uuid,
  email text,
  PRIMARY KEY (id)
)
```

In the preceding example, id is the primary key and also the partition key. There is no clustering. It is a simple key. Let's add a twist to the primary key:

```
CREATE TABLE country_states (
  country text,
  state text,
  population int,
  PRIMARY KEY (country, state)
)
```

In the preceding example, we have a composite key that uses country and state to uniquely define a CQL row. The country column is the partition key, so all the rows with the same country node will belong to the same node/machine. The rows within a partition will be sorted by the state names. So, when you query for states in the US, you will encounter the row with California before the one with New York. What if I want to partition by composition? Let's take a look at the following example:

```
CREATE TABLE country_chiefs (
  country text,
  prez_name text,
  num_states int,
  capital text,
  ruling_year int,
  PRIMARY KEY ((country, prez_name), num_states,
capital)
)
```

The preceding example has a composite key involving four columns: country, prez_name, num_states, and capital, with country and prez_name constituting composite partition key. This means the rows with the same country but different president will be in a different partition. Rows will be ordered by the number of states followed by the capital name.

Installing Cassandra locally

Installing Cassandra on your local machine for experimental or development purposes is as easy as downloading and unzipping the tarball (the `.tar` compressed file). For development purposes, Cassandra does not have any extreme requirements. Any modern computer with 1 GB of RAM and a dual-core processor is good to test the water. All the examples in this chapter are performed on a laptop with 4 GB of RAM, a dual-core processor, and the Ubuntu 14.04 operating system. Cassandra is supported on all major platforms; after all, it's Java. Here are the steps to install Cassandra locally:

1. Install Oracle Java 1.6 (Java 6) or higher. Installing the JVM is sufficient, but you may need the **Java Development Kit (JDK)** if you are planning to code in Java:

    ```
    # Check whether you have Java installed in your system
    $ java -version
    java version "1.7.0_21"
    Java(TM) SE Runtime Environment (build 1.7.0_21-b11)
    Java HotSpot(TM) 64-Bit Server VM (build 23.21-b01, mixed mode)
    ```

    If you do not have Java, you may want to follow the installation details for your machine from the Oracle Java website (http://www.oracle.com/technetwork/java/javase/downloads/index.html).

2. Download Cassandra 2.0.0 or a newer version from the Cassandra website (http://archive.apache.org/dist/cassandra/ or http://cassandra.apache.org/download/). This book uses Cassandra 2.1.2, which was the latest version at the time of writing this book. Decompress this file to a suitable directory:

    ```
    # Download Cassandra
    wget http://archive.apache.org/dist/cassandra/2.1.2/apache-cassandra-2.1.2-bin.tar.gz


    # Untar to your home directory
    tar xzf apache-cassandra-2.1.2-bin.tar.gz -C $HOME
    ```

    The unzipped file location is $HOME/apache-cassandra-2.1.2. Let's call this location CASSANDRA_HOME. Wherever we refer to CASSANDRA_HOME in this book, always assume it to be the location where Cassandra is installed.

3. You may want to edit $CASSANDRA_HOME/conf/cassandra.yaml to configure Cassandra. It is advisable to change the data directory to a writable location when you start Cassandra as a nonroot user.

4. To change the `data` directory, change the `data_file_directories` attribute in `cassandra.yaml`, as follows (here, the `data` directory is chosen as `/mnt/Cassandra/data`; you may want to set the directory where you want to put the data):

```
data_file_directories:
    - /mnt/cassandra/data
```

5. Set the commit log directory:

```
commitlog_directory: /mnt/cassandra/commitlog
```

6. Set the saved caches directory:

```
saved_caches_directory: /mnt/cassandra/saved_caches
```

7. Set the logging location. Edit `$CASSANDRA_HOME/conf/log4j-server.properties` as follows:

```
log4j.appender.R.File=/tmp/cassandra.log
```

With this, you are ready to start Cassandra. Fire up your shell and type in `$CASSANDRA_HOME/bin/cassandra -f`. In this command, `-f` stands for foreground. You can keep viewing the logs and press *Ctrl + C* to shut the server down. If you want to run it in the background, do not use the `-f` option. If your `data` or `log` directories are not set with the appropriate user permission, you may want to start Cassandra as superuser using the `sudo` command. The server is ready when you see statistics in the startup log:

```
INFO  14:55:37 system.schema_triggers                    0,0
INFO  14:55:37 system.local                              0,0
INFO  14:55:37 system.peers                            1,152
INFO  14:55:37 system.batchlog                           0,0
INFO  14:55:37 system.compactions_in_progress              0,0
INFO  14:55:37 system.schema_usertypes                   0,0
INFO  14:55:37 system.schema_keyspaces                 4,471
INFO  14:55:37 system.compaction_history             19,2573
INFO  14:55:37 system.paxos                              0,0
INFO  14:55:37 system.schema_columns               792,215617
INFO  14:55:37 system.schema_columnfamilies           433,97089
INFO  14:55:37 system.IndexInfo                          0,0
INFO  14:55:37 system.range_xfers                        0,0
INFO  14:55:37 system.peer_events                        0,0
INFO  14:55:37 system.hints                              0,0
INFO  14:55:37 system.sstable_activity                   0,0
INFO  14:55:37 hadoop_test.output                        0,0
INFO  14:55:37 hadoop_test.lines                         0,0
INFO  14:55:37 system_traces.sessions                    0,0
INFO  14:55:37 system_traces.events                      0,0
```

Cassandra in action

There is no better way to learn a technology than by performing a proof of concept of the technology. In this section, we will work on a very simple application to get you familiarized with Cassandra. We will build the backend of a simple blogging application, where a user can perform the following tasks:

- Create a blogging account
- Publish posts
- Tag the posts, and posts can be searched using those tags
- Have people comment on those posts
- Have people upvote or downvote a post or a comment

Modeling data

In the RDBMS world, you would glance over the entities and think about relations while modeling the application. Then, you will join tables to get the required data. There is no join option in Cassandra, so we will have to denormalize things. Looking at the previously mentioned specifications, we can say that:

- We need a blogs table to store the blog name and other global information, such as the blogger's username and password
- We will have to pull posts for the blog, ideally, sorted in reverse chronological order
- We will also have to pull all the comments for each post, when we see the post page
- We will have to maintain tags in such a way that tags can be used to pull all the posts with the same tag
- We will also have to have counters for the upvotes and downvotes for posts and comments

With the preceding details, let's see the tables we need:

- `blogs`: This table will hold global blog metadata and user information, such as blog name, username, password, and other metadata.

- `posts`: This table will hold individual posts. At first glance, `posts` seems to be an ordinary table with primary keys as post ID and a reference to the blog that it belongs to. The problem arises when we add the requirement of being able to be sorted by timestamp. Unlike RDBMS, you cannot just perform an `ORDER BY` operation across partitions. The work-around for this is to use a composite key. A composite key consists of a partition key and one or more column(s) that determines where the other columns are going to be stored. Also, the other columns in the composite key determine relative ordering for the set of columns that are being inserted as a row with the key.

  Remember that a partition is completely stored on a node. The benefit of this is that the fetches are faster, but at the same time a partition is limited by the total number of cells that it can hold, which is 2 billion cells. The other downside of having everything on one partition may cause lots of requests to go to only a couple of nodes (replicas), making them a hotspot in the cluster, which is not good. You can avoid this by using some sort of bucketing such as involving months and years in the partition key. This will make sure that the partition changes every month and each partition has only one month worth of records. This will solve both the problems: the cap on the number of records and the hotspot issue. However, we will still need a way to order buckets. For this example, we will have all the posts in one partition just to keep things simple. We will tackle the bucketing issues in *Chapter 3, Effective CQL*. The following figure shows how to write time series grouped data using composite columns:

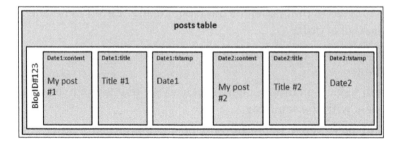

- `comments`: They have a similar property as post, except it is linked to a post instead of being linked to a blog.

- `tags`: They are a part of post. We use the `Set` data type to represent tags on the posts. One of the features that we mentioned earlier is to be able to search posts by tags. The best way to do it is to create an index on the `tags` column and make it searchable. Unfortunately, index on collections data types has not been supported until Cassandra Version 2.1 (`https://issues.apache.org/jira/browse/CASSANDRA-4511`). In our case, we will have to create and manage this sort of indexing manually. So, we will create a `tags` table that will have a compound primary key with tag and blog ID as its components.

- `counters`: Ideally, you would think that you want to put upvote and downvote counters as a part of the `posts` and `comments` tables' column definition, but Cassandra does not support a table that has a counter type column(s) and some other type column unless the counter is a part of the primary key definition. So, in our case, we will create two new tables just to keep track of votes.

With this, we are done with data modeling. The next step is inserting and getting data back.

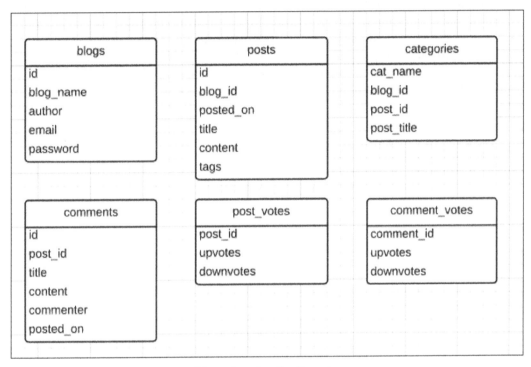

Schema based on the discussion

Writing code

Time to start something tangible! In this section, we will create the schema, insert the data, and make interesting queries to retrieve the data. In a real application, you will have a GUI with button and links to be able to log in, post, comment, upvote and downvote, and navigate. Here, we will stick to what happens in the backend when you perform those actions. This will keep the discussion from any clutter introduced by other software components. Also, this section contains **Cassandra Query Language** (CQL), a SQL-like query language for Cassandra. So, you can just copy these statements and paste them into your CQL shell ($CASSANDRA_HOME/bin/cqlsh) to see it working. If you want to build an application using these statements, you should be able to just use these statements in your favorite language via the CQL driver library that you can find at http://www.datastax.com/download#dl-datastax-drivers. You can also download a simple Java application that is built using these statements from my GitHub account (https://github.com/naishe/mastering-cassandra-v2).

Setting up

Setting up a project involves creating a keyspace and tables. This can be done via the CQL shell or from your favorite programming language.

Here are the statements to create the schema:

```
cqlsh> CREATE KEYSPACE weblog WITH REPLICATION = {'class':
'SimpleStrategy', 'replication_factor': 1};

cqlsh> USE weblog;

cqlsh:weblog> CREATE TABLE blogs (id uuid PRIMARY KEY, blog_name
varchar, author varchar, email varchar, password varchar);

cqlsh:weblog> CREATE TABLE posts (id timeuuid, blog_id uuid, posted_
on timestamp, title text, content text, tags set<varchar>, PRIMARY
KEY(blog_id, id));

cqlsh:weblog> CREATE TABLE categories (cat_name varchar, blog_id uuid,
post_id timeuuid, post_title text, PRIMARY KEY(cat_name, blog_id,
post_id));

cqlsh:weblog> CREATE TABLE comments (id timeuuid, post_id timeuuid,
title text, content text, posted_on timestamp, commenter varchar,
PRIMARY KEY(post_id, id));
```

```
cqlsh:weblog> CREATE TABLE post_votes(post_id timeuuid PRIMARY KEY,
upvotes counter, downvotes counter);

cqlsh:weblog> CREATE TABLE comment_votes(comment_id timeuuid PRIMARY
KEY, upvotes counter, downvotes counter);
```

Universally unique identifiers: uuid and timeuuid

In the preceding CQL statements, there are two interesting data types—uuid and timeuuid. uuid stands for universally unique identifier. There are five types of them. One of these uuid types is timeuuid, which is essentially uuid type 1 that takes timestamp as its first component. This means it can be used to sort things by time. This is what we wanted to do in this example: sort posts by the time they were published.

On the other hand, uuid accepts any of these five types of uuid as long as the format follows the standard uuid format.

In Cassandra, if you have chosen the uuid type for a column, you will need to pass uuid while inserting the data. With timeuuid, just passing timestamp is enough.

The first statement requests Cassandra to create a keyspace named weblog with replication factor 1 because we are running a single node Cassandra on a local machine. Here are a couple of things to notice:

- The column tags in the posts table is a set of strings.
- The primary key for posts, categories, and comments has more than one component. The first of these components is a partition key. Data with the same primary key in a table resides on the same machine. This means, all the posts' records that belong to one blog stays on one machine (not really; if the replication factor is more than one, the records get replicated to as many machines). This is true for all the tables with composite keys.
- Categories have three components in its primary key. One is the category name, which is the partition key, another is the blog ID, and then the post ID. One can argue that inclusion of the post ID in the primary key was unnecessary. You could just use the category name and blog ID. The reason to include the post ID in the primary key was to enable sorting by the post ID.
- Note that some of the IDs in the table definition are timeuuid. The timeuuid data type is an interesting ID generation mechanism. It generates a timestamp-based (provided by you) uuid, which is unique and you can use it in applications where you want things to be ordered by chronology.

Inserting records

This section demonstrates inserting the records in the schema. Unlike RDBMS, you will find that there are some redundancies in the system. You may notice that you cannot have a lot of rules enforced by Cassandra. It is up to the developer to make sure the records are inserted, updated, and deleted from appropriate places.

 Note that the CQL code is just for instruction purposes and is just a snippet. Your output may vary.

We will see a simple INSERT example now:

```
cqlsh:weblog> INSERT INTO blogs (id, blog_name, author, email,
password) VALUES ( blobAsUuid(timeuuidAsBlob(now())), 'Random
Ramblings', 'JRR Rowling', 'rowling@yahoo.com', 'someHashed#passwrd');


cqlsh:weblog> SELECT * FROM blogs;


 id             | author      | blog_name        | email              |
password

 ---------------+-------------+------------------+--------------------+---
-----------------

 83cec... | JRR Rowling | Random Ramblings | rowling@yahoo.com |
someHashed#passwrd


(1 rows)
```

Downloading the example code

You can download the example code files for all Packt books you have purchased from your account at http://www.packtpub.com. If you purchased this book elsewhere, you can visit http://www.packtpub.com/support and register to have the files e-mailed directly to you.

The application would generate uuid or you will get uuid from an existing record in the blogs table based on a user's e-mail address or some other criteria. Here, just to be concise, the uuid generation is left to Cassandra, and it is retrieved by running the SELECT statement. Let's insert some posts to this blog:

 # First post

```
cqlsh:weblog> INSERT INTO posts (id, blog_id, title, content, tags,
posted_on) VALUES (now(), 83cec740-22b1-11e4-a4f0-7f1a8b30f852, 'first
post', 'hey howdy!', {'random','welcome'}, 1407822921000);

cqlsh:weblog> SELECT * FROM posts;

 blog_id | id             | content   | posted_on                | tags
 | title

 -----------+-----------+-----------+--------------------------+-----
 ------------------+-----------

 83cec... | 04722... | hey howdy! | 2014-08-12 11:25:21+0530 |
{'random', 'welcome'} | first post

(1 rows)

cqlsh:weblog> INSERT INTO categories (cat_name, blog_id, post_id,
post_title) VALUES ( 'random', 83cec740-22b1-11e4-a4f0-7f1a8b30f852,
047224f0-22b2-11e4-a4f0-7f1a8b30f852, 'first post');

cqlsh:weblog> INSERT INTO categories (cat_name, blog_id, post_id,
post_title) VALUES ( 'welcome', 83cec740-22b1-11e4-a4f0-7f1a8b30f852,
047224f0-22b2-11e4-a4f0-7f1a8b30f852, 'first post');
```

 # Second post

```
cqlsh:weblog> INSERT INTO posts (id, blog_id, title, content, tags,
posted_on) VALUES (now(), 83cec740-22b1-11e4-a4f0-7f1a8b30f852,
'Fooled by randomness...', 'posterior=(prior*likelihood)/evidence',
{'random','maths'}, 1407823189000);

cqlsh:weblog> select * from posts;
```

```
 blog_id  | id           | content                                      |
posted_on                |  tags                  | title
-----------+-----------+------------------------------------------------+----
-------------------+----------------------+--------------------
---

 83cec.... | 04722... |                                       hey howdy! | 2014-
08-12 11:25:21+0530 | {'random', 'welcome'} |                    first post


 83cec... | c06a4... | posterior=(prior*likelihood)/evidence | 2014-
08-12 11:29:49+0530 |   {'maths', 'random'} | Fooled by randomness...

(2 rows)

cqlsh:weblog> INSERT INTO categories (cat_name, blog_id, post_id,
post_title) VALUES ( 'random', 83cec740-22b1-11e4-a4f0-7f1a8b30f852,
c06a42f0-22b2-11e4-a4f0-7f1a8b30f852, 'Fooled by randomness...');

cqlsh:weblog> INSERT INTO categories (cat_name, blog_id, post_id,
post_title) VALUES ( 'maths', 83cec740-22b1-11e4-a4f0-7f1a8b30f852,
c06a42f0-22b2-11e4-a4f0-7f1a8b30f852, 'Fooled by randomness...');
```

 You may want to insert more rows so that we can experiment with pagination in the upcoming sections.

You may notice that the primary key, which is of type `timeuuid`, is created using Cassandra's built-in `now()` function, and we repeated the title in the `categories` table. The rationale behind repetition is that we may want to display the title of all the posts that match a tag that a user clicked. These titles will have URLs to redirect us to the posts (a post can be retrieved by the blog ID and post ID). Alternatively, Cassandra does not support a relational connect between two tables, so you cannot join categories and posts to display the title. The other option is to use the blog ID and post ID to retrieve the post's title. However, that's more work, and somewhat inefficient.

Let's insert some comments and upvote and downvote some posts and comments:

```
# Insert some comments

cqlsh:weblog>  INSERT INTO comments (id, post_id, commenter,
title, content, posted_on) VALUES (now(), c06a42f0-22b2-11e4-a4f0-
7f1a8b30f852, 'liz@gmail.com', 'Thoughful article but...', 'It is too
short to describe the complexity.', 1407868973000);
```

```
cqlsh:weblog> INSERT INTO comments (id, post_id, commenter,
title, content, posted_on) VALUES (now(), c06a42f0-22b2-11e4-a4f0-
7f1a8b30f852, 'tom@gmail.com', 'Nice!', 'Thanks, this is good stuff.',
1407868975000);

cqlsh:weblog> INSERT INTO comments (id, post_id, commenter,
title, content, posted_on) VALUES (now(), c06a42f0-22b2-11e4-a4f0-
7f1a8b30f852, 'g@ouv.com', 'Follow my blog', 'Please follow my blog.',
1407868979000);

cqlsh:weblog> INSERT INTO comments (id, post_id, commenter,
title, content, posted_on) VALUES (now(), 047224f0-22b2-11e4-a4f0-
7f1a8b30f852, 'liz@gmail.com', 'New blogger?', 'Welcome to weblog
application.', 1407868981000);

# Insert some votes

cqlsh:weblog> UPDATE comment_votes SET upvotes = upvotes + 1 WHERE
comment_id = be127d00-22c2-11e4-a4f0-7f1a8b30f852;

cqlsh:weblog> UPDATE comment_votes SET upvotes = upvotes + 1 WHERE
comment_id = be127d00-22c2-11e4-a4f0-7f1a8b30f852;


cqlsh:weblog> UPDATE comment_votes SET downvotes = downvotes + 1 WHERE
comment_id = be127d00-22c2-11e4-a4f0-7f1a8b30f852;

cqlsh:weblog> UPDATE post_votes SET downvotes = downvotes + 1 WHERE
post_id = d44e0440-22c2-11e4-a4f0-7f1a8b30f852;

cqlsh:weblog> UPDATE post_votes SET upvotes = upvotes + 1 WHERE post_
id = d44e0440-22c2-11e4-a4f0-7f1a8b30f852;
```

Counters are always inserted or updated using the UPDATE statement.

Retrieving data

Now that we have data inserted for our application, we need to retrieve it. To blog applications, usually the blog name serves as the primary key in their database. So, when you request `cold-caffein.blogspot.com`, a blog metadata table with the blog ID as `cold-caffein` exists. We, on the other hand, can use the blog `uuid` to request to serve the contents. So, we assume that having the blog ID is handy.

Let's display posts. We should not load all the posts for the user upfront. It is not a good idea from the usability point of view. It demands more bandwidth, and it is probably a lot of reads for Cassandra. So first, let's pull two posts at a time from ones posted earlier:

```
cqlsh:weblog> select * from posts where blog_id = 83cec740-22b1-11e4-
a4f0-7f1a8b30f852 order by id desc limit 2;

 blog_id | id              | content               | posted_on
 | tags                    | title

-----------+-------------+-----------------+-------------------------
+-----------------------+--------------
83cec… | c2240… | posterior=(prior*likelihood)/evidence | 2014-08-12
11:29:49+0530 |    {'maths', 'random'} | Fooled by randomness...

83cec… | 965a2… |                                 hey howdy! | 2014-08-12
11:25:21+0530 | {'random', 'welcome'} |             first post

(2 rows)
```

This was the first page. For the next page, we can use an anchor. We can use the last post's ID as an anchor, as its `timeuuid` increases monotonically with time. So, posts older than that will have the post ID with smaller values, and this will work as our anchor:

```
cqlsh:weblog> select * from posts where blog_id = 83cec740-22b1-11e4-
a4f0-7f1a8b30f852 and id < 8eab0c10-2314-11e4-bac7-3f5f68a133d8 order
by id desc limit 2;


 blog_id | id              | content               | posted_on                      |
 tags                    | title

-----------+-------------+-----------------+-------------------------------+-
-----------------------+--------------

 83cec... | 83f16... | random content8 | 2014-08-13 23:33:00+0530 |
{'garbage', 'random'} | random post8


 83cec... | 76738... | random content7 | 2014-08-13 23:32:58+0530 |
{'garbage', 'random'} | random post7


(2 rows)
```

You can retrieve the posts on the next page as follows:

```
cqlsh:weblog> select * from posts where blog_id = 83cec740-22b1-11e4-
a4f0-7f1a8b30f852 and id < 76738dc0-2314-11e4-bac7-3f5f68a133d8 order
by id desc limit 2;
```

```
 blog_id | id              | content        | posted_on                 |
tags                      | title

-----------+-----------+-----------------+---------------------------+-
-----------------------+-------------

 83cec... | 6f85d... | random content6 | 2014-08-13 23:32:56+0530 |
{'garbage', 'random'} | random post6


 83cec... | 684c5... | random content5 | 2014-08-13 23:32:54+0530 |
{'garbage', 'random'} | random post5



(2 rows)
```

Now for each post, we need to perform the following tasks:

- Pull a list of comments
- Up and downvotes
- Load comments as follows:

```
cqlsh:weblog> select * from comments where post_id = c06a42f0-
22b2-11e4-a4f0-7f1a8b30f852 order by id desc;
```

```
 post_id  | id              | commenter      | content
| posted_on                | title
-----------+-----------+-----------------+-------------------------
-------------------+---------------------------+--------------------
-------


 c06a4... | cd5a8... |     g@ouv.com |                  Please
follow my blog. | 2014-08-13 00:12:59+0530 |        Follow my
blog
```

```
c06a4... | c6aff... | tom@gmail.com |                    Thanks,
this is good stuff. | 2014-08-13 00:12:55+0530 |
Nice!


c06a4... | be127... | liz@gmail.com | It is too short to describe
the complexity. | 2014-08-13 00:12:53+0530 | Thoughful article
but...
```

- Individually fetch counters for each post and comment as follows:

```
cqlsh:weblog> select * from comment_votes where comment_id =
be127d00-22c2-11e4-a4f0-7f1a8b30f852;
```

```
 comment_id    | downvotes | upvotes
---------------------+-----------+---------
 be127...            |         1 |       6

(1 rows)
```

```
cqlsh:weblog> select * from post_votes where post_id = c06a42f0-
22b2-11e4-a4f0-7f1a8b30f852;

 post_id | downvotes | upvotes
------------+-----------+---------
 c06a4... |         2 |       7

(1 rows)
```

Now, we want to facilitate the users of our blogging website with the ability to click on a tag and see a list of all the posts with that tag. Here is what we do:

```
cqlsh:weblog> select * from categories where cat_name = 'maths' and
blog_id = 83cec740-22b1-11e4-a4f0-7f1a8b30f852 order by blog_id desc;

 cat_name | blog_id| post_id   | post_title

----------+--------------+-----------+--------------------------

   maths | 83cec... | a865c... |                      YARA

   maths | 83cec... | c06a4... | Fooled by randomness...

(2 rows)
```

We can obviously use the pagination and sorting here. I think you have got the idea.

Sometimes, it is nice to see what people generally comment. It would be great if we could find all the comments by a user. To make a nonprimary key field searchable in Cassandra, you need to create an index on that column. So, let's do that:

```
cqlsh:weblog> CREATE INDEX commenter_idx ON comments (commenter);

cqlsh:weblog> select * from comments where commenter = 'liz@gmail.
com';

 post_id   | id           | commenter       | content
 | posted_on                      | title

------------+------------+---------------+----------------------------
------------------+-------------------------+----------------------
---

 04722... | d44e0... | liz@gmail.com |        Welcome to weblog
application. | 2014-08-13 00:13:01+0530 |        New blogger?

 c06a4... | be127... | liz@gmail.com | It is too short to describe the
complexity. | 2014-08-13 00:12:53+0530 | Thoughful article but...


(2 rows)
```

This completes all the requirements we stated. We did not cover the `update` and `delete` operations. They follow the same pattern as the insertion of records. The developer needs to make sure that the data is updated or deleted from all the places. So, if you want to update a post's title, it needs to be done in the `posts` and `category` tables.

Writing your application

Cassandra provides the API for almost all the main stream programming languages. Developing applications for Cassandra is nothing more than actually executing CQL through an API and collection result set or iterator for the query. This section will give you a glimpse of the Java code for the example we discussed earlier. It uses the DataStax Java driver for Cassandra. The full code is available at `https://github. com/naishe/mastering-cassandra-v2`.

Getting the connection

An application creates a single instance of the `Cluster` object and keeps it for its life cycle. Every time you want to execute a query or a bunch of queries, you ask for a `session` object from the `Cluster` object. In a way, it is like a connection pool. Let's take a look at the following example:

```java
public class CassandraConnection {
  private static Cluster cluster = getCluster();
  public static final Session getSession(){
    if ( cluster == null ){
      cluster = getCluster();
    }
    return cluster.connect();
  }

  private static Cluster getCluster(){
    Cluster clust = Cluster
        .builder()
        .addContactPoint(Constants.HOST)
        .build();
    return clust;
  }
[-- snip --]
```

Executing queries

Query execution is barely different from what we did in the command prompt earlier:

```java
private static final String BLOGS_TABLE_DEF =
    "CREATE TABLE IF NOT EXISTS "
+ Constants.KEYSPACE + ".blogs "
    + "("
    + "id uuid PRIMARY KEY, "
    + "blog_name varchar, "
    + "author varchar, "
    + "email varchar, "
    + "password varchar"
    + ")";
[-- snip --]
    Session conn = CassandraConnection.getSession();
[--snip--]
    conn.execute(BLOGS_TABLE_DEF);
[-- snip --]
    conn.close();
```

Object mapping

The DataStax Java driver provides an easy-to use, annotation-based object mapper, which can help you avoid a lot of code bloat and marshalling effort. Here is an example of the `Blog` object that maps to the `blogs` table:

```java
@Table(keyspace = Constants.KEYSPACE, name = "blogs")
public class Blog extends AbstractVO<Blog> {
  @PartitionKey
  private UUID id;
  @Column(name = "blog_name")
  private String blogName;
  private String author;
  private String email;
  private String password;

  public UUID getId() {
    return id;
  }
  public void setId(UUID id) {
    this.id = id;
  }
  public String getBlogName() {
    return blogName;
  }
  public void setBlogName(String blogName) {
    this.blogName = blogName;
  }
  public String getAuthor() {
    return author;
  }
  public void setAuthor(String author) {
    this.author = author;
  }
  public String getEmail() {
    return email;
  }
  public void setEmail(String email) {
    this.email = email;
  }
  public String getPassword() {
    return password;
  }
  public void setPassword(String password) {
/* Ideally, you'd use a unique salt with this hashing */
```

```
        this.password = Hashing
          .sha256()
          .hashString(password, Charsets.UTF_8)
          .toString();
    }

    @Override
    public boolean equals(Object that) {
      return this.getId().equals(((Blog)that).getId());
    }

    @Override
    public int hashCode() {
      return Objects.hashCode(getId(), getEmail(), getAuthor(),
getBlogName());
    }

    @Override
    protected Blog getInstance() {
      return this;
    }

    @Override
    protected Class<Blog> getType() {
      return Blog.class;
    }

    // ----- ACCESS VIA QUERIES -----

    public static Blog getBlogByName(String blogName,
  SessionWrapper sessionWrapper)
throws BlogNotFoundException {
    AllQueries queries = sessionWrapper.getAllQueries();
    Result<Blog> rs = queries.getBlogByName(blogName);
    if (rs.isExhausted()){
    throw new BlogNotFoundException();
    }
    return rs.one();
  }

  }
```

For now, forget about the `AbstractVO` super class. That is just some abstraction, where common things are thrown into `AbstractVO`. You can see the annotations that basically show which keyspace and table this class is mapped to. Each instance variable is mapped with a column in the table. For any column that has a different name than the attribute name in the class, you will have to explicitly state that. Getters and setters do not have to be dumb. You can get creative in there. For example, `setPassword` setter takes a plain text password and hashes it before storing. Note that you *must* mention which field acts as the partition key. You do not have to specify all the fields that consist of the primary key, just the first component. Now you can use DataStax's mapper to create, retrieve, update, and delete an object without having to marshal the results into the object. Here is an example:

```
Blog blog =
new MappingManager(session)
.mapper(Blog.class)
.get(blogUUID);
```

You can execute any arbitrary queries and map it to an object. To do that, you will have to write an interface that contains a method signature of what the query consumes as its argument and what it returns as the method return type, as follows:

```
@Accessor
public interface AllQueries {
[--snip--]

  @Query("SELECT * FROM " + Constants.KEYSPACE + ".blogs WHERE blog_
name = :blogName")
  public Result<Blog> getBlogByName(@Param("blogName") String
blogName);
[-- snip --]
```

This interface is annotated with `Accessor`, and it has methods that basically satisfy the `Query` annotation that it carries. The snippet of the `Blog` class uses this method to retrieve the names blog by blog.

Summary

We have started learning about Cassandra. You can set up your local machine, play with CQL3 in `cqlsh`, and write a simple program that uses Cassandra on the backend. It seems like we are all done. But, it's not so. Cassandra is not all about ease in modeling or simple to code around with (unlike RDBMS). It is all about speed, availability, and reliability. The only thing that matters in a production setup is how quickly and reliably your application can serve a fickle-minded user. It does not matter if you have an elegant database architecture with the third normal form or if you use a functional programming language and follow the **Don't Repeat Yourself** (**DRY**) principle religiously. Cassandra and many other modern databases, especially in the NoSQL space, are there to provide you with speed. Cassandra's performance increases almost linearly with the addition of new nodes, which makes it suitable for high throughput applications without committing a lot of expensive infrastructure to begin with. For more information, visit `http://vldb.org/pvldb/vol5/p1724_ tilmannrabl_vldb2012.pdf`. The rest of the book is aimed at giving you a solid understanding of the following aspects of Cassandra — one chapter at a time:

- You will learn the internals of Cassandra and the general programming pattern for Cassandra

- Setting up a cluster and tweaking Cassandra and Java settings to get the maximum out of Cassandra for your use

- Infrastructure maintenance — nodes going down, scaling up and down, backing the data up, keeping vigil monitoring, and getting notified about an interesting event on your Cassandra setup will be covered

- Cassandra is easy to use with the Apache Hadoop and Apache Pig tools and we will see simple examples of this

The best thing about these chapters is that there is no prerequisite. Most of these chapters start from the basics to get you familiar with the concept and then take you to an advanced level. So, if you have never used Hadoop, do not worry. You can still have a simple setup up and running with Cassandra.

In the next chapter, we will see Cassandra internals and what makes it so fast.

2
Cassandra Architecture

This chapter aims to set you into a perspective where you will be able to see the evolution of the NoSQL paradigm. It will start with a discussion of common problems that an average developer faces when the application starts to scale up and software components cannot keep up with it. Then, we'll see what can be assumed as a thumb rule in the NoSQL world: the CAP theorem that says to choose any two out of consistency, availability, and partition-tolerance. As we discuss this further, we will realize how much more important it is to serve the customers (availability), than to be correct (consistency) all the time. However, we cannot afford to be wrong (inconsistent) for a long time. The customers wouldn't like to see that the items are in stock, but that the checkout is failing. Cassandra comes into picture with its tunable consistency.

We will take a quick peep into all the actions that go on when a read or mutate happens. This leaves us with lots of fancy terms. Next, we will move on to see these terms in full glory with explanation as we discuss various parts of the Cassandra design. You will be amazed to see how close yet how far Cassandra is when compared with its precursors and inspiration databases, such as Google's BigTable and Amazon's Dynamo. We will meet with some of the modern and efficient data structures, such as bloom filters and Merkle trees, and algorithms, such as gossip protocol, phi accrual error detectors, and log-structured merge trees. Some of these discussions will help you rationalize the performance and constraints of Cassandra.

Problems in the RDBMS world

RDBMS is a great approach. It keeps data consistent, it's good for OLTP (http://en.wikipedia.org/wiki/Online_transaction_processing), it provides access to good grammar, and manipulates data supported by all the popular programming languages. It has been tremendously successful in the last 40 years (the relational data model was proposed in its first incarnation by Codd, E.F. (1970) in his research paper *A Relational Model of Data for Large Shared Data Banks*). However, in early 2000s, big companies such as Google and Amazon, which have a gigantic load on their databases to serve, started to feel bottlenecked with RDBMS, even with helper services such as Memcache on top of them. As a response to this, Google came up with BigTable (`http://research.google.com/archive/bigtable.html`), and Amazon with Dynamo (`http://www.cs.ucsb.edu/~agrawal/fall2009/dynamo.pdf`).

If you have ever used RDBMS for a complicated web application, you must have faced problems such as slow queries due to complex joins, expensive vertical scaling, and problems in horizontal scaling. Due to these problems, indexing takes a long time. At some point, you may have chosen to replicate the database, but there was still some locking, and this hurts the availability of the system. This means that under a heavy load, locking will cause the user's experience to deteriorate.

Although replication gives some relief, a busy slave may not catch up with the master (or there may be a connectivity glitch between the master and the slave). Consistency of such systems cannot be guaranteed. Consistency, the property of a database to remain in a consistent state before and after a transaction, is one of the promises made by relational databases. It seems that one may need to make compromises on consistency in a relational database for the sake of scalability. With the growth of the application, the demand to scale the backend becomes more pressing, and the developer teams may decide to add a caching layer (such as Memcached) at the top of the database. This will alleviate some load off the database, but now the developers will need to maintain the object states in two places: the database, and the caching layer. Although some **Object Relational Mappers** (ORMs) provide a built-in caching mechanism, they have their own issues, such as larger memory requirement, and often mapping code pollutes application code. In order to achieve more from RDBMS, we will need to start to denormalize the database to avoid joins, and keep the aggregates in the columns to avoid statistical queries.

Sharding or horizontal scaling is another way to distribute the load. Sharding in itself is a good idea, but it adds too much manual work, plus the knowledge of sharding creeps into the application code. Sharded databases make the operational tasks (backup, schema alteration, and adding index) difficult. To find out more about the hardships of sharding, visit `http://www.mysqlperformanceblog.com/2009/08/06/why-you-dont-want-to-shard/`.

There are ways to loosen up consistency by providing various isolation levels, but concurrency is just one part of the problem. Maintaining relational integrity, difficulties in managing data that cannot be accommodated on one machine, and difficult recovery, were all making the traditional database systems hard to be accepted in the rapidly growing big data world. Companies needed a tool that could support hundreds of terabytes of data on the ever-failing commodity hardware reliably. This led to the advent of modern databases like Cassandra, Redis, MongoDB, Riak, HBase, and many more. These modern databases promised to support very large datasets that were hard to maintain in SQL databases, with relaxed constrains on consistency and relation integrity.

Enter NoSQL

NoSQL is a blanket term for the databases that solve the scalability issues which are common among relational databases. This term, in its modern meaning, was first coined by Eric Evans. It should not be confused with the database named NoSQL (`http://www.strozzi.it/cgi-bin/CSA/tw7/I/en_US/nosql/Home%20Page`). NoSQL solutions provide scalability and high availability, but may not guarantee ACID: atomicity, consistency, isolation, and durability in transactions. Many of the NoSQL solutions, including Cassandra, sit on the other extreme of ACID, named BASE, which stands for basically available, soft-state, eventual consistency.

 Wondering about where the name, NoSQL, came from? Read Eric Evans' blog at `http://blog.sym-link.com/2009/10/30/nosql_whats_in_a_name.html`.

The CAP theorem

In 2000, Eric Brewer (`http://en.wikipedia.org/wiki/Eric_Brewer_%28scientist%29`), in his keynote speech at the ACM Symposium, said, "A distributed system requiring always-on, highly-available operations cannot guarantee the illusion of coherent, consistent single-system operation in the presence of network partitions, which cut communication between active servers". This was his conjecture based on his experience with distributed systems. This conjecture was later formally proved by Nancy Lynch and Seth Gilbert in 2002 (*Brewer's Conjecture and the Feasibility of Consistent, Available, Partition-Tolerant Web Services*, published in ACMSIGACT News, Volume 33 Issue 2 (2002), page 51 to 59 available at `http://webpages.cs.luc.edu/~pld/353/gilbert_lynch_brewer_proof.pdf`).

Let's try to understand this. Let's say we have a distributed system where data is replicated at two distinct locations and two conflicting requests arrive, one at each location, at the time of communication link failure between the two servers. If the system (the cluster) has obligations to be highly available (a mandatory response, even when some components of the system are failing), one of the two responses will be inconsistent with what a system with no replication (no partitioning, single copy) would have returned. To understand it better, let's take an example to learn the terminologies. These terms will be used frequently throughout this book.

Let's say you are planning to read George Orwell's book *Nineteen Eighty-Four* over the Christmas vacation. A day before the holidays start, you logged into your favorite online bookstore to find out there is only one copy left. You add it to your cart, but then you realize that you need to buy something else to be eligible for free shipping. You start to browse the website for any other item that you might buy. To make the situation interesting, let's say there is another customer who is trying to buy *Nineteen Eighty-Four* at the same time.

Consistency

A consistent system is defined as one that responds with the same output for the same request at the same time, across all the replicas. Loosely, one can say a consistent system is one where each server returns the right response to each request.

In our book buying example, we have only one copy of *Nineteen Eighty-Four*. So, only one of the two customers is going to get the book delivered from this store. In a consistent system, only one can check out the book from the payment page. As soon as one customer makes the payment, the number of *Nineteen Eighty-Four* books in stock will get decremented by one, and one quantity of *Nineteen Eighty-Four* will be added to the order of that customer. When the second customer tries to check out, the system says that the book is not available any more.

Relational databases are good for this task because they comply with the ACID properties. If both the customers make requests at the same time, one customer will have to wait till the other customer is done with the processing, and the database is made consistent. This may add a few milliseconds of wait to the customer who came later.

An eventual consistent database system (where consistency of data across the distributed servers may not be guaranteed immediately) may have shown availability of the book at the time of check out to both the customers. This will lead to a back order, and one of the customers will be paid back. This may or may not be a good policy. A large number of back orders may affect the shop's reputation and there may also be financial repercussions.

Availability

Availability, in simple terms, is responsiveness; a system that's always available to serve. The funny thing about availability is that sometimes a system becomes unavailable exactly when you need it the most.

In our example, one day before Christmas, everyone is buying gifts. Millions of people are searching, adding items to their carts, buying, and applying for discount coupons. If one server goes down due to overload, the rest of the servers will get even more loaded now, because the request from the dead server will be redirected to the rest of the machines, possibly killing the service due to overload. As the dominoes start to fall, eventually the site will go down. The peril does not end here. When the website comes online again, it will face a storm of requests from all the people who are worried that the offer end time is even closer, or those who will act quickly before the site goes down again.

Availability is the key component for extremely loaded services. Bad availability leads to bad user experience, dissatisfied customers, and financial losses.

Partition-tolerance

Network partitioning is defined as the inability to communicate between two or more subsystems in a distributed system. This can be due to someone walking carelessly in a data center and snapping the cable that connects the machine to the cluster, or may be network outage between two data centers, dropped packages, or wrong configuration. Partition-tolerance is a system that can operate during the network partition. In a distributed system, a network partition is a phenomenon where, due to network failure or any other reason, one part of the system cannot communicate with the other part(s) of the system. An example of network partition is a system that has some nodes in a subnet A and some in subnet B, and due to a faulty switch between these two subnets, the machines in subnet A will not be able to send and receive messages from the machines in subnet B. The network will be allowed to lose many messages arbitrarily sent from one node to another. This means that even if the cable between the two nodes is chopped, the system will still respond to the requests.

The following figure shows the database classification based on the CAP theorem:

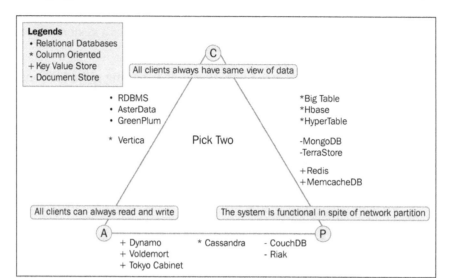

An example of a partition-tolerant system is a system with real-time data replication with no centralized master(s). So, for example, in a system where data is replicated across two data centers, the availability will not be affected, even if a data center goes down.

The significance of the CAP theorem

Once you decide to scale up, the first thing that comes to mind is vertical scaling, which means using beefier servers with a bigger RAM, more powerful processor(s), and bigger disks. For further scaling, you need to go horizontal. This means adding more servers. Once your system becomes distributed, the CAP theorem starts to play, which means, in a distributed system, you can choose only two out of consistency, availability, and partition-tolerance. So, let's see how choosing two out of the three options affects the system behavior as follows:

- **CA system**: In this system, you drop partition-tolerance for consistency and availability. This happens when you put everything related to a transaction on one machine or a system that fails like an atomic unit, like a rack. This system will have serious problems in scaling.

- **CP system**: The opposite of a CA system is a CP system. In a CP system, availability is sacrificed for consistency and partition-tolerance. What does this mean? If the system is available to serve the requests, data will be consistent. In an event of a node failure, some data will not be available. A sharded database is an example of such a system.

- **AP system**: An available and partition-tolerant system is like an always-on system that is at risk of producing conflicting results in an event of network partition. This is good for user experience, your application stays available, and inconsistency in rare events may be alright for some use cases. In the book example, it may not be such a bad idea to back order a few unfortunate customers due to inconsistency of the system than having a lot of users return without making any purchases because of the system's poor availability.

- **Eventual consistent (also known as BASE system)**: The AP system makes more sense when viewed from an uptime perspective—it's simple and provides a good user experience. But, an inconsistent system is not good for anything, certainly not good for business. It may be acceptable that one customer for the book *Nineteen Eighty-Four* gets a back order. But if it happens more often, the users would be reluctant to use the service. It will be great if the system could fix itself (read: repair) as soon as the first inconsistency is observed; or, maybe there are processes dedicated to fixing the inconsistency of a system when a partition failure is fixed or a dead node comes back to life. Such systems are called eventual consistent systems.

The following figure shows the life of an eventual consistent system:

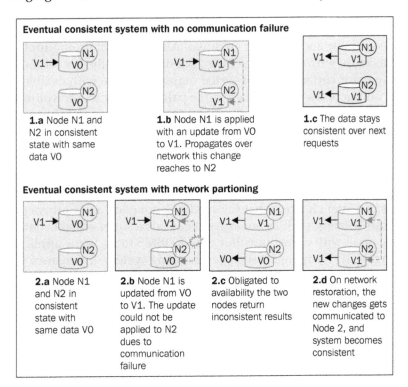

Quoting Wikipedia, "[In a distributed system] given a sufficiently long time over which no changes [in system state] are sent, all updates can be expected to propagate eventually through the system and the replicas will be consistent". (The page on eventual consistency is available at http://en.wikipedia.org/wiki/Eventual_consistency.)

Eventual consistent systems are also called BASE, a made-up term to represent that these systems are on one end of the spectrum, which has traditional databases with ACID properties on the opposite end.

Cassandra is one such system that provides high availability and partition-tolerance at the cost of consistency, which is tunable. The preceding figure shows a partition-tolerant eventual consistent system.

Cassandra

Cassandra is a distributed, decentralized, fault tolerant, eventually consistent, linearly scalable, and column-oriented data store. This means that Cassandra is made to easily deploy over a cluster of machines located at geographically different places. There is no central master server, so no single point of failure, no bottleneck, data is replicated, and a faulty node can be replaced without any downtime. It's eventually consistent. It is linearly scalable, which means that with more nodes, the requests served per second per node will not go down. Also, the total throughput of the system will increase with each node being added. And finally, it's column oriented, much like a map (or better, a map of sorted maps) or a table with flexible columns where each column is essentially a key-value pair. So, you can add columns as you go, and each row can have a different set of columns (key-value pairs). It does not provide any relational integrity. It is up to the application developer to perform relation management.

So, if Cassandra is so good at everything, why doesn't everyone drop whatever database they are using and jump start with Cassandra? This is a natural question. We'll discuss in a later chapter what Cassandra is not good at, but there may be several obvious reasons, such as not everyone needs a super scalable data store, and some are good with rather slow but cozy RDBMS tools. Some applications require strong ACID compliance, such as a booking system. If you are a person who goes by statistics, you'd ask how Cassandra fares with other existing data stores. TilmannRabl and others in their paper, *Solving Big Data Challenges for Enterprise Application Performance Management* (http://vldb.org/pvldb/vol5/p1724_tilmannrabl_vldb2012.pdf), said that, "In terms of scalability, there is a clear winner throughout our experiments. Cassandra achieves the highest throughput for the maximum number of nodes in all experiments with a linear increasing throughput from one to 12 nodes. This comes at the price of a high write and read latency. Cassandra's performance is best for high insertion rates".

If you go through the paper, Cassandra wins in almost all the criteria. Equipped with proven concepts of distributed computing, made to reliably serve from commodity servers, and simple and easy maintenance, Cassandra is one of the most scalable, fastest, and very robust NoSQL database. So, the next natural question is, "What makes Cassandra so blazing fast?". Let's dive deeper into the Cassandra architecture.

Understanding the architecture of Cassandra

Cassandra is a relative latecomer in the distributed data-store war. It takes advantage of two proven and closely similar data-store mechanisms, namely *Bigtable: A Distributed Storage System for Structured Data*, 2006 (http://static. googleusercontent.com/external_content/untrusted_dlcp/research. google.com/en//archive/bigtable-osdi06.pdf) and *Amazon Dynamo: Amazon's Highly Available Key-value Store*, 2007 (http://www.read.seas.harvard. edu/~kohler/class/cs239-w08/decandia07dynamo.pdf). The following diagram displays the read throughputs that show linear scaling of Cassandra:

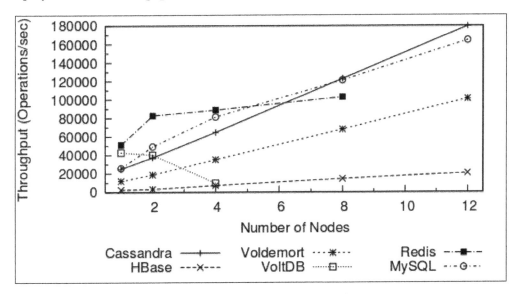

Like BigTable, it has a tabular data presentation. It is not tabular in the strictest sense. It is rather a dictionary-like structure where each entry holds another sorted dictionary/map. This model is more powerful than the usual key-value store and it is named a table, formerly known as a column family. The properties such as eventual consistency and decentralization are taken from Dynamo.

We'll discuss column family in detail in a later chapter. For now, assume a column family is a giant spreadsheet, such as MS Excel. But unlike spreadsheets, each row is identified by a row key with a number (token), and unlike spreadsheets, each cell may have its own unique name within the row. In Cassandra, the columns in the rows are sorted by this unique column name. Also, since the number of partitions is allowed to be very large (1.7*1038), it distributes the rows almost uniformly across all the available machines by dividing the rows in equal token groups. Tables or column families are contained within a logical container or name space called keyspace. A keyspace can be assumed to be more or less similar to database in RDBMS.

A word on max number of cells, rows, and partitions

A cell in a partition can be assumed as a key-value pair. The maximum number of cells per partition is limited by the Java integer's max value, which is about 2 billion. So, one partition can hold a maximum of 2 billion cells.

A row, in CQL terms, is a bunch of cells with predefined names. When you define a table with a primary key that has just one column, the primary key also serves as the partition key. But when you define a composite primary key, the first column in the definition of the primary key works as the partition key. So, all the rows (bunch of cells) that belong to one partition key go into one partition. This means that every partition can have a maximum of X rows, where X = (2*109/number_ of_columns_in_a_row). Essentially, rows * columns cannot exceed 2 billion per partition.

Finally, how many partitions can Cassandra hold for each table or column family? As we know, column families are essentially distributed hashmaps. The keys or row keys or partition keys are generated by taking a consistent hash of the string that you pass. So, the number of partitioned keys is bounded by the number of hashes these functions generate. This means that if you are using the default Murmur3 partitioner (range -263 to +263), the maximum number of partitions that you can have is 1.85*1019. If you use the Random partitioner, the number of partitions that you can have is 1.7*1038.

Ring representation

A Cassandra cluster is called a **ring**. The terminology is taken from Amazon Dynamo. Cassandra 1.1 and earlier versions used to have a token assigned to each node. Let's call this value the initial token. Each node is responsible for storing all the rows with token values (a token is basically a hash value of a row key) ranging from the previous node's initial token (exclusive) to the node's initial token (inclusive).

This way, the first node, the one with the smallest initial token, will have a range from the token value of the last node (the node with the largest initial token) to the first token value. So, if you jump from node to node, you will make a circle, and this is why a Cassandra cluster is called a ring.

Let's take an example. Assume that there is a hashing algorithm (partitioner) that generates tokens from 0 to 127 and you have four Cassandra machines to create a cluster. To allocate equal load, we need to assign each of the four nodes to bear an equal number of tokens. So, the first machine will be responsible for tokens one to 32, the second will hold 33 to 64, third 65 to 96, and fourth 97 to 127 and 0. If you mark each node with the maximum token number that it can hold, the cluster looks like a ring, as shown in the following figure:

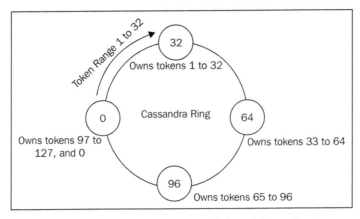

Token ownership and distribution in a balanced Cassandra ring

Virtual nodes

In Cassandra 1.1 and previous versions, when you create a cluster or add a node, you manually assign its initial token. This is extra work that the database should handle internally. Apart from this, adding and removing nodes requires manual resetting token ownership for some or all nodes. This is called **rebalancing**. Yet another problem was replacing a node. In the event of replacing a node with a new one, the data (rows that the to-be-replaced node owns) is required to be copied to the new machine from a replica of the old machine (we will see replication later in this chapter). For a large database, this could take a while because we are streaming from one machine. To solve all these problems, Cassandra 1.2 introduced **virtual nodes (vnodes)**.

The following figure shows 16 vnodes distributed over four servers:

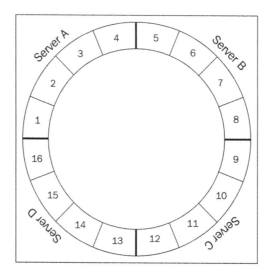

In the preceding figure, each node is responsible for a single continuous range. In the case of a replication factor of 2 or more, the data is also stored on other machines than the one responsible for the range. (**Replication factor** (**RF**) represents the number of copies of a table that exist in the system. So, RF=2, means there are two copies of each record for the table.) In this case, one can say one machine, one range. With vnodes, each machine can have multiple smaller ranges and these ranges are automatically assigned by Cassandra. How does this solve those issues? Let's see. If you have a 30 ring cluster and a node with 256 vnodes had to be replaced. If nodes are well-distributed randomly across the cluster, each physical node in remaining 29 nodes will have 8 or 9 vnodes (256/29) that are replicas of vnodes on the dead node. In older versions, with a replication factor of 3, the data had to be streamed from three replicas (10 percent utilization). In the case of vnodes, all the nodes can participate in helping the new node get up.

The other benefit of using vnodes is that you can have a heterogeneous ring where some machines are more powerful than others, and change the vnodes ' settings such that the stronger machines will take proportionally more data than others. This was still possible without vnodes but it needed some tricky calculation and rebalancing. So, let's say you have a cluster of machines with similar hardware specifications and you have decided to add a new server that is twice as powerful as any machine in the cluster. Ideally, you would want it to work twice as harder as any of the old machines. With vnodes, you can achieve this by setting twice as many `num_tokens` as on the old machine in the new machine's `cassandra.yaml` file. Now, it will be allotted double the load when compared to the old machines.

Yet another benefit of vnodes is faster repair. Node repair requires the creation of a Merkle tree (we will see this later in this chapter) for each range of data that a node holds. The data gets compared with the data on the replica nodes, and if needed, data re-sync is done. Creation of a Merkle tree involves iterating through all the data in the range followed by streaming it. For a large range, the creation of a Merkle tree can be very time consuming while the data transfer might be much faster. With vnodes, the ranges are smaller, which means faster data validation (by comparing with other nodes). Since the Merkle tree creation process is broken into many smaller steps (as there are many small nodes that exist in a physical node), the data transmission does not have to wait till the whole big range finishes. Also, the validation uses all other machines instead of just a couple of replica nodes.

> As of Cassandra 2.0.9, the default setting for vnodes is "on" with default vnodes per machine as 256. If for some reason you do not want to use vnodes and want to disable this feature, comment out the `num_tokens` variable and uncomment and set the `initial_token` variable in `cassandra.yaml`. If you are starting with a new cluster or migrating an old cluster to the latest version of Cassandra, vnodes are highly recommended.

The number of vnodes that you specify on a Cassandra node represents the number of vnodes on that machine. So, the total vnodes on a cluster is the sum total of all the vnodes across all the nodes. One can always imagine a Cassandra cluster as a ring of lots of vnodes.

How Cassandra works

Diving into various components of Cassandra without having any context is a frustrating experience. It does not make sense why you are studying SSTable, MemTable, and **log structured merge** (**LSM**) trees without being able to see how they fit into the functionality and performance guarantees that Cassandra gives. So first we will see Cassandra's write and read mechanism. It is possible that some of the terms that we encounter during this discussion may not be immediately understandable. The terms are explained in detail later in this chapter.

A rough overview of the Cassandra components is as shown in the following figure:

Cassandra API	Cassandra Tools
Storage Layer	
Partioner	Replicator
Failure Detector	Compaction Manager
Messaging Layer	

Main components of the Cassandra service

The main class of Storage Layer is `StorageProxy`. It handles all the requests. The messaging layer is responsible for inter-node communications, such as gossip. Apart from this, process-level structures keep a rough idea about the actual data containers and where they live.

There are four data buckets that you need to know. MemTable is a hash table-like structure that stays in memory. It contains actual cell data. SSTable is the disk version of MemTables. When MemTables are full, they are persisted to hard disk as SSTable. Commit log is an append only log of all the mutations that are sent to the Cassandra cluster.

 Mutations can be thought of as update commands. So, `insert`, `update`, and `delete` operations are mutations, since they mutate the data.

Commit log lives on the disk and helps to replay uncommitted changes. These three are basically core data. Then there are bloom filters and index. The bloom filter is a probabilistic data structure that lives in the memory. They both live in memory and contain information about the location of data in the SSTable. Each SSTable has one bloom filter and one index associated with it. The bloom filter helps Cassandra to quickly detect which SSTable does not have the requested data, while the index helps to find the exact location of the data in the SSTable file.

With this primer, we can start looking into how write and read works in Cassandra. We will see more explanation later.

Write in action

To write, clients need to connect to any of the Cassandra nodes and send a write request. This node is called the **coordinator node**. When a node in a Cassandra cluster receives a write request, it delegates the write request to a service called `StorageProxy`. This node may or may not be the right place to write the data. StorageProxy's job is to get the nodes (all the replicas) that are responsible for holding the data that is going to be written. It utilizes a replication strategy to do this. Once the replica nodes are identified, it sends the `RowMutation` message to them, the node waits for replies from these nodes, but it does not wait for all the replies to come. It only waits for as many responses as are enough to satisfy the client's minimum number of successful writes defined by `ConsistencyLevel`.

> `ConsistencyLevel` is basically a fancy way of saying how reliable a read or write you want to be. Cassandra has tunable consistency, which means you can define how much reliability is wanted. Obviously, everyone wants a hundred percent reliability, but it comes with latency as the cost. For instance, in a thrice-replicated cluster (replication factor = 3), a write time consistency level TWO, means the write will become successful only if it is written to at least two replica nodes. This request will be faster than the one with the consistency level THREE or ALL, but slower than the consistency level ONE or ANY.

The following figure is a simplistic representation of the write mechanism. The operations on node N2 at the bottom represent the node-local activities on receipt of the write request:

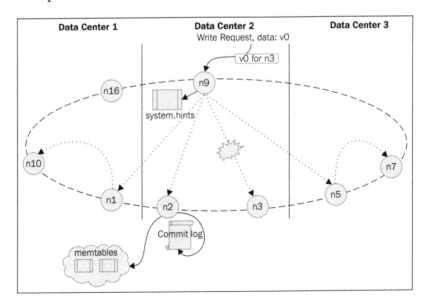

The following steps show everything that can happen during a write mechanism:

1. If the failure detector detects that there aren't enough live nodes to satisfy ConsistencyLevel, the request fails.

2. If the failure detector gives a green signal, but writes time-out after the request is sent due to infrastructure problems or due to extreme load, StorageProxy writes a local hint to replay when the failed nodes come back to life. This is called **hinted hand off**.

> One might think that hinted handoff may be responsible for Cassandra's eventual consistency. But it's not entirely true. If the coordinator node gets shut down or dies due to hardware failure and hints on this machine cannot be forwarded, eventual consistency will not occur. The anti-entropy mechanism is responsible for consistency, rather than hinted hand-off. Anti-entropy makes sure that all replicas are in sync.

3. If the replica nodes are distributed across data centers, it will be a bad idea to send individual messages to all the replicas in other data centers. Rather, it sends the message to one replica in each data center with a header, instructing it to forward the request to other replica nodes in that data center.

4. Now the data is received by the node which should actually store that data. The data first gets appended to the commit log, and pushed to a MemTable appropriate column family in the memory.

5. When the MemTable becomes full, it gets flushed to the disk in a sorted structure named SSTable. With lots of flushes, the disk gets plenty of SSTables. To manage SSTables, a compaction process runs. This process merges data from smaller SSTables to one big sorted file.

Read in action

Similar to a write case, when StorageProxy of the node that a client is connected to gets the request, it gets a list of nodes containing this key based on the replication strategy. The node's StorageProxy then sorts the nodes based on their proximity to itself. The proximity is determined by the snitch function that is set up for this cluster. Basically, the following types of snitches exist:

- SimpleSnitch: A closer node is the one that comes first when moving clockwise in the ring. (A ring is when all the machines in the cluster are placed in a circular fashion with each machine having a token number. When you walk clockwise, the token value increases. At the end, it snaps back to the first node.)

- PropertyFileSnitch: This snitch allows you to specify how you want your machines' location to be interpreted by Cassandra. You do this by assigning a data center name and rack name for all the machines in the cluster in the $CASSANDRA_HOME/conf/cassandra-topology.properties file. Each node has a copy of this file and you need to alter this file each time you add or remove a node. This is what the file looks like:

```
# Cassandra Node IP=Data Center:Rack
192.168.1.100=DC1:RAC1
192.168.2.200=DC2:RAC2
10.0.0.10=DC1:RAC1
10.0.0.11=DC1:RAC1
10.0.0.12=DC1:RAC2
10.20.114.10=DC2:RAC1
10.20.114.11=DC2:RAC1
```

- GossipingPropertyFileSnitch: The PropertyFileSnitch is kind of a pain, even when you think about it. Each node has the locations of all nodes manually written and updated every time a new node joins or an old node retires. And then, we need to copy it on all the servers. Wouldn't it be better if we just specify each node's data center and rack on just that one machine, and then have Cassandra somehow collect this information to understand the topology? This is exactly what GossipingPropertyFileSnitch does. Similar to PropertyFileSnitch, you have a file called $CASSANDRA_HOME/conf/cassandra-rackdc.properties, and in this file you specify the data center and the rack name for that machine. The gossip protocol makes sure that this information gets spread to all the nodes in the cluster (and you do not have to edit properties of files on all the nodes when a new node joins or leaves). Here is what a cassandra-rackdc.properties file looks like:

```
# indicate the rack and dc for this node
dc=DC13
rack=RAC42
```

- RackInferringSnitch: This snitch infers the location of a node based on its IP address. It uses the third octet to infer rack name, and the second octet to assign data center. If you have four nodes 10.110.6.30, 10.110.6.4, 10.110.7.42, and 10.111.3.1, this snitch will think the first two live on the same rack as they have the same second octet (110) and the same third octet (6), while the third lives in the same data center but on a different rack as it has the same second octet but the third octet differs. Fourth, however, is assumed to live in a separate data center as it has a different second octet than the three.

- `EC2Snitch`: This is meant for Cassandra deployments on Amazon EC2 service. EC2 has regions and within regions, there are availability zones. For example, us-east-1e is an availability zone in the us-east region with availability zone named 1e. This snitch infers the region name (us-east, in this case) as the data center and availability zone (1e) as the rack.

- `EC2MultiRegionSnitch`: The multi-region snitch is just an extension of `EC2Snitch` where data centers and racks are inferred the same way. But you need to make sure that `broadcast_address` is set to the public IP provided by EC2 and seed nodes must be specified using their public IPs so that inter-data center communication can be done.

- `DynamicSnitch`: This Snitch determines closeness based on a recent performance delivered by a node. So, a quick responding node is perceived as being closer than a slower one, irrespective of its location closeness, or closeness in the ring. This is done to avoid overloading a slow performing node. `DynamicSnitch` is used by all the other snitches by default. You can disable it, but it is not advisable.

Now, with knowledge about snitches, we know the list of the fastest nodes that have the desired row keys, it's time to pull data from them. The coordinator node (the one that the client is connected to) sends a command to the closest node to perform a read (we'll discuss local reads in a minute) and return the data. Now, based on `ConsistencyLevel`, other nodes will send a command to perform a read operation and send just the digest of the result. If we have read repairs (discussed later) enabled, the remaining replica nodes will be sent a message to compute the digest of the command response.

Let's take an example. Let's say you have five nodes containing a row key K (that is, RF equals five), your read `ConsistencyLevel` is three; then the closest of the five nodes will be asked for the data and the second and third closest nodes will be asked to return the digest. If there is a difference in the digests, full data is pulled from the conflicting node and the latest of the three will be sent. These replicas will be updated to have the latest data. We still have two nodes left to be queried. If read repairs are not enabled, they will not be touched for this request. Otherwise, these two will be asked to compute the digest. Depending on the `read_repair_chance` setting, the request to the last two nodes is done in the background, after returning the result. This updates all the nodes with the most recent value, making all replicas consistent.

Let's see what goes on within a node. Take a simple case of a read request looking for a single column within a single row. First, the attempt is made to read from MemTable, which is rapid fast, and since there exists only one copy of data, this is the fastest retrieval. If all required data is not found there, Cassandra looks into SSTable. Now, remember from our earlier discussion that we flush MemTables to disk as SSTables and later when the compaction mechanism wakes up, it merges those SSTables. So, our data can be in multiple SSTables.

The following figure represents a simplified representation of the read mechanism. The bottom of the figure shows processing on the read node. The numbers in circles show the order of the event. BF stands for bloom filter.

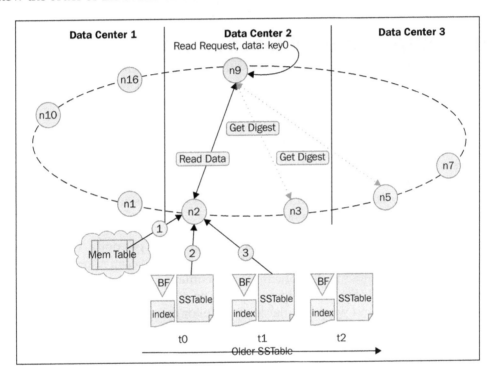

Each SSTable is associated with its bloom filter built on the row keys in the SSTable. Bloom filters are kept in the memory and used to detect if an SSTable may contain (false positive) the row data. Now, we have the SSTables that may contain the row key. The SSTables get sorted in reverse chronological order (latest first).

Apart from the bloom filter for row keys, there exists one bloom filter for each row in the SSTable. This secondary bloom filter is created to detect whether the requested column names exist in the SSTable. Now, Cassandra will take SSTables one by one from younger to older, and use the index file to locate the offset for each column value for that row key and the bloom filter associated with the row (built on the column name). On the bloom filter being positive for the requested column, it looks into the SSTable file to read the column value. Note that we may have a column value in other yet-to-be-read SSTables, but that does not matter, because we are reading the most recent SSTables first, and any value that was written earlier to it does not matter. So, the value gets returned as soon as the first column in the most recent SSTable is allocated.

The components of Cassandra

We have gone through how read and write takes place in highly distributed Cassandra clusters. It's time to look into the individual components of it a little deeper.

The messaging service

The messaging service is the mechanism that manages inter-node socket communication in a ring. Communications, for example gossip, read, read digest, write, and so on, processed via a messaging service, can be assumed as a gateway messaging server running at each node.

To communicate, each node creates two socket connections per node. This implies that if you have 101 nodes, there will be 200 open sockets on each node to handle communication with other nodes. The messages contain a verb handler within them that basically tells the receiving node a couple of things: how to deserialize the payload message and what handler to execute for this particular message. The execution is done by the verb handlers (sort of an event handler). The singleton class that orchestrates the messaging service mechanism is `org.apache.cassandra.net.MessagingService`.

Gossip

Cassandra uses the gossip protocol for inter-node communication. As the name suggests, the protocol spreads information in the same way an office rumor does. It can also be compared to a virus spread. There is no central broadcaster, but the information (virus) gets transferred to the whole population. It's a way for nodes to build the global map of the system with a small number of local interactions.

Cassandra uses gossip to find out the state and location of other nodes in the ring (cluster). The gossip process runs every second and exchanges information with, at the most, three other nodes in the cluster. Nodes exchange information about themselves and other nodes that they come to know about via some other gossip session. This causes all the nodes to eventually know about all the other nodes. Like everything else in Cassandra, gossip messages have a version number associated with them. So, whenever two nodes gossip, the older information about a node gets overwritten with newer information. Cassandra uses an anti-entropy version of the gossip protocol that utilizes Merkle trees (discussed later) to repair unread data.

Implementation-wise, the gossip task is handled by the `org.apache.cassandra.gms.Gossiper` class. The `Gossiper` class maintains a list of live and dead endpoints (the unreachable endpoints). At each one-second interval, this module starts a gossip round with a randomly chosen node. A full round of gossip consists of three messages. A node X sends a syn message to a node Y to initiate gossip. Y, on receipt of this syn message, sends an ack message back to X. To reply to this ack message, X sends an ack2 message to Y completing a full message round. The following figure shows the two nodes gossiping:

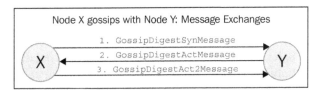

Syn and ack are also known as a **message handshake**. It is a mechanism that allows two machines trying to communicate to each other to negotiate the parameters of connection before transmitting data. Syn stands for "synchronize packet" and ack stands for "acknowledge packet".

The `Gossiper` module is linked to failure detection. The module, on hearing one of these messages, updates the failure detector with the liveness information that it has gained. If it hears `GossipShutdownMessage`, the module marks the remote node as dead in the failure detector.

The node to be gossiped with is chosen based on the following rules:

- Gossip to a random live endpoint
- Gossip to a random unreachable endpoint
- If the node in point 1 was not a seed node or the number of live nodes is less than the number of seeds, gossip to a random seed

Seed node

Seed nodes are the nodes that are first contacted by a newly joining node when they first start up. Seed nodes help the newly started node to discover other nodes in the cluster. It is suggested that to have more than one seed node in a `cluster`. `Seed` node is nothing like a master in a master-slave mechanism. It is just another node that helps newly joining nodes to bootstrap gossip protocol. So, seeds are not a **single point of failure** (SPOF) and neither has any other purpose that makes them superior.

Failure detection

Failure detection is one of the fundamental features of any robust and distributed system. A good failure detection mechanism implementation makes a fault-tolerant system, such as Cassandra. The failure detector that Cassandra uses is a variation of *The ϕ accrual failure detector (2004)* by Xavier Défago and others (`http://citeseerx.ist.psu.edu/viewdoc/summary?doi=10.1.1.106.3350`).

The idea behind a failure detector is to detect a communication failure and take appropriate actions based on the state of the remote node. Unlike traditional failure detectors, phi accrual failure detector does not emit a Boolean alive or dead (true or false, trust or suspect) value. Instead, it gives a continuous value to the application and the application is left to decide the level of severity and act accordingly. This continuous suspect value is called **phi** (ϕ). So, how does ϕ get calculated?

Let's say we are observing the heartbeat sent from a process on a remote machine. Assume that the latest heartbeat arrived at time T_{last}, current time t_{now}, and $P_{later}(t)$ is the probability that the heartbeat will arrive t time unit later than the last heartbeat. Then ϕ can be calculated as follows:

$$\phi(t_{now}) = -\log_{10}(P_{later}(t_{now} - T_{last}))$$

Let's observe this formula informally using common sense. On a sunny day, when everything is fine and the heartbeat is at a constant interval Δt, the probability of the next heartbeat will keep increasing towards ($t_{now} - T_{last}$) as one approaches Δt. So, the value of ϕ will go up. If a heartbeat is not received at Δt, the more we depart away, the lower the value of P_{later} becomes, and the value of ϕ keeps on increasing, as shown in the following figure:

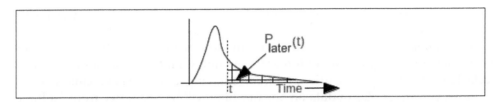

In the preceding figure, the curve shows the heartbeat arrival distribution estimate based on past samples. It is used to calculate the value of ϕ based on last arrival, T_{last}, and t_{now}.

One may question as to where a heartbeat is being sent in Cassandra. Gossip has it!

Gossip and failure detection

During gossip sessions, each node maintains a list of the arrival time stamps of gossip messages from the other nodes. This list is basically a sliding window, which, in turn, is used to calculate P_{later}. One may set the sensitivity of the ϕ_{thres} threshold.

ϕ_{thres} can be understood like this. Let's say we start to suspect whether a node is dead when $\phi >= \phi_{thres}$. When ϕ_{thres} is 1, it is equivalent to - log(0.1). The probability that we will make a mistake (that is, the decision that the node is dead will be contradicted in future by a late arriving heartbeat) is 0.1 or 10 percent. Similarly, with $\phi_{thres} = 2$, the probability of making a mistake goes down to 1 percent; with $\phi_{thres} = 3$, it drops to 0.1 percent; and so on, following log base 10 formula.

Partitioner

Cassandra is a distributed database management system. This means it takes a single logical database and distributes it over one or more machines in the database cluster. So, when you insert some data in Cassandra with a unique row key, based on that row key, Cassandra assigns that row to one of the nodes that's responsible for managing it.

Let's try to understand this. Cassandra inherits a data model from Google's BigTable (`http://research.google.com/archive/bigtable.html`). This means we can roughly assume that the data is stored in some sort of a table that has an unlimited number of columns (not really unlimited; Cassandra limits the maximum number of cells to be 2 billion per partition) with rows having a unique key, namely row key. Now, your terabytes of data on one machine will be restrictive from multiple points of view. One is disk space, and another is limited parallel processing, and if not duplicated, a source of single point of failure. What Cassandra does is, it defines some rules to slice data across rows and assigns which node in the cluster is responsible for holding which slice. This task is done by a partitioner. There are several types of partitioners to choose from. We'll discuss them in detail in *Chapter 4, Deploying a Cluster*. In short, Cassandra (as of Version 1.2) offers three partitioners, as follows:

- `Murmur3Partitioner`: This uses a Murmur hash to distribute the data. It performs somewhat better than `RandomPartitioner`. It is the default partitioner in Cassandra Version 1.2 onwards.

- `RandomPartitioner`: This uses MD5 hashing to distribute data across the cluster. Cassandra 1.1.x and precursors have this as the default partitioner.

- `ByteOrderPartitioner`: This keeps keys distributed across the cluster by key bytes. This is an ordered distribution, so the rows are stored in lexical order. This distribution is commonly discouraged because it may cause a hotspot. (A hotspot is a phenomenon where some nodes are heavily under load, (the hotspots), while others are not. Essentially, there is an uneven workload.)

One of the key benefits of partitioning data is that it allows the cluster to grow incrementally. What any partitioning algorithm does is it gives a consistent divisibility of data across all available nodes. The token that a node is assigned to by the partitioner also determines the node's position in the ring. Since the partitioner is a global setting, any node in the cluster can calculate which nodes to look for in a given row key. This ability to calculate data-holding nodes without knowing anything other than the row key, enables any node to calculate what node to forward requests to. This makes the node selection process a single-hop mechanism. The following figure shows a Cassandra ring with an alphabetical partitioner, which shows keys owned by the nodes and data replication:

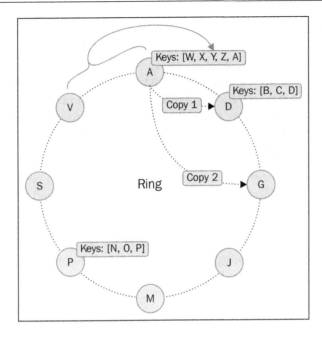

The previous figure shows what an Amazon Dynamo or Cassandra cluster looks like; it looks like a ring. In this particular figure, each node or virtual node is assigned with a letter as its token ID. Let's assume the partitioner in this example slices row keys based on the first letter of the row key (no such default partitioner exists, but you can write one by implementing IPartitioner interface which we will see in *Chapter 4, Deploying a Cluster*). So, node D will have all the rows whose row keys start with the letters B, C, and D. Since all nodes know about what partitioner and what snitch is being set, they know which nodes have which row keys.

Now that we have observed that partitioning has such a drastic effect on the data movement and distribution, one may think that a bad partitioner can lead to uneven data distribution. In fact, our example ring in the previous paragraph might be a bad partitioner. For a dataset where terms with a specific starting letter have a very high population than the terms with other letters, the ring will be lopsided. A good partitioner is one that is quick to calculate the position from the row key and distributes the row keys evenly; something like a partitioner based on a consistent hashing algorithm.

Replication

Cassandra runs on commodity hardware, and works reliably in network partitions. However, this comes with a cost: replication. To avoid data inaccessibility if a node goes down or becomes unavailable, one must replicate data to more than one node. Replication provides features such as fault tolerance and no single point of failure to the system. Cassandra provides more than one strategy to replicate the data, and one can configure the replication factor while creating key space. This will be discussed in detail in *Chapter 3, Effective CQL*.

Replication is tightly bound to **consistency level (CL)**. CL can be thought of as an answer to the question: How many replicas must respond positively to declare a successful operation? If you have a read consistency level three, that means a client will be returned a successful read as soon as three replicas respond with the data. The same goes for write. For write consistency three, at least three replicas must respond that the write to them was successful. Obviously, the replication factor must be greater than any consistency level, otherwise there will never be enough replicas to write to, or read from, successfully.

 Do not confuse replication factor with the number of nodes in the system. The replication factor is the number of copies of data. The number of nodes just affects how much data a node will hold based on the configured partitioner.

Replication should be thought of as an added redundancy. One should never have a replication factor one in their production environment. If you think having multiple writes to different replicas will slow down the writes, you can set up a favorable consistency level. Cassandra offers a set of consistency levels, including fire and forget, CL ZERO, and ensures all replica operations (read and write). This is where the so-called "tunable" consistency of Cassandra lies. The following table shows all the consistency levels:

WRITE		READ	
Consistency level	Meaning	Consistency level	Meaning
ZERO	Fire and forget		
ANY	Success on hinted hand off write		
ONE	First replica returned successfully	ONE	First replica returned successfully
QUORUM	N/2 + 1 replica success	QUORUM	N/2 + 1 replica success
ALL	All replica success	ALL	All replica success

The notorious R + W > N inequality

Imagine that the value of your replication factor is three. This means your data will be stored in three nodes. If you have a write consistency level as one, and a read consistency level as one, they may or may not be consistent. Here is why: when a write happens, the row mutation information is sent to all the nodes, but the user is returned a success message as soon as the first replica responds with a success message. Meanwhile, the data is being written to two other nodes. If a read request comes into those two nodes with a consistency level one, they would return the stale data. Or, if it is a heavy write-read scenario, all the three nodes may have different data at some instant of time, and read with CL=1, which may result in inconsistent reads for a very brief time. The following figure shows reads and writes, on an R + W > N system:

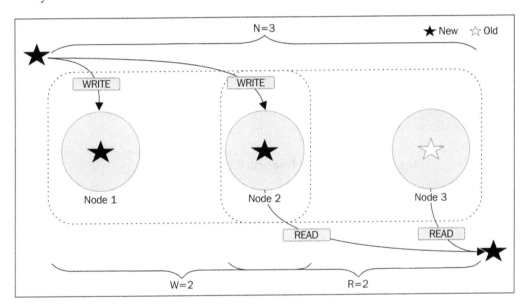

The concept of weak and strong consistencies comes here. Weak consistency is when reads may be wrong for a brief amount of time and strong consistency is when results are always consistent. Basically, weak consistency sometimes returns inconsistent results. If you have an N replica, to ensure that your reads always result in the latest value, you must write and read from as many nodes that ensure at least one node overlaps. So, if you write to W nodes and read from R nodes such that R+W > N, there must be at least one node that is common in both read and write. And this will ensure that you have the latest data. See the previous figure; ZERO and ANY consistency levels are weak consistency. ALL is strong. ONE for read and ALL for write, or vice versa, will make a strongly consistent system.

A system with QUORUM for both, read and write, is a strongly consistent system. Again, the idea is to make sure that between the reads and the writes, at least one node overlaps. While we are on this topic, it may be worth noticing that the higher the consistency level, the slower the operation. So, if you want a super-fast write and a not-so-fast read, and you also want the system to be strongly consistent, you can opt for consistency level ONE for the writes and ALL for the reads.

LSM tree

Cassandra (and HBase) is heavily influenced by LSM tree. It uses an LSM tree-like mechanism to store data on a disk. The writes are sequential (in append fashion) and the data storage is contiguous. This makes writes in Cassandra fast, because there is no disk-seek involved. Contrast this with an RBDMS system that is based on the B+ tree (http://en.wikipedia.org/wiki/B%2B_tree) implementation.

LSM tree advocates the following mechanism to store data: note down the arriving modification into a log file (commit log), push the modification/new data into memory (MemTable) for faster lookup, and when the system has gathered enough updates in memory, or after a certain threshold time, flush this data to a disk in a structured store file (SSTable). The logs corresponding to the updates that are flushed can now be discarded.

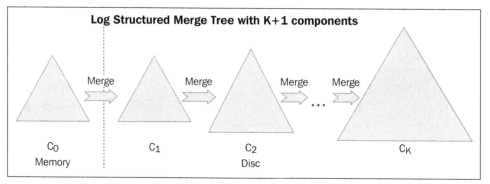

LSM trees

 For more information, refer to *The Log-Structured Merge-Tree (LSM-Tree) (1996)* by Patrick O'Neil and others at http://citeseerx.ist.psu.edu/viewdoc/summary?doi=10.1.1.44.2782.

The preceding paper suggests multi-component LSM trees, where data from memory is flushed into a smaller tree on disk for a quicker merge. When this tree fills up, it rolls them into a bigger tree. So, if you have K trees with the first tree being the smallest and the Kth being the largest, the memory gets flushed into the first tree, which when full, performs a rolling merge to the second tree, and so on. The change eventually lands up onto the Kth tree. This is a background process (similar to the compaction process in Cassandra). Cassandra differs a little bit where memory resident data is flushed into immutable SSTables, which are eventually merged into one big SSTable by a background process. Like any other disk-resident access tree, popular pages are buffered into memory for faster access. Cassandra has a similar concept with key cache and row cache (optional) mechanisms.

We'll see the LSM tree in action in the context of Cassandra in the next three sections.

Commit log

One of the promises that Cassandra makes to the end users is durability. In conventional terms (or in ACID terminology), durability guarantees that a successful transaction (write, update) will survive permanently. This means that once Cassandra says `write successful`, it means the data is persisted and will survive system failures. This is done the same way as in any DBMS that guarantees durability: by writing the replayable information to a file before responding to a successful write. This log is called the commit log in the Cassandra realm.

This is what happens under the hood: any write to a node gets tracked by `org. apache.cassandra.db.commitlog.CommitLog`, which writes the data with certain metadata into the commit log file in such a manner that replaying this will recreate the data. The purpose of this exercise is to ensure there is no data loss. If, due to some reason, the data cannot make it into MemTable or SSTable, the system can replay the commit log to recreate the data.

Commit log, MemTable, and SSTable in a node are tightly coupled. Any write operation gets written to the commit log first and then the MemTable gets updated. MemTable, based on certain criteria, gets flushed to a disk in immutable files called SSTable. The data in commit logs gets purged after its corresponding data in MemTable gets flushed to SSTable.

Also, there exists one single commit log per node server. Like any other logging mechanism, the commit log is set to rolling after a certain size. The following figure shows the commit log, MemTable, and SSTable in action:

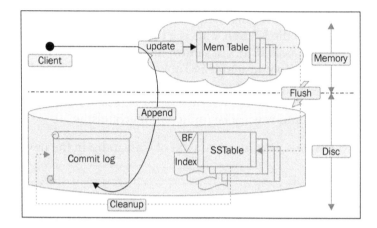

Let's quickly go a bit deeper into the implementation. All the classes that deal with the commit log management reside under the `org.apache.cassandra.db.commitlog` package. The commit log singleton is a facade for all the operations. The implementations of `ICommitLogExecutorService` are responsible for write commands to the commit log file. Then there is a `CommitLogSegment` class. It manages a single commit log file, writes serialized write (mutation) to the commit log, and it holds a very interesting property: `cfLastWrite`. The `cfLastWrite` property is a map with a key as the column family name and value as an integer that represents the position (offset) in the commit log file where the last mutation for that column family is written. It can be thought of as a cursor; one cursor per column family. When the MemTable of a column family is flushed, the segments containing those mutations are marked as clean (for that particular column family). And when a new write arrives, it is marked dirty with offset at the latest mutation.

In events of failure (hardware crash, abrupt shutdown), this is how the commit log helps the system to recover:

1. Each commit log segment is iterated in the ascending order of timestamp.
2. Lowest `ReplayPosition` (which is the offset in commit log that specifies the point till which the data is already stored in SSTables) is chosen from the SSTable metadata.
3. The log entry is replayed for a column family if the position of the log entry is greater than the replay position in the latest SSTable metadata.
4. After the log replay is done, all the MemTables are force flushed to a disk, and all the commit log segments are recycled.

MemTable

MemTable is an in-memory representation of a column family. It can be thought of as cached data. MemTable is sorted by key. Data in MemTable is sorted by row key. Unlike the commit log, which is append-only, MemTable does not contain duplicates. A new write with a key that already exists in the MemTable, overwrites the older record. This being in memory is both fast and efficient. The following is an example:

```
Write 1: {k1: [{c1, v1}, {c2, v2}, {c3, v3}]}

In CommitLog (new entry, append):
  {k1: [{c1, v1},{c2, v2}, {c3, v3}]}

In MemTable (new entry, append):
  {k1: [{c1, v1}, {c2, v2}, {c3, v3}]}

Write 2: {k2: [{c4, v4}]}

In CommitLog (new entry, append):
  {k1: [{c1, v1}, {c2, v2}, {c3, v3}]}
  {k2: [{c4, v4}]}

In MemTable (new entry, append):
  {k1: [{c1, v1}, {c2, v2}, {c3, v3}]}
  {k2: [{c4, v4}]}

Write 3: {k1: [{c1, v5}, {c6, v6}]}

In CommitLog (old entry, append):
  {k1: [{c1, v1}, {c2, v2}, {c3, v3}]}
  {k2: [{c4, v4}]}
  {k1: [{c1, v5}, {c6, v6}]}

In MemTable (old entry, update):
  {k1: [{c1, v5}, {c2, v2}, {c3, v3}, {c6, v6}]}
  {k2: [{c4, v4}]}
```

Cassandra Version 1.1.1 uses SnapTree (https://github.com/nbronson/snaptree) for MemTable representation, which claims to be "A drop-in replacement for ConcurrentSkipListMap, with the additional guarantee that clone() is atomic and iteration has snapshot isolation". See also, copy-on-write and compare-and-swap on the following sites:

- http://en.wikipedia.org/wiki/Copy-on-write
- http://en.wikipedia.org/wiki/Compare-and-swap

 SnapTree is very likely to be replaced by Btree implementation. It is implemented in Cassandra 2.1 beta version, so it is likely to be default in future. For more information, visit https://issues.apache.org/jira/browse/CASSANDRA-6271.

Any write gets first written to the commit log and then to MemTable.

SSTable

SSTable is a disk representation of the data. MemTables get flushed to disk to immutable SSTables. MemTables get flushed to individual SSTables, and all the writes are sequential, which makes this process fast. So, the faster the disk speed, the quicker the flush operation.

The SSTables eventually get merged in the compaction process and the data gets organized properly into one file. This extra work in compaction pays off during reads.

SSTables have three components: bloom filter, index files, and data files.

The bloom filter

The bloom filter is a litmus test for the availability of certain data in storage (collection). But unlike a litmus test, a bloom filter may result in false positives; that is, it says that data exists in the collection associated with the bloom filter, when it actually does not. A bloom filter never results in a false negative; that is, it never states that data is not there when it is. The reason to use a bloom filter, even with its false-positive defect, is because it is very fast and its implementation is really simple.

Cassandra uses bloom filters to determine whether an SSTable has the data for a particular row key. Bloom filters are unused for range scans, but they are good candidates for index scans. This saves a lot of disk I/O that might take in a full SSTable scan, which is a slow process. That's why it is used in Cassandra; to avoid reading many SSTables, which might have become a bottleneck.

How a bloom filter works

A bloom filter, in its simplest form, can be assumed as a bit array of length l, with all elements set to zero. It also has k predefined hash functions associated with it.

The following figure shows the bloom filter in action. It uses three hash functions and sets the corresponding bit in the array to 1 (it might already be 1).

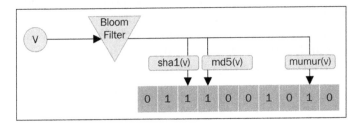

To add a key to a bloom filter (at the time of entering data in the associated collection), k hashes are calculated using k predefined hash functions. A modulus of each hash value is taken using array length l, and the value at this array position is set to 1.

The following pseudo code shows what happens:

```
//calculate hash, mod it to get location in bit array
arrayIndex1 = md5(v) % arrayLength
arrayIndex2 = sha1(v) % arrayLength
arrayindex3 = murmur(v) % arrayLength

//set all those indexes to 1
bitArray[arrayIndex1] = 1
bitArray[arrayIndex2] = 1
bitArray[arrayIndex3] = 1
```

To query the existence of a key in the bloom filter, the process is similar. Take the key and calculate the predefined hash values. Take modulus of the hash values with the length of the bit array. Look into those locations. If it turns out that at least one of those array locations have a zero value in them, it is certain that this value was never inserted in this bloom filter, and hence, does not exist in the associated collection. On the other hand, if all values are 1s, this means that the value may exist in the collection associated with this bloom filter. We cannot guarantee its presence in the collection because it is possible that there exist other k keys whose i^{th} hash function filled the same spot in the array as the jth hash of the key that we are looking for.

Removal of a key from a bloom filter as in its original avatar is not possible. One may break multiple keys because multiple keys may have the same index bit set to 1 in the array for different hashes. Counting bloom filter solves these issues by changing the bit array into an integer array where each element works as a counter; insertion increments the counter and deletion decrements it.

Effectiveness of the bloom filter depends on the size of the collection it is applied to. The bigger the collection associated with the bloom filter, the higher the frequency of false positives will be (because the array will be more densely packed with 1s). Another thing that governs bloom filter is the quality of a good hash function. A good hash function will distribute hash values evenly in the array, and it will be fast. One does not look at the cryptic strength of the hash function here, so the Murmur3 hash will be preferred over the SHA1 hash.

From Cassandra 1.2 onwards, bloom filters are stored off heap memory. This is done to alleviate pressure on heap memory because Java garbage collectors start to underperform for heap size 8 GB or more, and that affects Cassandra's performance.

Index files

Index files are companion files of SSTables. Similar to the bloom filter, there exists one index file per SSTable. It contains all the row keys in the SSTable and its offset is at the point where the row starts in the data file.

At startup, Cassandra reads every 128th key (configurable) into the memory (sampled index). When the index is looking for a row key (after the bloom filter hinted that the row key might be in this SSTable), Cassandra performs a binary search on the sampled index in memory. Followed by a positive result from the binary search, Cassandra will have to read a block in the index file from the disk starting from the nearest value lower than the value that we are looking for.

Let's take an example. See the figure in the *Read repair and anti-entropy* section, where Cassandra is looking for a row key 404. It is not in MemTable. On querying the bloom filter of a certain SSTable, Cassandra gets a positive nod that this SSTable may contain the row. The next step is to look into the SSTable. But before we start scanning the SSTable or the index file, we can get some help from the sampled index in memory. Looking through the sampled index, Cassandra finds out that there exists a row key 400 and another, 624. So, the row fragments may be in this SSTable. But more importantly, the sampled index tells the offset about the 400 entry in the index file. Cassandra now scans the SSTable from 400 and gets to the entry for 404. This tells Cassandra the offset of the entry for the 404 key in SSTable and it reads from there. The following figure shows the Cassandra SSTable index in action:

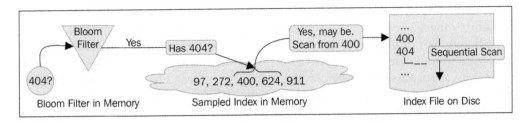

If you followed the example, you must have observed that the smaller the sampling size, the more the number of keys in the memory; the smaller the size of the block to read on the disk, the faster the results. This is a trade-off between memory usage and performance.

Data files

Data files are the actual data. They contain row keys, metadata, and columns (partial or full). Reading data from the data files is just one disk seek, followed by a sequential read, as the offset to a row key is already obtained from the associated index file.

Compaction

As we discussed earlier in the *Read in action* section, a read require may require Cassandra to read across multiple SSTables to get a result. This is wasteful, costs multiple (disk) seeks, may require a conflict resolution, and if there are too many SSTables, it may slow down the read. To handle this problem, Cassandra has a process in place, namely compaction. Compaction merges multiple SSTable files into one. Off the shelf, Cassandra offers two types of compaction mechanisms: size-tiered compaction strategy and level compaction strategy (refer to the *Read performance* section in *Chapter 5, Performance Tuning*). This section stays focused on a size-tiered compaction mechanism for better understanding.

The compaction process starts when the number of SSTables on disk reaches a certain threshold (configurable). Although the merge process is a little I/O intensive, it benefits in the long term with a lower number of disk seeks during reads. Apart from this, there are a few other benefits of compaction, as follows:

- Removal of expired tombstones (Cassandra v0.8+)
- Merging row fragments
- Rebuilds primary and secondary indexes

Merge is not as painful as it may seem because SSTables are already sorted. (Remember merge-sort?) Merge results into larger files, but old files are not deleted immediately. For example, let's say you have a compaction threshold set to four. Cassandra initially creates SSTables of the same size as MemTable. When the number of SSTables surpasses the threshold, the compaction thread triggers. This compacts the four equal-sized SSTables into one. Temporarily, you will have two times the total SSTable data on your disk. Another thing to note is that SSTables that get merged have the same size. So, when the four SSTables get merged to give a larger SSTable of size, say G, the buckets for the rest of the to-be-filled SSTables will be G each. So, the next compaction will take an even larger space while merging.

The SSTables, after merging, are marked as deletable. They get deleted at a garbage collection cycle of the JVM, or when Cassandra restarts.

The compaction process happens on each node and does not affect other nodes. This is called minor compaction. This is automatically triggered, system controlled, and regular. There is more than one type of compaction setting that exists in Cassandra. Another league of compaction is called, obviously, **major compaction**.

What's a major compaction? A major compaction takes all the SSTables, and merges them into one single SSTable. It is somewhat confusing when you see that a minor compaction merges SSTables and a major one does it too. There is a slight difference. For example, if we take the size-tiered compaction strategy, it merges the tables of the same size. So, if your threshold is four, Cassandra will start to merge when it finds four same sized SSTables. If your system starts with four SSTables of size X, after the compaction you will end up with one SSTable of size 4X. Next time when you have four X-sized SSTables, you will end up with two 4X tables, and so on. (These larger SSTables will get merged after 16 X-sized SSTables get merged into four 4X tables.) After a really long time, you will end up with a couple of really big SSTables, a handful of large SSTables, and many smaller SSTables. This is a result of continuous minor compaction. So, you may need to hop a couple of SSTables to get data for a query. Then, you run a major compaction and all the big and small SSTables get merged into one. This is the only benefit of major compaction.

Major compaction may not be the best idea after Cassandra v0.8+. There are a couple of reasons for this. One reason is that automated minor compaction no longer runs after a major compaction is executed. So, this adds up manual intervention or doing extra work (such as setting a cron job) to perform regular major compaction. The performance gain after major compaction may deteriorate with time. Probably because of the larger the SSTable, which is what we get after major compaction, it is more likely to get more bloom filter false positive. And then, it will take longer to perform binary search on the index, which is very big.

Tombstones

Cassandra is a complex system with its data distributed among commit logs, MemTables, and SSTables on a node. The same data is then replicated over replica nodes. So, like everything else in Cassandra, deletion is going to be eventful. Deletion, to an extent, follows an update pattern, except Cassandra tags the deleted data with a special value, and marks it as a tombstone. This marker helps future queries, compaction, and conflict resolution. Let's step further down and see what happens when a column from a column family is deleted.

A client connected to a node (a coordinator node may not be the one holding the data that we are going to mutate), issues a delete command for a column C, in a column family CF. If the consistency level is satisfied, the delete command gets processed. When a node, containing the row key receives a delete request, it updates or inserts the column in MemTable with a special value, namely tombstone. The tombstone basically has the same column name as the previous one; the value is set to the Unix epoch. The timestamp is set to what the client has passed. When a MemTable is flushed to SSTable, all tombstones go into it as any regular column will.

On the read side, when the data is read locally on the node and it happens to have multiple versions of it in different SSTables, they are compared and the latest value is taken as the result of reconciliation. If a tombstone turns out to be a result of reconciliation, it is made a part of the result that this node returns. So, at this level, if a query has a deleted column, this exists in the result. But the tombstones will eventually be filtered out of the result before returning it back to the client. So, a client can never see a value that is a tombstone.

For consistency levels more than one, the query is executed on as many replicas as the consistency level. The same as a regular read process, data from the closest node and a digest from the remaining nodes is obtained (to satisfy the consistency level). If there is a mismatch, such as the tombstone not yet being propagated to all the replicas, a partial read repair is triggered, where the final view of the data is sent to all the nodes that were involved in this read, to satisfy the consistency level.

One thing where `delete` differs from `update` is a compaction. A compaction removes a tombstone only if its (the tombstone's) garbage collection's grace seconds (t) are over. This t is called `gc_grace_seconds` (configurable). So, do not expect that a major deletion will free up a lot of space immediately.

What happens to a node that was holding data that was deleted (in other live replicas) when this node was down? If a tombstone still exists in any of the replica nodes, the delete information will eventually be available to the previously dead node. But a compaction occurs at `gc_grace_seconds`, after the deletion will kick the old tombstones out. This is a problem, because no information about the deleted column is left. Now, if a node that was dead all the time during `gc_grace_seconds` wakes up and sees that it has some data that no other node has, it will treat this data as fresh data, and assuming a write failure, it will replicate the data over all the other replica nodes. The old data will resurrect and replicate, and may reappear in client results.

`gc_grace_seconds` is 10 days by default, before which any sane system admin will bring the node back in, or discard the node completely. But it is something to watch out for and repair nodes occasionally.

Hinted handoff

When we last talked about durability, we observed that Cassandra provides a commit log to provide write durability. This is good. But what if the node, where the writes are going to be, is itself dead? No communication will keep anything new to be written to the node. Cassandra, inspired by Dynamo, has a feature called "hinted handoff". In short, it's the same as taking a quick note locally that X cannot be contacted; here is the mutation, M, that will be required to be replayed when it comes back.

The coordinator node (the node which the client is connected to) on receipt of a mutation/write request forwards it to appropriate replicas that are alive. If this fulfills the expected consistency level, the write is assumed successful. The write requests a node that does not respond to a write request or is known to be dead (via gossip) and is stored locally in the `system.hints` table. This hint contains the mutation. When a node comes to know, via gossip, that a node is recovered, it replays all the hints it has in store for that node. Also, every 10 minutes, it keeps checking any pending hinted handoffs to be written.

Why worry about hinted hand off when you have written to satisfy the consistency level? Wouldn't it eventually get repaired? Yes, that's right. Also, hinted handoff may not be the most reliable way to repair a missed write. What if the node that has hinted handoff dies? This is a reason we do not count on hinted handoff as a mechanism to provide consistency (except for the case of the consistency level, ANY) guarantee; it's a single point of failure. The purposes of hinted handoff are one- to make restored nodes quickly consistent with the other live ones; and two to provide extreme write availability when consistency is not required.

The way extreme write availability is obtained is at the cost of consistency. One can set consistency level for writes to ANY. What happens next is that if all the replicas that are meant to hold this value are down, Cassandra will just write a local hinted handoff and return write success to the client. There is one caveat; the handoff can be on any node. So, a read for the data that we have written as a hint will not be available as long as the replicas are dead plus until the hinted handoff is replayed. But it is a nice feature.

> There is a slight difference where hinted handoff is stored in Cassandra's different versions. Prior to Cassandra 1.0, hinted handoff is stored on one of the replica nodes that can be communicated with. From Version 1.0+ (including 1.0), handoff can be written on the coordinator node (the node that the client is connected to).

Removing a node from a cluster causes deletion of hinted handoff stored for that node. All hints for deleted records are dropped.

Read repair and anti-entropy

Cassandra promises eventual consistency and read repair is the process that does this part. Read repair, as the name suggests, is the process of fixing inconsistencies among the replicas at the time of read. What does that mean? Let's say we have three replica nodes, A, B, and C, that contain a data X. During an update, X is updated to X1 in replicas A and B, but it fails in replica C for some reason. On a read request for data X, the coordinator node asks for a full read from the nearest node (based on the configured snitch) and digest of data X from other nodes to satisfy consistency level. The coordinator node compares these values (something like digest(full_X) == digest_from_node_C). If it turns out that the digests are the same as the digests of the full read, the system is consistent and the value is returned to the client. On the other hand, if there is a mismatch, full data is retrieved and reconciliation is done and the client is sent the reconciled value. After this, in the background, all the replicas are updated with the reconciled value to have a consistent view of data on each node. The following figure shows this process:

- Client queries for data X, from a node C (coordinator)
- C gets data from replicas R1, R2, and R3 reconciles
- Sends reconciled data to client
- If there is a mismatch across replicas, a repair is invoked

The following figure shows the read repair dynamics:

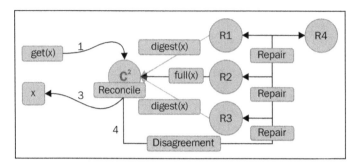

So, we have got a consistent view on read. What about the data that is inserted, but never read? Hinted handoff is there, but we do not rely on hinted handoff for consistency. What if the node containing hinted handoff data dies, and the data that contains the hint is never read? Is there a way to fix them without read? This brings us to the anti-entropy architecture of Cassandra (borrowed from Dynamo).

Anti-entropy compares all the replicas of a column family and updates the replicas to the latest version. This happens during major compaction. It uses Merkle trees to determine discrepancies among the replicas and fixes them.

Merkle tree

Merkle tree is a hash tree where leaves of the tree hashes hold actual data in column family and non-leaf nodes hold hashes of their children. For more information, refer to *A digital signature Based On A Conventional Encryption Function* by Merkle, R. (1988), available at http://link.springer.com/chapter/10.1007%2F3-540-48184-2_32. The unique advantage of a Merkle tree is that a whole subtree can be validated just by looking at the value of the parent node. So, if nodes on two replica servers have the same hash values, then the underlying data is consistent and there is no need to synchronize. If one node passes the whole Merkle tree of a column family to another node, it can determine all the inconsistencies.

The following figure shows the Merkle tree to determine a mismatch in hash values at the parent nodes due to the difference in the underlying data:

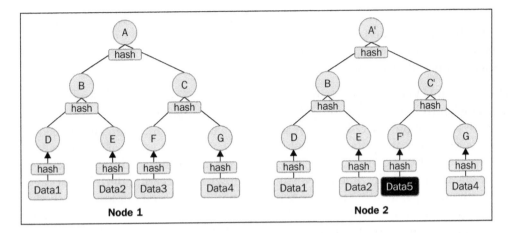

To exemplify this, the preceding figure shows the Merkle tree from two nodes with inconsistent data. A process comparing these two trees would know that there is something inconsistent, because the hash values stored in the top nodes do not match. It can descend down and knows that the right subtree is likely to have an inconsistency. And then, the same process is repeated until it finds out that all the data is mismatched.

Summary

By now, you should be familiar with all the nuts and bolts of Cassandra. We have discussed how the pressure to make data stores to web scale inspired a rather not-so-common database mechanism to become mainstream, and how the CAP theorem governs the behavior of such databases. We have seen that Cassandra shines out among its peers. Then, we dipped our toes into the big picture of Cassandra read and write mechanisms. This left us with lots of fancy terms. Furthermore, we looked into the definition of these words, the components that drive Cassandra, and their influence on its behavior.

It is understandable that it may be a lot to take in for someone new to NoSQL systems. It is okay if you do not have complete clarity at this point. As you start working with Cassandra, tweaking it, experimenting with it, and going through the Cassandra mailing list discussions or talks, you will start to come across stuff that you have read in this chapter and it will start to make sense, and perhaps you may want to come back and refer to this chapter to improve your clarity.

It is not required that you understand this chapter fully to be able to write queries, set up clusters, maintain clusters, or do anything else related to Cassandra. A general sense of this chapter will take you far enough to work extremely well with Cassandra-based projects.

How does this knowledge help us in building an application? Isn't it just about learning Thrift or CQL API and getting going? You might be wondering why you need to know about the compaction and storage mechanism, when all you need to do is to deliver an application that has a fast backend. It may not be obvious at this point why you are learning this, but as we move ahead with developing an application, we will come to realize that knowledge about underlying storage mechanism helps. In later chapters, when we will learn about deploying a cluster, performance tuning, maintenance, and integrating with other tools such as Apache Hadoop, you may find this chapter useful. At this point, we are ready to learn some of the commonly used cases, and how they utilize various features of Cassandra.

3
Effective CQL

This chapter will introduce you to the underlying data structure of tables in Cassandra. Let's set some development rules of thumb before we dive into CQL. With CQL 3, Cassandra development team has done a commendable job of almost entirely eliminating any chance of using an antipattern, and at the same time bringing an interface that is SQL people friendly.

If you are a developer, this is probably the most important chapter for you. You will get a sense of things that are possible and not possible when working with Cassandra. You may also want to refer *Chapter 8, Integration with Hadoop*, to understand how to use Cassandra with various big data technologies such as the Hadoop ecosystem and Spark/Shark.

When dealing with Cassandra, keep the following things in mind:

- **Denormalize, denormalize, and denormalize**: Forget about old school 3NF in Cassandra; the fewer the network trips, the better the performance. Denormalize wherever you can for quicker retrieval and let the application logic handle the responsibility of reliably updating all the redundancies.

- **Rows are gigantic and sorted**: The giga-sized rows (a row can accommodate 2 billion cells per partition) can be used to store sortable and sliceable columns. Need to sort comments by timestamp? Need to sort bids by quoted price? Put in a column with the appropriate comparator (you can always write your own comparator).

- **One row, one machine**: Each row stays on one machine. Rows are not sharded across nodes. So beware of this. A high-demand row may create a hotspot.

- **From query to model**: Unlike RDBMS, where you model most of the tables with entities in the application and then run analytical queries to get data out of it, Cassandra has no such provision. So you may need to denormalize your model in such a way that all your queries stay limited to a bunch of simple commands such as `get`, `slice`, `count`, `multi_get`, and some simple indexed searches.

The Cassandra data model

From Version 1.2 onwards, Cassandra has CQL as its primary way to access and alter the database. CQL is an abstraction layer that makes you feel like you are working with RDBMS, but the underlying data model does not support all the features that a traditional database or SQL provides. There is no group by, no relational integrity, foreign key constraints, and no join. There is some support for order, distinct, and triggers. There are things such as **time to live** (TTL) and write time functions. So Cassandra, like most of the NoSQL databases, is generally less featured compared to the number of features traditional databases provide.

Cassandra is designed for extremely high-read and high-write speed and horizontal scalability. Without some of the analytical features of traditional systems, developers need to work around Cassandra's shortcomings by planning ahead. In the Cassandra community, it is generally referred to as modeling the database based on what queries you will run in future. Let's take an example. If you have a people database and you wanted to draw a bar chart that shows the number of people from different cities, in Cassandra, you cannot just run the `select count(*), city from people group by city` statement. Instead, you will have to create a different table that has `city` as its primary key and a counter column that holds the number of records of persons. Every time a people record is added or removed, you increase or decrease the counter for the specific city. Understanding underlying the data structure can help you rationalize why Cassandra can or cannot do some things.

If you remove all the complexity, the data in Cassandra is stored in a nested hash map– a hash map containing another hash map. Realistically speaking, it is a distributed, nested, sorted hash map where the outer sorted hash map is distributed across the machines and the inner one stays on one machine. The following figure shows the Cassandra data model:

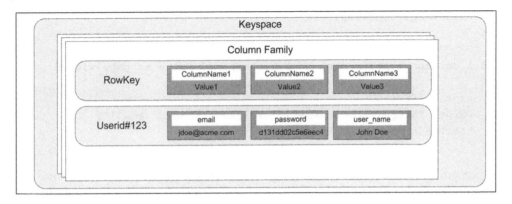

Cassandra has two ways of viewing its data: one is viewing data as maps within a map, the other is viewing it as a table. The former is the old way, and more closer to actually how the data is stored; and the latter is the new way, the way CQL represents the data. In this section, since we are trying to understand how the data is stored in Cassandra, we will go the old way. Then in the next section, we will see how this maps to CQL.

At the heart of Cassandra lies two structures: column family and cell. There is a container entity for these entities called keyspace.

> Previously, we used to call a cell a column. From Cassandra 1.2 onward, the nomenclature has been changed a bit to avoid confusion with columns as defined in CQL3. Columns in CQL3 are more in line with columns in the traditional database. "Column family" is the old name for a table. There is still a slight difference between the column family and table, but for the most part, we can use them interchangeably.

A cell is the smallest unit of the Cassandra data model. Cells are contained within a column family. A cell is essentially a key-value pair. The key of a cell is called **cell name** and value is called **cell value**. A cell can be represented as a triplet of the cell name, value, and timestamp. The timestamp is used to resolve conflicts during read repair or to reconcile two writes that happen to the same cell at the same time; the one written later wins. It's worth noting that the timestamp is client-supplied data, and since it is critical to write a resolution, it is a good idea to have all your client application servers clock synchronized. How? Read about **network time protocol daemon (NTPD)**.

```
# A column, which is much like a relational system
{
  name: "username",
  value: "Carl Sagan",
```

```
    timestamp: 1366048948904
}


# A column with its name as timestamp and value as page-viewed
{
  name: 1366049577,
  value: "http://foo.com/bar/view?itemId=123&ref=email",
  timestamp: 1366049578003
}
```

The preceding code snippet is an example of two cells; the first looks more like a traditional cell, and one would expect each row of the `users` column family to have one `username` cell. The latter is more like a dynamic cell. Its name is `timestamp` when a user accesses a web page, and the value is the URL of the page.

Later in this book, we'll ignore the `timestamp` field whenever we refer to a cell because it is generally not needed for application use, and is used by Cassandra internally. A cell can be viewed as shown in the following figure:

Representing a cell

The counter column (cell)

A counter column is a special purpose cell to keep count. A client application can increment or decrement it by an integer value. Counter columns cannot be mixed with regular or any other cell types (as of Cassandra v2.0.9). So, a counter column always lives in a table that has all the cells of type counter. Let's call this type of table a counter table. When we have to use a counter, we either plug it into an existing counter table or create a separate table with columns (CQL3 columns) as the counter type.

Counters require tight consistency, and this makes it a little complex for Cassandra. Under the hood, Cassandra tracks distributed counters and uses system-generated timestamps. So clock synchronization is crucial.

The counter tables behave a little differently than the regular ones. Cassandra makes a read once in the background when a write for a counter column occurs. So it reads the counter value before updating, which ensures that all the replicas are consistent. Since we know this little secret, we can leverage this property while writing since the data is always consistent. While writing to a counter column, we can use a consistency level of ONE. We know from *Chapter 2, Cassandra Architecture*, in the *Replication* topic that the lower the consistency level, the faster the read/write operation. The counter writes can be very fast without risking a false read.

 Clock synchronization can easily be achieved with NTPD (http://www.ntp.org). In general, it's a good idea to keep your servers in sync.

Here's an example of a table with counter columns in it and the way to update it:

```
cqlsh:mastering_cassandra> CREATE TABLE demo_counter_cols (city_name
varchar PRIMARY KEY, count_users counter, count_page_views counter);

cqlsh:mastering_cassandra> UPDATE demo_counter_cols SET count_users =
count_users + 1, count_page_views = count_page_views + 42 WHERE city_
name = 'newyork';

cqlsh:mastering_cassandra> UPDATE demo_counter_cols SET count_users =
count_users + 13  WHERE city_name = 'washingtondc';

cqlsh:mastering_cassandra> UPDATE demo_counter_cols SET count_users =
count_users + 1, count_page_views = count_page_views + 0 WHERE city_
name = 'baltimore';

cqlsh:mastering_cassandra> SELECT * FROM demo_counter_cols;
```

city_name	count_page_views	count_users
washingtondc	null	13
baltimore	0	1
newyork	42	1

```
(3 rows)

cqlsh:mastering_cassandra> UPDATE demo_counter_cols SET count_page_
views = count_page_views - 22 WHERE city_name = 'newyork';

cqlsh:mastering_cassandra> SELECT * FROM demo_counter_cols;
```

city_name	count_page_views	count_users
washingtondc	null	13
baltimore	0	1
newyork	20	1

(3 rows)

A couple of things to notice here. First, instead of using the INSERT statement, we have used the UPDATE statement to insert the data. If you try to insert, it will fail with an error saying, Bad Request: INSERT statement are not allowed on counter tables, use UPDATE instead. Second, an uninitiated column is set to null by default. You can initiate to any value just by passing an appropriate value in the UPDATE statement.

> Note that counter updates are not idempotent. In the event of a write failure, the client will have no idea if the write operation succeeded. A retry to update the counter columns may cause the columns to be updated twice—leading to the column value to be incremented or decremented by twice the value intended.

The expiring cell

Every once in a while, you find yourself in a situation where the data gets stale after a given time, and you want to delete it because it does not have a future value or will possibly mess up with the result set. One such example could be a user session object or a password reset request that expires in a day, or maybe you are streaming out word frequency analysis on tweets posted in the last week (moving average). Cassandra gives you the power to make any cell (and hence row) expire after a given time. And if later, before the data is expired, you want to further change the expiry time, you can do that too. This expiry time is commonly referred to as TTL.

On insertion or the update of a TTL-containing cell, the coordinator node sets a deletion timestamp by adding the current local time to the TTL provided. The column expires when the local time of a querying node goes past the set expiration timestamp. The deleted node is marked for deletion with a tombstone and is removed during a compaction after the expiration timestamp or during repair. Expiring columns take 8 bytes of extra space to record the TTL. Here's an example:

```
# Create a regular table
cqlsh:mastering_cassandra> CREATE TABLE demo_ttl ( id int PRIMARY KEY,
expirable_col varchar, column2 int );

# Insert data as usual
```

```
cqlsh:mastering_cassandra> INSERT INTO demo_ttl (id, expirable_col,
column2) VALUES (1, 'persistent_row', 10);
```

 # Insert a row with TTL equals to 30 seconds
```
cqlsh:mastering_cassandra> INSERT INTO demo_ttl (id, expirable_col,
column2) VALUES (2, 'row_with_30sec_TTL', 30) using TTL 30;
```
 # Observe decreasing TTL with time
```
cqlsh:mastering_cassandra> SELECT ttl(expirable_col), ttl(column2)
FROM demo_ttl WHERE id = 2;
```

```
 ttl(expirable_col) | ttl(column2)
--------------------+--------------
                 23 |           23


  (1 rows)
```

```
cqlsh:mastering_cassandra> SELECT ttl(expirable_col), ttl(column2)
FROM demo_ttl WHERE id = 2;
```

```
 ttl(expirable_col) | ttl(column2)
--------------------+--------------
                  2 |            2


(1 rows)
```

 # The row is deleted
```
cqlsh:mastering_cassandra> SELECT ttl(expirable_col), ttl(column2)
FROM demo_ttl WHERE id = 2;
```

```
(0 rows)
```

 # No row, no TTL, obviously
```
cqlsh:mastering_cassandra> SELECT ttl(expirable_col), ttl(column2)
FROM demo_ttl;
```

```
 ttl(expirable_col) | ttl(column2)
--------------------+--------------
               null |         null


(1 rows)
```

 # The TTL is not carried forward to new values on the same row that had a TTL previously

```
cqlsh:mastering_cassandra> INSERT INTO demo_ttl (id, expirable_col,
column2) VALUES (2, 'single_cell_TTL', 30);

cqlsh:mastering_cassandra> SELECT ttl(expirable_col), ttl(column2)
FROM demo_ttl WHERE id = 2;

 ttl(expirable_col) | ttl(column2)
--------------------+--------------
               null |         null

(1 rows)

# Setting TTL is CELL LEVEL, so you need to set it individually
cqlsh:mastering_cassandra> UPDATE demo_ttl USING TTL 60 SET expirable_
col = 'single_cell_TTL' WHERE id = 2;

cqlsh:mastering_cassandra> SELECT ttl(expirable_col), ttl(column2)
FROM demo_ttl WHERE id = 2;

 ttl(expirable_col) | ttl(column2)
--------------------+--------------
                 56 |         null

(1 rows)

# Only the cell with TTL is deleted
cqlsh:mastering_cassandra> SELECT * FROM demo_ttl;

 id | column2 | expirable_col
----+---------+----------------
  1 |      10 | persistent_row
  2 |      30 |           null

(2 rows)

# You CANNOT really just update TTL of a whole row without actually
manually updating each cell!
cqlsh:mastering_cassandra> UPDATE demo_ttl USING TTL 60 WHERE id = 2;

Bad Request: line 1:29 mismatched input 'WHERE' expecting K_SET

# You can reset a TTL
cqlsh:mastering_cassandra> INSERT INTO demo_ttl (id, expirable_col,
column2) VALUES (3, 'some_more_time_please', 40);
```

```
cqlsh:mastering_cassandra> UPDATE demo_ttl USING TTL 30 SET expirable_
col = 'some_more_time_please' WHERE id = 3;

cqlsh:mastering_cassandra> SELECT ttl(expirable_col) FROM demo_ttl
WHERE id = 3;

 ttl(expirable_col)
--------------------
                 12

(1 rows)
```

 # Do the same things that you do to assign a TTL

```
cqlsh:mastering_cassandra> UPDATE demo_ttl USING TTL 60 SET expirable_
col = 'some_more_time_please' WHERE id = 3;

cqlsh:mastering_cassandra> SELECT ttl(expirable_col) FROM demo_ttl
WHERE id = 3;

 ttl(expirable_col)
--------------------
                 59

(1 rows)
```

#Dismiss a TTL by setting it to zero

```
cqlsh:mastering_cassandra> UPDATE demo_ttl USING TTL 60 SET expirable_
col = 'some_more_time_please' WHERE id = 3;

cqlsh:mastering_cassandra> SELECT ttl(expirable_col) FROM demo_ttl
WHERE id = 3;

 ttl(expirable_col)
--------------------
                 55

(1 rows)

cqlsh:mastering_cassandra> UPDATE demo_ttl USING TTL 0 SET expirable_
col = 'some_more_time_please' WHERE id = 3;

cqlsh:mastering_cassandra> SELECT ttl(expirable_col) FROM demo_ttl
WHERE id = 3;

 ttl(expirable_col)
```

```
-------------------
             null

(1 rows)
```

The following are a few things to be noted about expiring columns:

- The TTL is in seconds, so the smallest TTL can be 1 second
- You can change the TTL by updating the column (that is, read the column, update the TTL, and insert the column)
- You can dismiss TTL by setting it to zero
- Although the client does not see the expired column, the space is kept occupied until the compaction process after `gc_grace_seconds` is triggered; but note that tombstones take a rather small space

Expiring cells can have some good uses; they remove the need for constantly watching cron-like tasks that delete the data that has expired or is not required any more. For example, an expiring shopping coupon or a user session can be stored with a TTL.

Where is my super column?

People who have used Cassandra in version 1.1 or older must have heard of a super column which is nothing but a cell that can have subcells. It was overly hyped and was considered bad practice, the reason being, it was not automatically sorted like other cells. You have to fetch all the subcolumns and it was adding unnecessary special casing in the Cassandra code base. From Cassandra 1.2 onward, super columns were removed. The Thrift request was still supported in 1.2, but it was internally using collections instead of subcolumns.

As we will see, Cassandra 2.0 and later versions have much richer, better, and faster ways to do all that you could do with super columns and more.

The column family

In CQL3 grammar, the column family and table are used interchangeably. In this particular section, when we say column family we mean the older representation of data storage. This representation is much closer to how the data is stored in Cassandra. We will discuss how this representation maps to the new CQL3 representation when we learn about CQL3 later in this chapter. Understanding this section will help you to understand concepts such as wide rows, and how collections work in CQL3.

A column family is a collection of rows where each row is a key-value pair. The key to a row is called a **row key** and the value is a sorted collection of cells. Essentially, a column family is a map with its keys as row keys and values as an ordered collection of cells.

Internally, each column family is stored in a file of its own, and there is no relational integrity between two column families. So you should keep all related information that the application might require in the column family.

In a column family, the row key is unique and serves as the primary key. It is used to identify and get/set records to a particular row of a column family.

Although a column family looks like a table from the relational database world, it is not. When you use CQL, it is treated as a table, but having an idea about the underlying structure helps in designing—how the cells are sorted, sliced, and persisted, and the fact that it's a schema-free map of maps. A dynamic column family showing daily hits on a website is displayed in the following figure. Each column represents a city and the column value is the number of hits from that city:

daily_hits				
2013-04-17	CA / 9502	LA / 102	NY / 31415	SF / 11011
2013-04-18	CA / 2	SF / 9		
• • •				

You can define a column family in such a way that it behaves as a standard RDBMS table or as a sequence of key-value pairs. The former is called **static** or **narrow column family** and the latter is known as **dynamic** or **wide row column family**. The concept of dynamic column family (table) is not overly stated in CQL3, but whenever you create a table with a compound key, you get a wide row. Let's demonstrate that.

To show how static tables and wide row tables differ in their underlying presentations, we will use `cassandra-cli`, a previous generation utility that uses the Thrift protocol to connect to Cassandra and assumes the column families are just sorted hash maps containing sorted hash maps.

Here's how you create a static column family:

```
# Using cqlsh
cqlsh:mastering_cassandra> CREATE TABLE demo_static_cf (id int PRIMARY
KEY, name varchar, age int);

cqlsh:mastering_cassandra> INSERT INTO demo_static_cf (id, name, age)
VALUES ( 1, 'Jennie', 39);

cqlsh:mastering_cassandra> INSERT INTO demo_static_cf (id, name, age)
VALUES ( 2, 'Samantha', 23);

cqlsh:mastering_cassandra> SELECT * FROM demo_static_cf;

 id | age | name
----+-----+----------
  1 |  39 |    Jennie
  2 |  23 |  Samantha

(2 rows)
```

This is how it is stored:

```
# View using cassandra-cli
[default@mastering_cassandra] LIST demo_static_cf;

Using default limit of 100
Using default cell limit of 100
-------------------
RowKey: 1
=> (name=, value=, timestamp=1410338723286000)
=> (name=age, value=00000027, timestamp=1410338723286000)
=> (name=name, value=4a656e6e6965, timestamp=1410338723286000)
-------------------

RowKey: 2
=> (name=, value=, timestamp=1410338757669000)
=> (name=age, value=00000017, timestamp=1410338757669000)
=> (name=name, value=53616d616e746861, timestamp=1410338757669000)

2 Rows Returned.

Elapsed time: 197 msec(s).
```

Pretty neat! Two rows with two different unique keys go into two different rows. So, the CQL representation is the same as the way the data is actually stored (Thrift representation). But this would not hold true for tables with a compound key. Here's how you create a table with a compound key:

```
# Using cqlsh
cqlsh:mastering_cassandra> CREATE TABLE demo_wide_row (id timestamp
, city varchar, hits counter, primary key(id, city)) WITH COMPACT
STORAGE;

cqlsh:mastering_cassandra> UPDATE  demo_wide_row SET hits = hits + 1
WHERE id = '2014-09-04+0000' AND city = 'NY';

cqlsh:mastering_cassandra> UPDATE  demo_wide_row SET hits = hits + 5
WHERE id = '2014-09-04+0000' AND city = 'Bethesda';

cqlsh:mastering_cassandra> UPDATE  demo_wide_row SET hits = hits + 2
WHERE id = '2014-09-04+0000' AND city = 'SF';

cqlsh:mastering_cassandra> UPDATE  demo_wide_row SET hits = hits + 3
WHERE id = '2014-09-05+0000' AND city = 'NY';

cqlsh:mastering_cassandra> UPDATE  demo_wide_row SET hits = hits + 1
WHERE id = '2014-09-05+0000' AND city = 'Baltimore';

cqlsh:mastering_cassandra> SELECT * FROM demo_wide_row;

 id                        | city      | hits
---------------------------+-----------+------
 2014-09-05 05:30:00+0530  | Baltimore |    1
 2014-09-05 05:30:00+0530  |        NY |    3
 2014-09-04 05:30:00+0530  |  Bethesda |    5
 2014-09-04 05:30:00+0530  |        NY |    1
 2014-09-04 05:30:00+0530  |        SF |    2

(5 rows)
```

One would expect that there should be five rows on a disk, but there are actually just two rows one for each unique ID. Here is what you get from `cassandra-cli`:

```
[default@mastering_cassandra] LIST demo_wide_row;

Using default limit of 100
Using default cell limit of 100

-------------------
```

```
RowKey: 2014-09-05 05:30+0530
=> (counter=Baltimore, value=1)
=> (counter=NY, value=3)
-------------------
RowKey: 2014-09-04 05:30+0530
=> (counter=Bethesda, value=5)
=> (counter=NY, value=1)
=> (counter=SF, value=2)


2 Rows Returned.

Elapsed time: 194 msec(s).
```

So why this discrepancy? We know that the data model of Cassandra is basically a hash map. When you create a table with a compound key, the first component of the key is treated as a row key and other components are treated as the cell name. This provides a couple of major benefits because unlike the row key, which is distributed across the machines, rows stay on one machine and are sorted by names. So, you can perform range queries as follows:

```
cqlsh:mastering_cassandra> SELECT * FROM demo_wide_row WHERE id =
'2014-09-04+0000' AND city > 'Baltimore' AND city < 'Rockville';

 id                        | city     | hits
---------------------------+----------+------
 2014-09-04 05:30:00+0530  | Bethesda |    5
 2014-09-04 05:30:00+0530  |       NY |    1


(2 rows)
```

However, this is not the only way to get range queries working. We will say later that we could do the same using a secondary index. So, why wide rows? Wide rows are traditionally useful for things like data series. An example of data series is time series where data is ordered by time such as a Twitter feed or Facebook timeline. In these cases, you may have user_id as a row key (partition key, which is the first component of a composite key), and timestamp as the cell names (the second component of a composite key), and the cell value is the data (a tweet or a timeline item).. It can be used to store sensor data in your Internet of Things application where row-key, cell name, and cell data are sensor ID, timestamp of data generated, and data from the sensor, respectively.

Keyspaces

Keyspaces are the outermost shells of Cassandra containers. It is the logical container of tables. It can be roughly imagined as a database of a relational database system. Its purpose is to group tables. In general, one application uses one keyspace, much like RDBMS.

Keyspaces hold properties such as replication factors and replica placement strategies, which are globally applied to all the tables in the keyspace. Keyspaces are global management points for an application.

Data types

Cassandra supports all data types any standard relational database supports and more. Here's the list of data types Cassandra 2.x supports:

CQL type	Java equivalent	Description
ascii	String	US-ASCII character string
bigint	Long	64-bit signed long
blob	ByteBuffer	Arbitrary bytes (no validation), expressed as hexadecimal (Java type: `java.nio.ByteBuffer`)
boolean	Boolean	True or false
counter	Long	Distributed counter value (64-bit long)
decimal	BigDecimal	Variable-precision decimal (Java type: `java.math.BigDecimal`)
double	Double	64-bit IEEE-754 floating point (Java type: `java.lang.Double`)
float	Float	32-bit IEEE-754 floating point (Java type: `java.lang.Float`)
inet	InetAddress	IP address string in IPv4 or IPv6 format, used by the python-cql driver and CQL native protocols (Java type: `java.net.InetAddress`)
int	Integer	32-bit signed integer
list	List<T>	A collection of one or more ordered elements (Java type: `java.util.List<T>`)
map	Map<K,V>	Map of unique key to value (Java type: `java.util.Map<K,V>`)
set	Set<T>	A collection of one or more elements (Java type: `java.util.Set<T>`)
text	String	UTF-8 encoded string

CQL type	Java equivalent	Description
timestamp	Date	Date plus time, encoded as 8 bytes since epoch
timeuuid	UUID	Type 1 UUID only
tuple	TupleType	Cassandra 2.1 and later; a group of 2-3 fields (Java type: `com.datastax.driver.core.TupleType`)
uuid	UUID	A UUID in the standard UUID format
varchar	String	UTF-8 encoded string
varint	BigInteger	Arbitrary-precision integer (Java type: `java.math.BigInteger`)

Apart from these data types, you can mix and match these data types to create your own data type much like a struct in the C language. We will see this later in this chapter when we discuss CQL3.

The primary index

A primary key or row key is the unique identifier of a row, in much the same way as the primary key of a table from a relational database system. It provides quick and random access to the rows. Since the rows are sharded (distributed) among the nodes, and each node just has a subset of rows, the primary keys are distributed too. Cassandra uses the partitioner (cluster-level setting) and replica placement strategy (keyspace-level setting) to locate the nodes that own a particular row. On a node, an index file and sample index is maintained locally and can be looked up via binary search followed by a short sequential read. (For more information, refer to *Chapter 2, Cassandra Architecture*.)

The problem with primary keys is that their location is governed by partitioners. Partitioners use a hash function to convert a row key into a unique number (called **token**) and then read/write happens from the node that owns this token. This means that if you use a partitioner that does not use a hash that follows the key's natural ordering, chances are that you can't sequentially read the keys just by accessing the next token on the node.

The following code snippet shows an example of this. The row keys `1234` and `1235` should naturally fall next to each other if they are not altered (or if an order preserving partitioner is used). However, if we take a consistent MD5 hash of these values, we can see that the two values are far away from each other. There's a good chance that they might not even live on the same machine. Here is an example of how two seemingly consecutive row keys have MD5 hash that is far apart:

```
ROW KEY | MD5 HASH VALUE
--------+------------------------------------
1234    | 81dc9bdb52d04dc20036dbd8313ed055
1235    | 9996535e07258a7bbfd8b132435c5962
```

Let's take an example of two partitioners: `ByteOrderPartitioner` that preserves lexical ordering by bytes, and `RandomPartitioner` that uses an MD5 hash to generate a row key. Let's assume that we have a `users_visits` table with a row key, `<city>_<userId>`. `ByteOrderPartioner` will let you iterate through rows to get more users from the same city in much the same way as a `SortedMap` interface does (for more detail, visit http://docs.oracle.com/javase/6/docs/api/java/util/SortedMap.html). However, in `RandomPartioner`, the key being the MD5 hash value of `<city>_<userId>`, the two consecutive `userIds` from the same city may be such that there are records for a different city in between. So, we cannot just iterate and expect grouping to work, like accessing entries of HashMap. (Ideally, you would not want to use a row key `<city>_<userId>` for grouping. You would create a compound key with `<city>` and `<userId>`. The purpose of the preceding example was just to show that consecutive row keys may have records between them.)

We will see partitioners in further detail in *Chapter 4, Deploying a Cluster*. But using the obviously better looking partitioner `ByteOrderPartitioner` is assumed to be a bad practice. There are a couple of reasons for this; the major reason being an uneven row key distribution across nodes. This can potentially cause a hotspot in the ring.

CQL3

CQL3 provides a SQL-like grammar to access data in a tabular manner. In the previous section, we saw how the data is actually stored in Cassandra. The CQL representation may not look like that especially when you use a composite key. In this section, we will discuss all the features of CQL3.

In this section, a typographic convention is used to indicate syntactic information. Here's the list of stylization used:

- Capital letter means literal or keyword.
- Curly brackets with the pipe character within them means that you must use at least one of those keywords in the query. Curly brackets are also used to specify a map, but they do not have the pipe character in them and they follow JSON notation.
- Square brackets show options settings.
- Lowercase means variables are to be provided by the developer.

Let's try to interpret an example:

```
CREATE { KEYSPACE | SCHEMA } [IF NOT EXISTS] keyspace_name

WITH REPLICATION = json_object

[AND DURABLE_WRITES = { true | false }]
```

The preceding query pattern suggests that after CREATE, we must use either KEYSPACE or SCHEMA followed by an optional IF NOT EXISTS setting, followed by the name of your choosing for the keyspace, followed by WITH REPLICATION. After this, you fill in a JSON object that specifies replication behavior and finally, we may choose to set DURABLE_WRITES. If we do choose to set DURABLE_WRITES, we must assign it a true or a false value.

Creating a keyspace

Keyspace is the logical container of tables just like a databaseor a schema in a RDBMS. Keyspace also holds some of the global settings applied to all the tables in it.

Cassandra needs two things from you to specify when creating a keyspace; one, the name of the keyspace, and the other is the replication strategy. Optionally, you can specify IF EXISTS clause if you are writing a script that adds tables to an existing keyspace and do not want to error out on the first line that creates the keyspace. You may want to specify whether you wanted a durable write. Note that switching off the durable write may be a bad idea. And generally, you would not want to disable durable write. While I agree that there is some performance gain by disabling durable write as it bypasses the commit log, it does so at the cost of possible data loss. You may get some performance gain just by moving commit log to a separate disk by changing the setting in cassandra.yaml. Here is how you create a keyspace:

```
CREATE { KEYSPACE | SCHEMA } [IF NOT EXISTS]
```

The REPLICATION setting takes a map. If you are using cqlsh, you need to type a JSON object to specify it. This setting is to specify how you want your data to be replicated across the nodes. There are two options to do this: SimpleStrategy and NetworkTopologyStrategy.

SimpleStrategy

SimpleStrategy is used when you have single data center or you want all nodes to be treated as they are in a single data center. In this setting, data is placed on one node and its replica is placed on the consecutive next node when moving clockwise (increasing token number side). SimpleStrategy is specified as follows:

```
{ 'class' : 'SimpleStrategy', 'replication_factor' : <positive_
integer> }
```

Here, <positive_integer> is the number of copies of data you want and it should be greater than zero.

NetworkTopologyStrategy

NetworkTopologyStrategy, as the name suggests, stores data depending on how the nodes are placed. Replicas should be stored on nodes that are on different racks in the data center to avoid a failure in case a rack dies. In this strategy, you can specify how many replicas you want in a data center if you have your nodes spanning across various data centers. It may be worth noting that each data center has a full set of data with specified replica. So, if you choose a DC1 to have the replication factor of 2 and DC2 to have the replication factor of 3, the whole corpus exists in DC1 and DC2 with DC1 having two copies of your data and DC2 having three. In the event of a complete data center failure, you can still work from the other data center.

This strategy is a recommended setting for production setup even if you have just one data center to start with. To specify this strategy, you should do the following:

```
{ 'class' : 'NetworkTopologyStrategy'[, '<datacenter_name>' :
<positive_integer>, '<datacenter_name>' : <positive_integer>, ...] }
```

Here are a couple of examples:

```
# Single data center, replication factor: 3
{ 'class' : 'NetworkTopologyStrategy', 'DC1' : 3}


# Three data centers, with RF as 3, 2, and 1
{ 'class' : 'NetworkTopologyStrategy', 'DC_NY' : 3, 'TokyoDC' : 2,
'DC_Hadoop': 1}


# Two data centers with three replica each
{ 'class' : 'NetworkTopologyStrategy', 'DC1' : 3, 'DC2' : 3}
```

Now, how would each node know which data center it belongs to? Snitch; you configure snitch in Cassandra's configuration file `cassandra.yaml`. We have already seen snitch and how it works and configured in *Chapter 2, Cassandra Architecture*, and we will see them again in *Chapter 4, Deploying a Cluster*.

Note that while you may still create a keyspace without any data center configuration when using `NetworkTopologyStrategy`, you may get an error when writing data to Cassandra.

Here are two examples of what your standard keyspace creation looks like:

```
# Keyspace with SimpleStrategy
CREATE KEYSPACE IF NOT EXISTS demo_keyspace
WITH REPLICATION = { 'class' : 'SimpleStrategy', 'replication_factor'
: 3 }


# Keyspace with NetworkTopologyStrategy
CREATE KEYSPACE IF NOT EXISTS demo_keyspace1
WITH REPLICATION = {'class': 'NetworkTopologyStrategy', 'DC1': 3,
'DC2': 1}


# Keyspace with no durable writes
CREATE KEYSPACE IF NOT EXISTS demo_keyspace2
WITH REPLICATION = {'class': 'NetworkTopologyStrategy', 'DC1': 3,
'DC2': 1}
AND DURABLE_WRITES = 'false'
```

Note that `class` and `replication_factor` in the REPLICATION setting must be in lowercase.

Altering a keyspace

You can alter keyspace properties like REPLICATION and DURABLE_WRITES, but the names cannot be altered. Here is the CQL syntax for that:

```
ALTER {KEYSPACE | SCHEMA} keyspace_name
WITH {
  REPLICATION = json_object |
  DURABLE_WRITES =  {true | false} |
  REPLICATION = json_object AND DURABLE_WRITES = {true | false}
}
```

Creating a table

Table creation in CQL3 is similar to how it's done in SQL. At the very least, you need to specify the table name, the name and types of the columns, and the primary key. The primary key can be single valued (made of a single column) or composite (made of more than one column). For more detail on keys, refer to the *A brief introduction to the data model* section in *Chapter 1, Quick Start*. In the former case, the primary key works as a partition key (or shard key). So, rows of such a table are distributed across the nodes based on the hash value of the primary key. In the latter case, where primary key constitutes of more than one column, the first column works as partition key. That means rows with same partition key stay in one wide row. (Refer to the *The column family* section.) This can be handy when you want to group things naturally. The following code snippet can be used to create a table:

```
CREATE TABLE [ IF NOT EXISTS ] [keyspace_name.]table_name
( column_definition, column_definition, ...)
[WITH property [ AND property ... ]]
```

Column definition, in most of the common cases, will be as follows:

```
column_name column_type [STATIC | PRIMARY KEY]
```

Let's take a look at the following example:

```
CREATE TABLE mytab (id int PRIMARY KEY, name varchar, article text,
is_paying_user boolean, phone_numbers set <varchar>);
```

You may define PRIMARY KEY separately, like we do in the case of the compound key:

```
CREATE TABLE team_match (city varchar, team_name varchar, is_
participating boolean, player_id set <int>, PRIMARY KEY(city, team_
name));
```

With Cassandra 2.1, you could create tables that have custom types, and on the same working principle it lets you create tuples. There is a special way to declare a tuple or custom type. You use the `frozen` keyword for them. The pattern is as follows:

```
column_name frozen<tuple<type [, type, ...]>> [PRIMARY KEY]
column_name frozen<user_defined_type> [PRIMARY KEY]
```

So, what does `frozen` signify? Cassandra serializes the tuple or user defined type into one cell. It may be noted that although the collections live in separate cells, if you have nested collections, the inner collections are serialized into one cell. This means when you update a user defined type or tuple, it pulls the whole thing, updates it, and inserts it again. But Cassandra might allow individual updates in version 3.0 and above. So, the `frozen` keyword is just a safety feature to avoid conflicts when you migrate to the third version. For now, you cannot create a column of user defined type, or tuple type without adding the `frozen` keyword. For more details on `frozen`, look at the Jira ticket (`https://issues.apache.org/jira/browse/CASSANDRA-7857`). Let's see the `frozen` keyword in action:

```
cqlsh:demo_cql> CREATE TYPE address (line1 varchar, line2 varchar,
city varchar, state varchar, postalcode int);

cqlsh:demo_cql> CREATE TABLE customer (id int PRIMARY KEY, name
varchar, addr address);

code=2200 [Invalid query] message="Non-frozen User-Defined types are
not supported, please use frozen<>"

cqlsh:demo_cql> CREATE TABLE customer (id int PRIMARY KEY, name
varchar, addr frozen<address>);

cqlsh:demo_cql> CREATE TABLE purchase_ability(id int PRIMARY KEY,
customer_id int, purchase_rating tuple<float, float, int, boolean>);

code=2200 [Invalid query] message="Non-frozen tuples are not
supported, please use frozen<>"

cqlsh:demo_cql> CREATE TABLE purchase_ability(id int PRIMARY KEY,
customer_id int, purchase_rating frozen<tuple<float, float, int,
boolean>>);
```

You can specify a non-clustering column as static and this column stays static across all the rows with the same partition key (row key). This only applies to the columns not involved in compound key. The static column does not make sense in a setting where you do not have a compound key because in those cases, you have row key as the primary key and hence each row lives in a separate partition, so each column is essentially a static column. Here's an example:

```
# We wanted to have one university per ID
CREATE TABLE static_col (id int, city varchar, university varchar
static, name varchar, PRIMARY KEY(id, city));

# Insert some data
INSERT INTO static_col (id, city, university, name ) VALUES ( 1,
'Seattle', 'Seattle University', 'Barry Kriple');
INSERT INTO static_col (id, city, university, name ) VALUES ( 2,
'Washington', 'Washington University', 'Rose Byrne');

INSERT INTO static_col (id, city, university, name ) VALUES ( 1,
'Washington', 'Seattle University', 'Nick Jonas');

# So far so good
SELECT * FROM static_col;
```

```
 id | city        | university            | name

----+-------------+-----------------------+--------------
  1 |     Seattle |     Seattle University | Barry Kriple
  1 |  Washington |     Seattle University |   Nick Jonas
  2 |  Washington |  Washington University |   Rose Byrne

(3 rows)
```

```
# Just insert another record to id=1 with a different university name
INSERT INTO static_col (id, city, university, name ) VALUES ( 1, 'New
York', 'Coursera', 'John Hacker Doe');

# All the records in that row key are updated
cqlsh:demo_cql> SELECT * FROM static_col;
```

```
 id | city        | university            | name

----+-------------+-----------------------+-----------------
  1 |    New York |              Coursera | John Hacker Doe
  1 |     Seattle |              Coursera |     Barry Kriple
  1 |  Washington |              Coursera |       Nick Jonas
  2 |  Washington | Washington University |       Rose Byrne
```

(4 rows)

The static column can be useful when you want to store a common global record of a column across all the records that share the same row key. It can be thought of as a static variable in Java, which is shared among all the instances of the class. An application of such a case could be a game where you are given initial credit coins, and you can use these coins to purchase things in the game. When you buy something, a purchase record is added with `balance_coins` as the static column. However, one might argue to use counter, which makes sense. Another example could be a static `Set<text>` to keep a set of ever changing tags of a product of a category available to all the products. For more rationale on static type, you can review the Jira ticket for this feature at `https://issues.apache.org/jira/browse/CASSANDRA-6561`.

Table properties

Table or column family is the center of the Cassandra universe. CQL3 provides you with options to tweak things to meet your requirements—both performance and functional, both. Here's a list of attributes that you set as your table properties.

As discussed in *Chapter 2, Cassandra Architecture*, the bloom filter is an in memory data structure to test whether the requested row exists in an SSTable before making a disk seek. It's a neat idea to avoid hitting disk read and hence reduces latency. The bloom filter is a probabilistic data structure and it may return a false positive result when asked. That means, when you ask a bloom filter if the SSTable it is associated with has a row it may say yes, while the SSTable does not have the row. But if it says no, the SSTable definitely does not have the row. You can configure the probability of getting the false positive result by setting `bloom_filter_fp_chance`. The tradeoff is that the lower the value of false-positive probability, the higher the amount of memory the bloom filter will consume. So, you can set `bloom_filter_fp_chance` to 0 for no false positive result, which will result in the largest bloom filter array for the table.

On the other hand, you can set it to 1, to say you want all false positive results, basically disabling the bloom filter. In practice, you would not want any of those extreme cases. The recommended and default value is 0.01 (if you choose LeveledCompactionStrategy, the default value get set to 0.1). Ideally, you wouldn't touch this configuration unless you are really concerned about 10 percent reads that might be hitting the disk. Let's take a look at the following example:

```
CREATE TABLE tiny_tiny_table (
  tab_id uuid,
  tab_details text,
  PRIMARY KEY (tab_id)
) WITH bloom_filter_fp_chance = 0.001;
```

If you have caching enabled in cassandra.yaml, Cassandra automatically caches data based on frequency of its access and size of the data. You can tune it for individual tables if you want. All you need to do is to specify caching in table creation or update CQL.

There are two types of caching: row caching, which is similar to the caching that object-relational mappers provide on top of RDBMS. Row caching caches the whole row and returns it from the memory if it is cached. The data gets cached after its first access. The other type of caching is key caching where just the key is cached in the memory. It takes much smaller memory, so we can have lots of keys caches without burning a lot of memory. Unlike row caching, this does require a disk seek to read the actual data. But data retrieval is much more efficient with key caching enabled than without it. It is suggested to keep key caching on unless you have a specific reason not to.

If you are using Cassandra 2.1, you can set both the caching individually using the following property:

```
caching = { 'keys' : '{NONE|ALL}', 'rows_per_partition' :
'{NONE|ALL|positive_int}' };
```

Here's an example:

```
CREATE TABLE searched_pages (
  page_id uuid,
  page_text text,
  metadata text,
  advertisement_count int,
  PRIMARY KEY (page_id)
) WITH caching = { 'keys' : 'ALL', 'rows_per_partition' : '31415' };
```

For Cassandra 2.0.x releases, the query looks a bit different. You specify it as
`caching = {'all'|'keys_only'|'rows_only'|'none'}`.

Here's an example:

```
CREATE TABLE searched_pages (
  page_id uuid,
  page_text text,
  metadata text,
  advertisement_count int,
  PRIMARY KEY (page_id)
) WITH caching = 'keys_only';
```

As you can see here, in Cassandra 2.0.x, we cannot set the number of rows per partition to be cached. By default, Cassandra has key caching enabled.

You can add comments to describe the specifics of a table to clarify the purpose of the table. Here's an example:

```
CREATE TABLE pigeon_hole (
  pigeon_id uuid,
  pigeon_offense text,
  pigeon_age int,
  is_it_a_fun_pigeon boolean,
  PRIMARY KEY(pigeon_id)
) WITH comment = 'Pigeon hole is a table for criminal pigeons. They
cannot see or talk to each other but if they are fun, we may want to
feed them once in a while';
```

As we know from *Chapter 2, Cassandra Architecture*, Memtables eventually get flushed to disk as immutable SSTables. But with time, we get lots of SSTables that may make data retrieval slow, and data mutation operations such as `update` and `delete` render rows living in an old SSTable useless. Cassandra performs compaction where it merges SSTables to solve these issues. We will see compaction in a little more detail in *Chapter 5, Performance Tuning*. For now, you should know that there are two types of compaction strategies:

- `SizeTieredCompactionStrategy`: This favors a write-intensive load where updates are less frequent.

- `LeveledCompactionStrategy`: Inspired by Google's LevelDB, this strategy is good for the cases where data is mutated more frequently. This strategy is a bit disk I/O intensive.

An example of setting a compaction strategy is as follows:

```
CREATE TABLE compaction_demo (id uuid PRIMARY KEY, name varchar)
WITH
COMPACTION  = {
'class': 'SizeTieredCompactionStrategy',
'tombstone_compaction_interval':43200,
'tombstone_threshold': 0.1
};
```

As you can see in the preceding code snippet, we have specified some other properties that are related to compaction in the query. Cassandra provides a very detailed configuration parameter to tweak the way you want the compaction process to take place. Here's the list of properties that you can specify within the JSON object for the COMPACTION keyword:

- enabled: This takes a Boolean value. This property tells Cassandra to enable or disable compaction on the particular table. You would probably never want to disable it, so likely you are not going to use it.

- tombstone_threshold: This is the ratio of cells (columns) in an SSTable that are eligible for deletion (garbage collectable) to the total number of columns in the SSTable. Essentially, it is the percentage of discarded columns in the SSTable expressed in decimal. By default, when 20 percent of SSTable columns become garbage collectable, it becomes a candidate for tombstone_compaction.

- tombstone_compaction_interval: This is the minimum amount of wait time (in seconds) before the SSTable is considered for tombstone compaction. If tombstone_threshold is reached, the SSTable is compacted; otherwise, Cassandra retries again after tombstone_compaction_interval. So, it may not be wise to set this value too small. The default is 86400 seconds (one day).

- unchecked_tombstone_compaction: If the data from the partition that the tombstone belongs to exists in other data files, the tombstone cannot be discarded; it works as an indicator of deletion. This check is performed every time before a tombstone compaction is attempted. This is extra work and is exactly why you would not want to keep tombstone_compaction_interval too low. By setting this option as true, you are telling Cassandra to try to compact without performing this check. Compaction may fail in this case, but if you have a situation where you have immutable rows that get discarded as a whole, you may opt for this option.

- `min_sstable_size` (specific to `SizeTieredCompactionStrategy`): This defines SSTables of similar sizes into one big SSTable. So, one can think of the compaction process as bucketed or batch process where SSTables that fall into one bucket get merged into one. If your SSTables are really small, you may end up in many tiny buckets, which may be inefficient. `min_sstable_size` is to specify the minimum size of SSTable, below which, all the SSTables are assumed to be in one bucket and compacted. The unit of `min_sstable_size` is bytes and the default value is 50 MB.

- `min_threshold` and `max_threshold` (specific to `SizeTieredCompactionStrategy`): This defines the minimum number of similar sized SSTables to start compaction. `max_threshold` is the maximum number of SSTables to consider in a compaction process. The default value of `min_threshold` is 4 and the default value of `max_threshold` is 32.

- `bucket_high` and `bucket_low` (specific to `SizeTieredCompactionStrategy`): When we mentioned similar sizes in the previous point, what we meant is explained here. A set of SSTables are assumed to be in the same bucket to be compacted if their size lies within the range described by this formula: `[average_size*bucket_low, average_size*bucket_high]`. Ideally, `bucket_low` should be a positive decimal fraction value less than one, and `bucket_high` is a decimal fraction more than one. Default values for `bucket_low` and `bucket_high` are 0.5 and 1.5 respectively.

- `cold_reads_to_omit` (specific to `SizeTieredCompactionStrategy`): Cassandra keeps track of which SSTable contributes to how many reads. So there may be cases where some SSTables contribute very little to nothing to the reads. It may not be worth the additional effort to compact those "cold" SSTables because they are accessed once in a while. For example, you have a table that has total 200 reads per second overall, of which 100 are contributed by SSTable S1, 85 by S2, 10 by S3, and 5 by S4. If you have `cold_reads_to_omit` as 0.1, then SSTables that cumulatively contribute to 200*0.1 or 20 reads will not be considered for compaction. Adding from the tiniest ones, S4 and S3 contribute to only 15 reads per second, so they will not be considered a candidate for compaction. Values for `cold_reads_to_omit` can be anything between 0.0 and to 1. However, you would not want to set it to 1, ignoring all the SSTables. Setting it to zero disabled discriminating the SSTables' eligibility to compact based on its contribution in reads. The default in Cassandra 2.1 and onwards is 0.05 and in the previous versions it is 0.

- `sstable_size_in_mb` (specific to `LeveledCompactionStrategy`): This is the target size for SSTable in `LeveledCompactionStrategy`. Cassandra tries to keep SSTable size less than or equal to this value, but SSTable may be larger than this value in exceptional cases where a partition key holds very large data. The default value is 160 MB.

- `Compression`: There are three compression algorithms available in Cassandra out of the box, `LZ4Compressor`, `SnappyCompressor`, and `DeflateCompressor`, in the decreasing order of read performance and increasing order disk space saving. So, why would one want a degraded performance for disk space? Consider a case where you have a table just for archival purposes. Here's an example of setting compression:

```
CREATE TABLE compression_demo (id uuid PRIMARY KEY, name varchar)
WITH
COMPRESSION = {
'sstable_compression': 'SnappyCompressor',
'chunk_length_kb': 128
};
```

To disable compression, use the empty string (`' '`) as the value for the `sstable_compression` attribute. Compression has a couple of other properties that can be tuned:

- `chunk_length_kb`: A chunk is the minimum quantum of data that is read by Cassandra. Depending on how much data is read on an average and the mean size of the rows of the table, this property may be tweaked. The higher value for this may improve compression performance, but it will also increase the minimum size of data read. In general, you wouldn't touch the default value of 64, unless you are familiar with data and its access pattern in the future.

- `crc_check_chance`: Cyclic Redundancy Check or CRC is a way to validate if the uncompressed data is exactly the same as the original. In cases when you have compression enabled for a table, each compressed block holds a checksum for CRC to avoid any data corruption. This property tells the probability by which reads are verified for any errors. By default, it is set to 1, so all reads are first validated for data integrity. If it is set to 0.25, every fourth read is validated.

- `time_to_live`: You have seen previously in this chapter that you can set TTL for individual row or cell, but there may be cases where you want all the rows to be deleted after some time. For example, if you have a table that is used to aggregate data for the last 24 hours, you may just want to keep the data for the last 24 hours or may be a little bit longer. You can do this by specifying `default_time_to_live` in seconds when creating or updating a table. To disable TTL, set this property to 0. The default is zero.

```
CREATE TABLE ttl_demo (id uuid PRIMARY KEY, name varchar)
WITH
default_time_to_live = 86400;
```

- `read_repair_chance`: The `dc_local_read_repair_chance` specifies the probability of performing a repair (making all replicas consistent) only in the data center that received the read request. If it is set to 0.25, every fourth read request will sync the whole data center. The default is 0.1.

  There is a global version of `dc_local_read_repair_chance`, that is, `read_repair_chance`. The `read_repair_chance` denotes the probability by which repairs across all the data centers take place. By default, this value is set to zero.

- `gc_grace_seconds`: When a cell or a row is deleted, it is marked so by writing a tombstone. These tombstones aren't immediately removed on compaction. Tombstones live till `gc_grace_seconds` before they become eligible to be removed. The reason for the wait is to avoid deleted data from respawning. You may ask how does it respawn. Let us assume that tombstones get removed immediately. This is fine when all nodes are up. In a case where there is a dead node carrying the data that was deleted, comes an issue. When the dead node comes back to the life, it communicates with the other nodes to repair data. Since there is no information about the deleted data as there is no tombstone, the dead node thinks it has the only copy of the data, and it updates all the other nodes with the data that should have been deleted. This would cause resurrection of a deleted record, which would be undesired. The default `gc_grace_seconds` is 864,000 or 10 days, which is probably enough time to notice a dead node and take appropriate action before garbage collection begins. On a single node setup this may be set to zero.

- `index_interval`: Each SSTable has an index summary loaded in the memory that keeps a sample of row keys index in that SSTable. Cassandra 2.0.x releases have a parameter named `index_interval` that basically dictates the number of primary key or row key skipped in the sample. The default value for this is 128. This means that the index of every 128th record in the SSTable is kept in memory. Talking of trade off, obviously the smaller the `index_interval`, the larger the number of rows indexes store in memory, which means a larger memory footprint and faster row retrieval.

Cassandra 2.1.0 and onwards, introduced two intervals: `min_index_interval` and `max_index_interval`. This is slightly smarter than the previous version. Based on the frequency of access of an SSTable, it determines the index interval to use. So, for a rarely accessed SSTable, the index interval will be equal to `max_index_interval`, and for an in-demand SSTable, the index interval will be `min_index_interval`. For the SSTables that are neither in high demand nor in low demand, the index interval will be set to somewhere between the min and max values. The index interval also depends on the availability of free memory in the index summary memory pool.

- `memtable_flush_period`: Memtables are serialized to SSTable after a time period defined by this attribute. This represents the number of milliseconds after which a Memtable is forced to be flushed to the disk. The default is zero.

- `replicate_on_write`: This is the only feature in Cassandra 2.0.x. When `replicate_on_write` is set to `true`, the data is written to all the replicas irrespective of the consistency level setting. It is true for counter tables by default.

- `speculative_retry`: Cassandra makes only as many requests as consistency level dictates. If a node dies during a read, Cassandra waits till timeout and then responds with a timeout error message. With `speculative_retry`, Cassandra avoids failure by sensing the unusual delay that a replica takes, and retries on a different replica. Here are the available settings:

  - `ALWAYS`: Cassandra reads from all the replicas and returns as soon as the consistency level is met.

  - `Xpercentile`: Retry triggers if the read operation takes more time than what the fastest X percent of reads took in the past. For example, if it is set to `99percentile`, the retry will trigger if a read operation takes more time than the fastest 99 percent of the queries took.

  - `Xms`: Retry triggers if the read did not return after X milliseconds of sending the request. So, if you wanted a speculative retry to happen if a replica did not respond in under 42 ms, set `speculative_retry` to `42 ms`.

  - `NONE`: No retries.

Here's an example:

```
CREATE TABLE speculative_retries_demo (id uuid PRIMARY KEY, name
varchar)
WITH
speculative_retry = '99percentile';
```

Altering a table

Altering a table is similar to creating one. You can add, rename, change type, drop columns, and you can also change various table properties that we saw in the previous section. Let's take a simple table and play with it:

```
CREATE TABLE modify_me (id uuid PRIMARY KEY, name varchar);
```

Adding a column

Adding a column has a syntax as follows:

```
ALTER TABLE table_name ADD new_column_name column_type;
```

However, you cannot mix a counter column in a non-counter table. Let's take a look at the following examples:

```
ALTER TABLE modify_me ADD phone_numbers map <varchar, varchar>;
```

```
ALTER TABLE modify_me ADD count_sheep counter;
```

```
<ErrorMessage code=2300 [Query invalid because of configuration issue]
message="Cannot add a counter column (count_sheep) in a non counter
column family">
```

Renaming a column

Renaming has very limited capability. Cassandra 2.1.0 only allows renaming columns that are a part of a primary key. The syntax is as follows:

```
ALTER TABLE table_name RENAME old_name TO new_name;
```

Changing the data type

Changing the data type of a column is possible as long the new data type is compatible with the old (existing) one, ideally superset. For example, ASCII can be converted to VARCHAR and VARCHAR to TEXT. Here's an example:

```
# A table with a clustering column and index
CREATE TABLE type_changer (id int, name ascii, age ascii, primary
key(id, age));

CREATE INDEX tc_idx ON type_changer (name);


# Alter the clustering column
```

```
ALTER TABLE type_changer ALTER age TYPE varchar;


# Insert some data
INSERT INTO type_changer (id, age, name) VALUES ( 1, '12',
'Mercedes');


# Alter everything
ALTER TABLE type_changer ALTER age TYPE text;
ALTER TABLE type_changer ALTER name TYPE varchar;
ALTER TABLE type_changer ALTER id TYPE varint;
```

Dropping a column

Dropping an existing column is simple. Adding the dropped column again does not bring the data back. You drop a column as follows:

```
ALTER TABLE table_name DROP column_name;
```

Updating the table properties

Table properties can be updated the same way they are done when the table is created. Here is the query format:

```
ALTER TABLE table_name WITH property [ AND property ...];
```

Let's take a look at the following example:

```
ALTER TABLE modify_me
WITH
default_time_to_live = 3600
AND
compaction = {
'class': 'LeveledCompactionStrategy',
'sstable_size_in_mb': 314
}
AND
speculative_retry = '75percentile'
AND
comment = 'New and improved formula';
```

Dropping a table

Dropping a table is the simplest of all the commands. All you have to do is execute a query in the following pattern:

```
DROP TABLE IF EXISTS table_name;
```

Creating an index

Unlike relational databases, if you try to perform a search on a column that is not the primary key, it will not work. One may argue the feasibility of going through all the rows sequentially and finding out the records matching the criteria, but Cassandra is meant for large datasets and performing a linear search on hundreds of gigabytes of records is just impractical. Allowing so may cause malpractice. So, consider a simple table like this:

```
SELECT * FROM searchable_tab;
 id | age | name         | phones
----+-----+--------------+------------------------------------------
  1 |  21 |  Misa Amane  | {'111-222-3333', '111-223-4444'
  2 |  26 | Light Yagami |                       {'111-277-0563'}
  3 | 666 |         Ryuk |                       {'000-000-0000'}

(3 rows)
```

Here, a simple query like this wouldn't work:

```
SELECT * FROM searchable_tab WHERE name = 'Light Yagami';

code=2200 [Invalid query] message="No indexed columns present in by-
columns clause with Equal operator"
```

So, we create index on that to make this search work:

```
CREATE INDEX searchable_tab_name_idx ON searchable_tab (name);
SELECT * FROM searchable_tab WHERE name = 'Light Yagami';


 id | age | name         | phones
----+-----+--------------+------------------
  2 |  26 | Light Yagami | {'111-277-0563'}

(1 rows)
```

Indexes are of great help in Cassandra. So why not just go ahead and create indexes for all the columns? There are a couple of reasons to that. First, indexes are not free. Indexes are maintained in separate columns' families, and extra work is needed to be done every time one mutates a column that has an index on it. The second thing is cardinality, which is true to the database indexes in general. The way Cassandra stores indexes is by creating a reverse index in a separate table; let's call it an index table. Let's also define the table on which the index is created as a parent table. The index table can be assumed as a table with very large rows where each cell can have any arbitrary name. (Traditionally, this is a wide row column family.) The index table contains primary keys of the parent table as the cell names and the values of the column of the parent table as primary keys. Let's see an example of a table with the primary key as `user_id` and an indexed column, `city`:

```
user_id | city
-----------+---------------------------
1          | Cape Town
2          | Kabul
3          | Mogadishu
4          | Cape Town
5          | Baghdad
6          | Kabul
```

The index table will look like this:

```
Baghdad              |  5  |
-------------------+-------------------------------------------
Cape Town            |  1  |   4  |
-------------------+-------------------------------------------
Kabul                |  2  |   6  |
-------------------+-------------------------------------------
Mogadishu            |  3  |
-------------------+-------------------------------------------
```

So, indexes are basically wide-rows or dynamic rows with row keys as values in the column being indexed (remember wide rows from the previous section?). These indexes are stored locally, which means an index table on node X will have an index created only for the rows that exist on node X. This means, every search that includes an indexed column makes a query on the index table on all the nodes, but do not worry about it, it is fast. The other things that you should keep in mind are as follows:

- **Avoid high cardinality columns**: Cardinality is the number of unique values. In our user's case, we have 40,000 or fewer cities across the world. If you have 40 million users, you have 1,000 users per city on average. If you have 25 nodes, you are making 25 reads (one on each node) from the index table, and then 1,000 reads for 1,000 rows. This looks okay; 1,025 reads for 1,000 records is about one read per record. Cities compared to users have low cardinality, so this helps us to optimize a read request. What happens when we use something that has high cardinality? Let's say we use the user's phone number as the index. Each user has a unique phone number. So, it is likely that when we search by phone number, we will get at most one record. The read process makes 25 read requests to the nodes to look into their local indexes; then if it exists, it will make one read request to the node that has the row. So, we are basically making 26 read requests read one row.

  We have seen that high cardinality columns are not good for indexes and hence, we should avoid them. It may be acceptable if it is a very low volume query (accessed once in a while), but it may be wise to create another table manually that has a phone number as the row key (primary key) and one of the columns as `user_id` from the `users` table. This way, we will make two read request fetch one record. The downside of this approach is, it is an extra effort on the developer side.

- **Extremely low cardinality might not add any value**: Extremely low cardinality like a Boolean field (cardinality: 2), or the number of seasons (cardinality: 4) may not be a good choice as it does not effectively reduce the number of rows to be pulled drastically. If you have a Boolean column and create an index on it, you will end up in two gigantic rows in your index table, one for true and another for false. If the data is evenly distributed for this column, each row in the index table will hold 50 percent of the rows. For a 40 million record table, you might end up pulling 20 million records, which might bog down the servers.

- **Extremely frequently updated or deleted columns are a bad choice**:
  Cassandra queries fail when tombstone counts exceed the configured value
  (default: 100,000 cells). This means that if you have a very fast changing
  column, it may not be the best idea to use it as an index column. This may
  change in future. For more information, visit `https://issues.apache.org/`
  `jira/browse/CASSANDRA-6117`.

After understanding the introduction , let's now see the index creation syntax:

```
CREATE [ CUSTOM ] INDEX [ IF NOT EXISTS ] [ index_name]
ON table_name ( { KEYS ( column_name ) | column_name } )
[ USING class_name ] [ WITH OPTIONS = json_object ];
```

As usual, `IF NOT EXISTS` is to avoid an error in case it already exists. Most
commonly, the version is used as follows:

```
CREATE INDEX IF NOT EXISTS my_simple_index
ON my_table(my_column);
```

Note that from Cassandra 2.1 onward, you are able to create an index on collections
as well. In case of map, by default, the index is created on map values. To create an
index on map keys, you will have to use the KEYS keyword. Here are some examples:

```
CREATE TABLE index_demo (id int PRIMARY KEY, name text, age int,
address map<text, text>, phones set <text>);
CREATE INDEX IF NOT EXISTS index_demo_name_idx ON index_demo (name);
CREATE INDEX index_demo_age_idx ON index_demo (age);
CREATE INDEX IF NOT EXISTS index_demo_phones_idx ON index_demo
(phones);
CREATE INDEX IF NOT EXISTS index_demo_address_key_idx ON index_demo
(KEYS(address));
CREATE INDEX IF NOT EXISTS index_demo_address_val_idx ON index_demo
(address);
code=2200 [Invalid query] message="Cannot create index on address
values, an index on address keys already exists and indexing a map on
both keys and values at the same time is not currently supported"
```

Something worth noticing; you can create an index on map keys or map values, but
not on both.

Also, the preceding example, with all the columns having indexes, is made up. The
decision to create an index is usually a requirement-driven one; so you may decide to
create an index later in the application development when you actually need it.

Cassandra allows users to create a custom indexing algorithm. You can create your own indexing mechanism, wrap it into a jar, and drop it into Cassandra's `lib` folder. You will have to mention the details of this new index when you are creating an index. The options can be used to pass parameters to the class. The CUSTOM, USING, and OPTIONS keywords are for the custom index. Here's an example:

```
CREATE CUSTOM INDEX index_name
ON
table_name (column_name)
USING 'fully.qualified.index.class.Name'
WITH OPTIONS = {
'param1': 'val1',
'param2': 'val2'
};
```

Dropping an index

Dropping an index is simple:

```
DROP INDEX [ IF EXISTS ] index_name;
```

You may have noticed that you can create indexes without providing a name. For those cases, Cassandra assigned an automated name that has the following pattern:

```
{table_name}_{column_name}_idx;
```

So, for an unnamed index on the `users` table on the `browsing_history` column, you would use the following query:

```
DROP INDEX IF EXISTS users_browsing_history_idx;
```

Creating a data type

Cassandra gives you freedom to compose your own data type using the basic types that Cassandra provides you with. Much like `struct` in C, it gives you relief in cases where you have to denormalize data because Cassandra does not support the `join` queries. The most common example of this is putting multiple shipping addresses in a map within a users' table. In RDBMS, you would probably just create two tables: `users` and `addresses`. You'd make `user_id` a foreign key in the `addresses` table. Then, you use a `join` query to retrieve a `User` object that has `Map<String, Address>` that lists all the shipping address of the user. In Cassandra, we have two options to go about it. The first option is to create a custom data type, which is **User Defined Type (UDT)**, for the `address` object, and save it as a part of row in the `users` table. This is denormalization using UDT.

The other option is to have a separate `addresses` table and store the primary keys of these addresses in the `users` table. When retrieving, the former just needs to fetch the data from the `users` table to get a user's data along with its addresses. In the latter case, however, you will need to pull the user's records and then use the primary keys of the addresses to execute another `IN` query on the `addresses` table to get addresses. It's a lot of work. We would go with the former, the custom data type with the denormalization approach.

Creating a type has the same syntax as creating a table without properties. Here's the query pattern:

```
CREATE TYPE [ IF NOT EXISTS ] type_name
( field_name field_type [, field_name field_type, ... ] );
```

Let's take a look at the following example:

```
# Create a UDT
CREATE TYPE address ( address text, country varchar, postal_code
varchar, preference int );

# Use the UDT in a table in a map
CREATE TABLE users ( user_id int PRIMARY KEY, name varchar, age int,
addresses map <text, frozen<address>> );

# Insert some records
INSERT INTO users (user_id, name, age, addresses ) VALUES ( 1, 'Willy
Wonka', 42, {'office': {address: 'The Choco Factory', country: 'US',
postal_code: '123', preference: 1}, 'home': {address: 'NA'}} );

SELECT * FROM users;

 user_id | age | name         | addresses
---------+-----+--------------+--------------------------    1 |
42 | Willy Wonka | {
                            'home': {
                              address: 'NA',
                              country: null,
                              postal_code: null,
                              preference: null
                              },
                            'office': {
                              address: 'The Choco Factory',
                              country: 'US',
```

```
                                 postal_code: '123',
                                 preference: 1
                               }
                             }
```

```
(1 rows)
```

A couple of things worth noticing:

- The UDT does not require all fields to be filled. The fields that are left unassigned will be set to `null`.

- UDTs, as of Cassandra 2.1, have to be defined as `frozen` as they are serialized and crammed into one cell. One may argue that `frozen` is just extraneous, but Cassandra 3 has plans to make UDTs as free as collections. So this is basically future proofing.

You can have collections within a UDT. Also, obviously, creating a UDT of a type that is provided by Cassandra out of the box will throw an error. Ideally, avoid all reserved keywords as a rule of thumb.

Altering a custom type

You cannot drop an attribute but you can practically do everything that you can do while altering a table. You can change type name, change attributes within the type's type, change the attributes' name, and append a new attribute.

Here are the patterns followed by an example:

```
ALTER TYPE old_type_name RENAME TO new_type_name;
```

At the time of writing, the preceding code was failing in Cassandra 2.1.

```
# Rename a type attribute
ALTER TYPE type_name RENAME old_column_name TO new_column_name;
ALTER TYPE address RENAME postal_code TO zipcode;

# Change a type attribute's type
ALTER TYPE type_name ALTER column_name TYPE new_type;
ALTER TYPE address ALTER country TYPE blob;

# Add a new attribute to the type
ALTER TYPE type_name ADD new_column column_type;
ALTER TYPE address ADD default_address Boolean;

# Final type
```

```
DESC TYPE address
CREATE TYPE address (
  address text,
  country blob,
  zipcode text,
  preference int,
  default_address boolean
);
```

Dropping a custom type

A custom type that is not used by any table can be dropped. The familiar drop syntax is as follows:

```
DROP TYPE [ IF EXISTS ] user_defined_type_name;
```

Creating triggers

Cassandra provides a way to act upon when a mutation request is made on a table. It is called **trigger**. Triggers are Java classes that implement org.apache.cassandra. triggers.ITrigger. You are provided with full mutation details, and you may return a collection of mutation objects if you wanted to take some actions. However, you are not limited to returning mutation; you may decide to send a mail as a trigger. Remember to keep your logic fast because it may affect the latency.

To create a trigger class, you must implement the Itrigger interface. Compile it then place the .class file or if packaged, the .jar file in $CASSANDRA_HOME/lib along with any external libraries that the trigger class needed. You need to copy this file to all the nodes and then reboot the Cassandra service. Once Cassandra is up, you may go ahead and use that trigger.

Here's the skeleton of a trigger:

```java
package com.mycompany.cassandra;

import java.nio.ByteBuffer;
import java.util.Collection;
import org.apache.cassandra.db.ColumnFamily;
import org.apache.cassandra.db.Mutation;
import org.apache.cassandra.triggers.ITrigger;

public class DummyTrigger implements ITrigger {

  /**
  * key: is the row key of incoming mutation
```

```
   * cf is map-like structure that holds column-name and mutation to
applied
   * Collection<Mutation> is the collection of mutations that you want
to execute. If there is no new mutation, return null
   **/
   public Collection<Mutation> augment(ByteBuffer key, ColumnFamily cf)

      /*
       * TRIGGER LOGIC GOES HERE
       */
      return null;
   }
}
```

To use this trigger, you need to follow this syntax:

```
# Pattern to create a trigger
CREATE TRIGGER trigger_name
ON
table_name
USING 'fully.qualified.trigger.Name';

# Create a trigger
CREATE TRIGGER dummy_trigger_on_users
ON
users
USING 'com.mycompany.cassandra.DummyTrigger';
```

Triggers are executed before the mutation request is performed. Triggers can be helpful in scenarios where you need to update another table based on mutations on a table, logging specific mutation or creating notification on certain events, or anything that is specific to your application.

There is an excellent example of trigger that generates an inverse index. The code can be found in Cassandra 2.1 source code at https://git-wip-us.apache.org/repos/asf?p=cassandra.git;a=blob_plain;f=examples/triggers/src/org/apache/cassandra/triggers/InvertedIndex.java;hb=HEAD.

Dropping a trigger

A trigger can be dropped using the following pattern:

```
DROP TRIGGER trigger_name ON table_name;
```

Creating a user

Cassandra, by default, ships with authentication or authorization settings disabled. To be able to create a user, you need to first enable it. Here is what you need to do:

1. Edit $CASSANDRA_HOME/conf/cassandra.yaml; look for this line:

   ```
   authenticator: AllowAllAuthenticator
   ```

   Change the authenticator to the following line:

   ```
   authenticator: PasswordAuthenticator
   ```

2. Restart Cassandra nodes. It is suggested to change the system_auth keyspace replication factor to more than one, so that your authentication does not fail when the node containing data goes down.

3. The user's username and password is cassandra to log in the first time. For security reasons, it is suggested to create a new superuser then discard the Cassandra user's superuser privilege.

To be on the safe side, you may also want to change the Cassandra user's password. From now on, use the new superuser to perform tasks.

Here's how one uses cqlsh for the first login after setting up authentication.

```
$CASSANDRA_HOME/bin/cqlsh -u cassandra -p cassandra localhost 9042
```

We will see more authentication and authorization in *Chapter 4, Deploying a Cluster*. Coming back to query definition, the following is the pattern to create a user:

```
CREATE USER [ IF NOT EXISTS ] user_name
[ WITH PASSWORD 'password' ]
[ NOSUPERUSER | SUPERUSER ];
```

Let's take a look at the following example:

```
CREATE USER oracle WITH PASSWORD 'X10n' SUPERUSER;
```

A couple of things to notice here are as follows:

- Password must be provided within single quotes.
- By default, the query creates a NOSUPERUSER user. To create a superuser who can create new users, you should explicitly mention SUPERUSER.

Altering a user

There are two things you can do with a user: alter its superuser status, and change its password. The syntax goes like this:

```
ALTER USER user_name
[ WITH PASSWORD 'new_password' ][ NOSUPERUSER | SUPERUSER ];
```

Let's take a look at the following example:

```
ALTER USER oracle WITH PASSWORD 'FollowTheWhileRabbitN30';
```

Dropping a user

Dropping a user follows a simple known syntax:

```
DROP USER [ IF EXISTS ] user_name;
```
Let's take a look at the following example:

```
DROP USER IF EXISTS oracle;
```

The granting permission

On a shared database with multiple users, it is usually a good idea to limit the number of users who can mutate objects, and have only a couple of users who can change permissions and create users. This is the best practice in general, applicable to all databases. Cassandra provides a SQL-like GRANT command that can be used to authorize users to perform chosen tasks on chosen entities. But before you go ahead and start altering users' capabilities, you need to enable authorization in the cassandra.yaml file.

1. Edit $CASSANDRA_HOME/conf/cassandra.conf to change the authorizer attribute to CassandraAuthorizer:

   ```
   authorizer: CassandraAuthorizer
   ```

2. Make sure that system_auth keyspace has a replication factor of more than 1 to avoid failures in cases a node with authorization data goes down. (Obviously, this does not hold true when you have a single node cluster or are just experimenting on your local machine.)

3. Restart the Cassandra node for this to take effect.

The syntax to grant permission is as follows:

```
GRANT permission_type
ON
{ ALL KEYSPACES | KEYSPACE ks_name | TABLE ks_name.table_name }
TO
user_name;
```

So basically, you can either specify a specific permission type or just provide all the permissions on an entity. An entity could be a keyspace, all keyspaces, or a table:

```
cqlsh> CREATE USER testuser WITH PASSWORD 'abc';

cqlsh> GRANT SELECT ON ALL KEYSPACES TO testuser;

cqlsh> exit

$CASSANDRA_HOME/bin/cqlsh -u testuser -p abc -k demo_cql -e 'select *
from grant_test'


 id | name

----+-------------

  1 | Mocking Jay

  2 |  Henry Ford



(2 rows)



$CASSANDRA_HOME/bin/cqlsh -u testuser -p abc -k demo_cql -e "insert
into grant_test (id, name) values (42, 'fail me')"

<stdin>:1:code=2100 [Unauthorized] message="User testuser has no
MODIFY permission on <table demo_cql.grant_test> or any of its
parents"
```

Permission types and their scopes are as follows:

- ALL: This allows all types of queries to run on the entity or entities specified.
- SELECT: This allows just SELECT statements to be run by the specified user on the specified entity.
- CREATE: This allows CREATE statements. The user can create a table in a keyspace if the user is given the CREATE permission to the keyspace. To create a keyspace, the user needs to have the CREATE permission to all keyspaces.
- MODIFY: This allows the statements such as INSERT, DELETE, UPDATE, and TRUNCATE. Users permitted to modify an entity can run these statements/commands without any constraints like the ones that the CREATE statement has.
- ALTER: This allows users to execute the ALTER statements and CREATE or DROP indexes.
- DROP: This allows you to drop keyspaces and tables.
- AUTHORIZE: This is a special permission. This permission can be provided only to the users that have the SUPERUSER privilege. It allows you to GRANT or REVOKE permission on an entity.

Revoking permission using REVOKE

The REVOKE permission basically undoes what GRANT did. There are a couple of gotchas that you should be aware of:

- **Superuser is a super user**: You cannot revoke permissions from a superuser.
- **Mind the hierarchy**: From bottom to top, table is the lowest level then keyspace, and ALL KEYSPACES are over and above all. So, if you have a user that has the SELECT permission across ALL KEYSPACES, you cannot remove the permission on a single table or on a single keyspace.

The syntax for REVOKE is as follows:

```
REVOKE { permission_type | REVOKE ALL PERMISSIONS }
ON
{ ALL KEYSPACES | KEYSPACE ks_name | TABLE ks_name.table_name }
FROM
user_name;
```

The details stay the same as GRANT.

Inserting data

With the platform created, now we are ready to do what we will be doing the most in an application: inserting and retrieving records. Inserting in Cassandra is similar to SQL with a couple of extra options. Here's the pattern:

```
INSERT INTO table_name ( column_name1, column_name1, ...)
VALUES
( column_value1, column_value2, ... )
[ IF NOT EXISTS ]
[ USING [ TTL ttl_in_sec ] [ [ AND ] TIMESTAMP ts_in_microsec ];
```

So the format is, after the INSERT INTO keyword, goes the table name, then a comma-separated list of columns, then the VALUES keyword, then a comma-separated list of values of appropriate types in the same order as the list of the columns. In case you want to avoid concurrently writing threads to overwrite a row, you should use IF NOT EXISTS. So, why not do this for all the insert queries? The answer is performance hit. We will come to see why this happens soon in this section. You can set a TTL for the row. TTL is a precondition that states the row will be deleted automatically after the specified time. You can also optionally set TIMESTAMP; this timestamp is used in conflict resolution. It is also worth noting that the INSERT statements are not applicable to counter tables. So, here are some examples:

```
# Create a simple table to insert data into
CREATE TABLE demo_insert (id int PRIMARY KEY, name text, phone
set<text>);

# Insert a simple row
INSERT INTO demo_insert (id, name, phone) VALUES ( 1, 'Harry Potter',
{'44-234-0495','44-234-9845'});

# Insert a row with the same primary key
# check for duplicates this time
INSERT INTO demo_insert (id, name, phone) VALUES ( 1, 'Draco malfoy',
{'44-234-0495','44-234-9845'}) IF NOT EXISTS;

 [applied] | id | name          | phone

-----------+----+---------------+-----------------------------------

     False |  1 | Harry Potter | {'44-234-0495', '44-234-9845'}
```

```
# Insert the same row with a different primary key; set its life as 30
seconds
INSERT INTO demo_insert (id, name, phone) VALUES ( 2, 'Draco malfoy',
{'44-234-4398'}) IF NOT EXISTS USING TTL 30;


 [applied]
-----------


       True


# Immediately after
SELECT * FROM demo_insert;


 id | name          | phone

----+---------------+--------------------------------

  1 | Harry Potter  | {'44-234-0495', '44-234-9845'}

  2 | Draco malfoy  |                 {'44-234-4398'}



(2 rows)



# 30 seconds later
SELECT * FROM demo_insert;


 id | name          | phone

----+---------------+--------------------------------

  1 | Harry Potter  | {'44-234-0495', '44-234-9845'}



(1 rows)
```

```
# Insert a record with a timestamp far into the future
INSERT INTO demo_insert (id, name) VALUES ( 3, 'Ginevra Weasley')
USING TIMESTAMP 2147483647000000;

# Check the insertion timestamp
SELECT id, name, phone, WRITETIME(name) FROM demo_insert;
```

```
 id | name          | phone                               |
writetime(name)

----+---------------+-------------------------------------+--------------
-----

  1 |    Harry Potter | {'44-234-0495', '44-234-9845'} |
1411919467570135

  3 | Ginevra Weasley |                              null |
2147483647000000


(2 rows)
```

Note that you cannot use IF NOT EXISTS if you manually set TIMESTAMP.

Collections in CQL

As we have seen in the past, collections use a special pattern. Collections are sort of dynamically created columns with a column name either as index (list), or keys (map), or the value itself (sets). So essentially, unlike tuples or UDTs, they are not serialized into one cell. Instead, each item lives in its individual cell. And you will see that you can pretty much do whatever you can do with a cell. Let's quickly go through how collections work.

Lists

Lists are like arrays in JSON. They can have duplicate items:

```
[item1, item2, ...]
```

You can append to them using the + operator, replace an item either by index or value, and delete items by index:

```
# Create a table with a list of integer column
CREATE TABLE list_demo (id int PRIMARY KEY, list_col list <int>);

# Insert some values with duplicates in the list
INSERT INTO list_demo (id, list_col ) VALUES ( 1, [1, 2, 1]);
select * from list_demo;


 id | list_col

----+-----------

  1 | [1, 2, 1]



(1 rows)




# Updating value in at index 1
UPDATE list_demo set list_col[1] = 3 WHERE id = 1;

select * from list_demo;


 id | list_col

----+-----------

  1 | [1, 3, 1]



(1 rows)




# Appending and prepending a column
UPDATE list_demo SET list_col = list_col + [4,5] WHERE id = 1;
UPDATE list_demo SET list_col = [0] + list_col WHERE id = 1;
```

```
SELECT * FROM list_demo;


 id | list_col

----+--------------------

  1 | [0, 1, 3, 1, 4, 5]



(1 rows)
```

Delete an item by the index
```
delete list_col[2] from list_demo WHERE id = 1;

SELECT * FROM list_demo;


 id | list_col

----+-----------------

  1 | [0, 1, 1, 4, 5]



(1 rows)
```

Deleting an item in the list by value deletes all copies of it
```
UPDATE list_demo SET list_col = list_col - [1] WHERE id = 1;

SELECT * FROM list_demo;


 id | list_col

----+-----------
```

```
 1 |  [0, 4, 5]
```

(1 rows)

Sets

Sets are comma-separated values in curly brackets. Sets cannot have duplicates:

```
{item1, item2, …}
```

Apart from the fact that a set is not ordered and contains unique values, it behaves the same way as a list, except that you cannot use an index to delete or update items. In reality, you do not need an index when items are unique, because their values are going to work as an identifier to them.

Here are some example operations:

```
# Create a simple table and insert a set with duplicates
CREATE TABLE set_demo (id int PRIMARY KEY, set_col set<text>);
INSERT INTO set_demo (id, set_col ) VALUES ( 1, {'head', 'tail',
'head'});
SELECT * FROM set_demo;


 id | set_col

----+------------------

  1 | {'head', 'tail'}



(1 rows)


# You can append, but cannot prepend, but order is not preserved. So,
it does not matter.
UPDATE set_demo SET set_col = set_col + { 'right' }  WHERE id = 1;
SELECT * FROM set_demo;


 id | set_col
```

```
----+---------------------------

  1 | {'head', 'right', 'tail'}
```

```
(1 rows)
```

```
# Removing an element is similar to adding one
UPDATE set_demo SET set_col = set_col - { 'head' }  WHERE id = 1;
SELECT * FROM set_demo;
```

```
 id | set_col

----+-------------------

  1 | {'right', 'tail'}
```

```
(1 rows)
```

Maps

Maps are represented as JSON objects. They do not support duplicate keys but you can have duplicate values. If you insert two or more entries with the same key, only one of them will persist.

```
{'key1': value1, 'key2': value2, …}
```

You can add values using a key or appending another map. You can delete values by key or by another map.

```
# Create a table and insert a map with duplicate keys
CREATE TABLE map_demo (id int PRIMARY KEY, map_col map<int, text> );
INSERT INTO map_demo (id, map_col ) VALUES ( 1, {1:'one', 2: 'two', 1:
'dupe'} );
SELECT * FROM map_demo;
```

```
 id | map_col

----+----------------------
```

```
1 | {1: 'one', 2: 'two'}
```

```
(1 rows)
```

Update the value of a key
```
UPDATE map_demo SET map_col[3] = 'three' WHERE id = 1;
SELECT * FROM map_demo;
```

```
 id | map_col

----+--------------------------------

  1 | {1: 'one', 2: 'two', 3: 'three'}
```

```
(1 rows)
```

Delete a key
```
DELETE map_col[2] FROM map_demo WHERE id = 1;
SELECT * FROM map_demo;
```

```
 id | map_col

----+-----------------------

  1 | {1: 'one', 3: 'three'}

(1 rows)
```

Lightweight transactions

Support for transaction is introduced in Cassandra 2.0. In the previous version of this book, we discussed how cages and other libraries can be used to lock specific mutations and allow other entries only when the previous operations have been executed. It was too much work and the system was brittle. But Cassandra 2.0 and onwards supports lightweight transactions using the Paxos consensus protocol. It is a part of CQL, and much more simple to use. To learn more about Paxos, visit http://www.cs.utexas.edu/users/lorenzo/corsi/cs380d/past/03F/notes/ paxos-simple.pdf.

Coming back to insert, we noted earlier that using IF NOT EXISTS has a negative impact on performance. To make sure the writes go linearly, Cassandra uses the Paxos consensus protocol. It basically make builds an agreement across the nodes before starting mutation. The whole process takes four round trips from all the replica nodes, which is concerning. This is the reason it is suggested to use light weight transaction, where it is a must.

One such example can be the case where users are registering with unique usernames. You will not want two users inserting the same name, because being unique it will act as an identifier, which is used to fetch user records or log them in.

Light weight transactions can be used during insert or update. Here's an example:

```
# Create an ordinary table
CREATE TABLE lwt_demo (id int PRIMARY KEY, name text, passwd text);

# Insert only iof the id column wasn't already taken
INSERT INTO lwt_demo (id, name, passwd) VALUES ( 1, 'Derek', 's3cr3t')
IF NOT EXISTS;


 [applied]

 -----------

      True



# If it is taken, the query returns the existing value with a hint
that this query/mutation was not applied
INSERT INTO lwt_demo (id, name, passwd) VALUES ( 1, 'Maverick',
'0p3ns3cr3t') IF NOT EXISTS;
```

```
[applied] | id | name | passwd

----------+----+-------+--------

   False |  1 | Derek | s3cr3t
```

```
# In update you do not need to depend on the primary key. Any column
can be validated in the IF block.
UPDATE lwt_demo SET name = 'Maverick', passwd = '0p3ns3cr3t' WHERE id
= 1 IF name = 'Derek';
```

```
[applied]

-----------

   True
```

```
# In case, the mutation failed, you are notified with the condition
that failed
UPDATE lwt_demo SET name = 'Maverick', passwd = '0p3ns3cr3t' WHERE id
= 1 IF name = 'Derek';
```

```
[applied] | name

----------+----------

   False | Maverick
```

Updating a row

Update follows a very similar construct to SELECT, and under the hood, UPDATE and INSERT are the same thing. As we have seen in the previous section, the counter column family only gets updated and cannot be inserted. Here is the syntax:

```
UPDATE [ table_name ]

[ USING [ TTL ttl_in_sec ] [ [ AND ] TIMESTAMP ts_in_microsec ] ]
```

```
SET column_name = column_value_or_expression [, column_name = column_
value_or_expression, ... ]

WHERE primary_key_name { = pk_value | IN ( pk_value1, pk_value2, ... )
}

IF column_name = col_val [ AND column_name = column_value ... ];
```

Most of the things in the previous expression follow the same rule as we have seen in the previous sections under *Inserting data, Collections in CQL,* and *Lightweight transactions.*

So, you can update to set TTL or TIMESTAMP of an individual or a set of columns. In simple cases like regular columns or collection columns with full replacement, you just go ahead and provide the value. But in cases like adding or removing collections, we use the + or - operator and sometime the DELETE query as we have seen in the *Collections in CQL* section previously.

Here are a couple of examples:

```
# Create a table and insert some data
CREATE TABLE update_demo ( id int PRIMARY KEY, name text, movies list
<text> );
INSERT INTO update_demo (id, name, movies) VALUES ( 1, 'imdb',
['Beautiful Mind', 'Se7en', '1984'] );

INSERT INTO update_demo (id, name, movies) VALUES ( 10, 'rotten
tomato', ['Star Wars', 'Donnie darko'] );

# Update a couple of rows
UPDATE update_demo SET name = 'Movie Website' WHERE id in (1,10);
SELECT * FROM update_demo;


 id | movies                                  | name

----+-----------------------------------------+--------------

 10 |        ['Star Wars', 'Donnie darko'] | Movie Website

  1 | ['Beautiful Mind', 'Se7en', '1984'] | Movie Website


(2 rows)
```

```
# Update a collection
UPDATE update_demo SET movies[2] = 'Amelie' WHERE id = 1;
SELECT * FROM update_demo;
```

```
 id | movies                                    | name

----+-------------------------------------------+---------------

 10 |          ['Star Wars', 'Donnie darko']    | Movie Website

  1 | ['Beautiful Mind', 'Se7en', 'Amelie']     | Movie Website
```

```
(2 rows)
```

```
# Lightweight transaction not applied as the condition did not match
UPDATE update_demo SET name  = 'Reviews' WHERE id = 1 IF movies[2] =
'1984';
```

```
 [applied] | movies

-----------+---------------------------------------

    False | ['Beautiful Mind', 'Se7en', 'Amelie']
```

Deleting a row

Deleting a row is a little more complicated than all the DROP statements that we have seen so far. All you have to do is specify the column or a member of a collection to delete, followed by table name and optionally, you can specify TIMESTAMP if you wanted it to be a check. And finally, you need to identify the row. Here's the scheme:

```
DELETE [ column_identifier ]
FROM table_name
[ USING TIMESTAMP ts_in_microsec ]
WHERE row_identifier
[ IF { EXISTS | condition [ AND condition [ AND condition ... ] ] } ];
```

Here are some examples, continuing from the previous section:

```
# Delete an element from a collection
DELETE movies[1] FROM update_demo WHERE id = 1;
SELECT * FROM update_demo;
```

```
 id | movies                          | name

----+--------------------------------+---------------

 10 | ['Star Wars', 'Donnie darko'] |          null

  1 |   ['Beautiful Mind', 'Amelie'] | Movie Website



(2 rows)
```

```
# Delete using the lightweight transaction
DELETE name FROM update_demo WHERE id = 1 IF movies[1] = 'Amelie';
```

```
 [applied]

-----------

      True
```

```
SELECT * FROM update_demo;
```

```
 id | movies                          | name

----+--------------------------------+------

 10 | ['Star Wars', 'Donnie darko'] | null
```

```
 1 |  ['Beautiful Mind', 'Amelie'] | null


(2 rows)



# Delete the whole row when columns are not specified
DELETE FROM update_demo WHERE id = 10;

SELECT * FROM update_demo;


 id | movies                          | name

----+--------------------------------+------

  1 |  ['Beautiful Mind', 'Amelie'] | null


(1 rows)
```

Executing the BATCH statement

Cassandra provides batch processing which is remotely similar to stored procedures in SQL. You can have multiple mutation (INSERT, UPDATE, or DELETE) statements in a BATCH statement and execute them. Cassandra guarantees that batch operations will be atomic; that means that if any of the queries in the batch are executed, all the queries will be executed. However, it does not provide a transactional guarantee. For example, a client can see the effect of execution of the first query in the batch, while others are yet to be applied. Note that it does not alter lightweight transaction queries in the batch by any way, but those queries still stay transactional.

Here's the syntax for BATCH:

```
BEGIN [ UNLOGGED | COUNTER ]  BATCH

  [ USING TIMESTAMP timestamp ]

  query1;

  query2;
```

. . .

```
APPLY BATCH;
```

The BATCH statement is written to a system table before being applied to make sure that the batch completes, even in the event of death of the coordinator node. This record gets removed when the batch gets processed. This may cause some performance issues. If you wanted to skip this persistence of the batch, use the UNLOGGED keyword. The UNLOGGED keyword should also be used if the batch contains any query that updates the counter. In Cassandra 2.0.9 or earlier, however, you should use COUNTER instead of UNLOGGED. It is important to note that counters are not idempotent. This means that if the same query is run twice, the results will be different. For example, if a batch contains a statement that increases credit_balance of a user by 1,000 and if for some reason the update block failed and retry was attempted, credit_balance will be updated again. Now if the batch failed after the counter was applied, the user will have credit_balance as 2,000, which is undesired.

By default, all the mutations hold the same system timestamp. If you wanted to supply something different, you could provide it by specifying USING TIMESTAMP <timestamp_in_microseconds>. It should be noted that the batch level timestamp does not overwrite the query level timestamp. So, if a query has a different timestamp than the batch, that query timestamp will be applied on that mutation.

Other CQL commands

CQL provides some commands to quickly get an overview, obtain information, or perform operations.

USE

The USE command is used to switch to a keyspace. All the examples in this chapter assume that the client is switched to the keyspace in question. In case you do not want to use the USE command, you will have to provide a fully-qualified table name or type name to address any command that involves a table or type.

A fully-qualified table name is the keyspace name followed by a dot followed by the table name. For example, in the university_ks keyspace, a table named departments will have a fully-qualified table name as university_ks.departments.

The usage of the USE keyword is as follows:

```
USE keyspace_name
```

TRUNCATE

The TRUNCATE command is the same as delete from table_name in SQL. It deletes all the data from a table, irreversibly. The syntax of this command is as follows:

```
TRUNCATE table_name
```

LIST USERS

The LIST USERS command lists all the users in the system and their status. Note that you must have authentication enabled and be logged in as a user to run the following query. Here's an example:

```
cqlsh:demo_cql> LIST USERS;
```

```
    name      | super

 -----------+-------

     oracle  | False

  cassandra  |  True

   testuser  | False


 (3 rows)
```

LIST PERMISSIONS

The LIST PERMISSIONS command lists all the permissions on an entity and the entities under it. The syntax is as follows:

```
LIST [ permission_name PERMISSION | ALL PERMISSIONS ]

[ ON { ALL KEYSPACES | KEYSPACE ks_name | TABLE ks_name.table_name} ]

[ OF user_name ]

[ NORECURSIVE ]
```

Here, `permission_name` is the same as we have seen in GRANT. The entity name can be the keyspace name or table name or all keyspaces. The username is one of the existing users; and if NORECURSIVE is used, it will not print all the entities under the requested entity. Here's an example:

```
LIST ALL PERMISSIONS


 username | resource                        | permission


----------+---------------------------------+------------

   oracle |            <keyspace demo_cql>  |     SELECT

   oracle | <table demo_cql.grant_test>     |     SELECT

 testuser |            <all keyspaces>      |     SELECT

 testuser | <table demo_cql.grant_test>     |     SELECT

 testuser |            <keyspace system>    |     CREATE
```

CQL shell commands

CQL shell or `cqlsh` comes with many little utilities. In this section, we will see them.

DESCRIBE

The DESCRIBE command is used to get details of container objects. You can use DESC in place of DESCRIBE. So, one can describe a keyspace, table, or cluster. There are five variants of this command:

```
# Describe the whole cluster
DESCRIBE CLUSTER
# Display the CQL command to regenerate all the keyspaces in the
cluster
DESCRIBE SCHEMA
# List all the keyspaces names
DESCRIBE KEYSPACES
# List the CQL statement that can be used to recreate the keyspace
DESCRIBE KEYSPACE <keyspace_name>
# Show tables names in the current keyspace
# Show all the tables across all the keyspaces if not using any
keyspace
```

```
DESCRIBE TABLES
# Print CQL to create a table
DESCRIBE TABLE <table_name>
```

TRACING

The TRACING command is a convenient tool to view the steps that your queries go through and possibly use it to optimize the query. It displays how much time is spent on what step at which node.

Use TRACING ON to turn tracing on, on every subsequent query. To turn TRACING off, use TRACING OFF.

CONSISTENCY

The CONSISTENCY command can be used to view or set current consistency level.

```
# To view the consistency level
CONSISTENCY
# To set the consistency level for all the following queries in
cqlsh's current session
CONSISTENCY <level>
```

COPY

The COPY command is a handy utility to load data to a table from a file or the command prompt (standard input). It can also be used to copy data from a table to an external CSV file or to the command prompt (standard output):

```
# To copy from a CSV file or stdin
COPY table_name ( column1, column2, …)
FROM ( 'file_name' | STDIN )
[ WITH option = 'value' [ AND option = 'value' [ AND option = 'value'
…]]]
```

```
# To copy to a CSV file or stdout
COPY table_name ( column1, column2, …)
TO ( 'file_name' | STDIN )
[ WITH option = 'value' [ AND option = 'value' [ AND option = 'value'
…]]]
```

The options are described as follows:

- HEADER: This option is to inform Cassandra whether the CSV has a header (the names of the columns) as the first row.

- DELIMITER: The character to be used to separate fields in one line. The default delimiter is a comma.

- QUOTE: The character to be used to surround each field value. Any delimiter within the quotes will not be treated as a delimiter, rather a regular character. The default is the double quote character.

- ESCAPE: The escape character is used to mark any QUOTE character within the field value as normal character. The default is a backslash.

- NULL: This is the string that one uses to represent NULL in text. The default is an empty string, but one can opt to choose NA or NIL if they wanted to.

- ENCODING: This is used by the COPY TO command.

CAPTURE

The CAPTURE command copies the output of a query to the file specified:

```
# Capture to /home/username/Desktop/testqueries.txt
CAPTURE '/home/username/Desktop/testqueries.txt'


# Turn off capturing
CAPTURE OFF
```

ASSUME

The ASSUME command is a feature from past versions. With the CQL definition, one does not need to explicitly set column types to view the result. The ASSUME command is used to tell the CQL shell to treat column names as a certain data type, or treat column values as a certain data type.

Here's an example where a table tabx is set to interpret the column names and values as various types:

```
# Treat column names as int and values as text
ASSUME tabx NAMES ARE int, VALUES ARE text;
# Treat the tabid column as UUID
ASSUME tabx(tabid) VALUES ARE uuid
```

SOURCE

The SOURCE command like the MySQL SOURCE command reads the contents of a file and tries to execute it. So, one can have a bunch of CQL statements in the file and then call the SOURCE command with the file location, and the CQL shell will execute it:

```
# Execute the contents of /home/username/Desktop/create_dev_envt.txt
SOURCE '/home/username/Desktop/create_dev_envt.txt'€
```

SHOW

The SHOW command displays system information. There are three variants of this command:

```
SHOW VERSION;
SHOW HOST;
SHOW ASSUMPTIONS;
```

EXIT

The EXIT or QUIT command stops the CQL shell session.

Summary

The ability to effectively utilize a database's potential is more of an art than science. This chapter is probably the most important chapter from the perspective of an application developer. CQL 3 is de facto standard to work with Cassandra and Cassandra has evolved much more beyond the older Thrift protocol. CQL3 makes sure that a developer can never go wrong or use an antipattern. Addition of collections, tuples, UDTs, and lightweight transactions helped a lot to avoid exceptional coding and handling from the developer side and working with third party libraries.

Although the Cassandra client layer has been completely revamped, at its core, the data representation has stayed more or less the same. Working with CQL3, it is easy to forget about underlying storage and start thinking in terms of SQL. Then, at some point, you hit an exceptional behavior and wonder why it works this way—why indexes are like that, why compound keys behave in that way, how collections are stored, how could we put a time series in a table, and much more. Most of these questions can be quickly answered if you have a rough idea of how the data storage is modeled. This chapter tried to show you some of that.

Having applications ready to perform at their best is a good idea, and it is equally important to have a capable infrastructure to serve the expectations. Setting up a Cassandra cluster is simple and easier than most of the distributed software deployments. Out of the box, Cassandra comes with good defaults for most of the cases. So, if you have deployed your cluster before reading the next chapter, chances are that you are not far away from your optimal setting, and you just need to read the next chapter to make sure everything is fine.

4
Deploying a Cluster

So, you have played a bit with Cassandra on your local machine and read something about how great it scales. Now it's time to evaluate all the tall claims that Cassandra makes.

This chapter deals with cluster deployment and the decision that you need to make that will affect a number of nodes, types of machines, and tweaks in the Cassandra configuration file. We start with hardware evaluations and then dive into OS-level tweaks, followed by the prerequisite software applications and how to install them. Once the base machine is ready, we will discuss the Cassandra installation—which is fairly easy. The rest of the chapter discusses various settings available, what fits in which situation, the pros and cons, and so on. Having been equipped with all this information, you are ready to launch your first cluster. The chapter provides working code that deploys Cassandra on n number of nodes, sets the entire configuration, and starts Cassandra, effectively launching each node in about 40 seconds, thus enabling you to get going with an eight-node cluster in about 5 minutes.

Code pattern

All the shell commands mentioned in this chapter follow a pattern. Each line starting with a # sign is just a comment to clarify the context. Each line starting with a $ sign is a command. Some longer commands may be broken into multiple lines for reading clarity. If a command is broken, the end of the line contains a line-continuation character—a backslash (\). Each line that does not have either of these symbols is the output of a command. Please follow this pattern unless specified otherwise.

Evaluating requirements

It is generally a good idea to examine what kind of load Cassandra is going to face when deployed on a production server. It does not have to be accurate, but some sense of traffic can give a little more clarity to what you expect from Cassandra (criteria for load tests), whether you really need Cassandra (the halo effect), or whether you can bear all the expenses that a running Cassandra cluster can incur on a daily basis (the value proposition). Let's see how to choose various hardware specifications for a specific need.

Hard disk capacity

A rough disk space calculation of the user that will be stored in Cassandra involves adding up data stored in four data components on disk: commit logs, SSTable, an index file, and a bloom filter. When the incoming data is compared with the data on the disk, you need to take account of the database overheads associated with each type of data. The data on disk can be about two times as large as raw data. Disk usage can be calculated using the following code snippet:

```
# Size of one normal column
column_size (in bytes) = column_name_size + column_val_size
                         + 15

# Size of an expiring or counter column
col_size (in bytes) = column_name_size + column_val_size
                      + 23

# Size of a row
row_size (bytes) = size_of_all_columns + row_key_size + 23

# Primary index file size
index_size (bytes) = number_of_rows * (32 + mean_key_size)

# Addition space consumption due to replication
replication_overhead = total_data_size *
                       (replication_factor - 1)
```

Apart from this, the disk also faces high read-write during compaction. Compaction is the process that merges SSTables to improve search efficiency. The important thing about compaction is that it may, in the worst case, utilize as much space as occupied by user data. Therefore, it is a good idea to have a lot of space left. We'll discuss this again, but it depends on the choice of `compaction_strategy` that is applied. For `LeveledCompactionStrategy`, a balance of 10 percent is enough. On the other hand, `SizeTieredCompactionStrategy` requires 50 percent free disk space in the worst case. Here are some rules of thumb with regard to disk choice and disk operations:

- **Commit logs and data files on separate disks**: Commit logs are updated on each write and are read-only for startups, which is rare. A `data` directory, on the other hand, is used to flush MemTables into SSTables asynchronously. It is read through and written on during compaction, and most importantly, it might be looked up by a client to satisfy the consistency level. Having the two directories on the same disk may potentially cause the client operation to be blocked. Their I/O patterns are quite different too. Commit log is basically an append-only write operation, whereas SSTable is basically random access.

> It is important to note that keeping `commitlog` and `data` directories only matters if you have a spinning disk. For **Solid State Drives (SSDs)**, you can keep them on the same disk. However, if you have an SSD and a spinning disk as your storage devices, it is recommended that you keep commit log on the spinning disk, and `data` directory on the SSD.

- **RAID 0**: Cassandra performs inbuilt replication by means of a replication factor. Therefore, it does not possess any sort of hardware redundancy. If one node dies completely, the data is available on other replica nodes, with no difference between the two. This is the reason that RAID 0 (`http://en.wikipedia.org/wiki/RAID#RAID_0`) is the most preferred RAID level. Another reason is improved disk performance and extra space.

- **Filesystem**: If one has choices, XFS is the most preferred filesystem for Cassandra deployment. XFS supports 16 TB on a 32-bit architecture, and a whopping 8 EiB (Exabibyte) on 64-bit machines. Owing to storage space limitations, the `ext4`, `ext3`, and `ext2` filesystems (in that order) can be considered to be used for Cassandra.

- **SCSI and SSD**: With disks, the guideline is the faster, the better. SCSI is faster than SATA, and SSD is faster than SCSI. SSDs are extremely fast as there are no moving parts. It is recommended that you use rather low-priced consumer SSD for Cassandra, as enterprise-grade SSD has no particular benefit over it.

- **No EBS on EC2**: This is specific to **Amazon Web Services (AWS)** users. **Elastic Block Store (EBS)** from AWS is strongly discouraged for the purpose of storing Cassandra data—either of data directories or commit log storage. Poor throughput and issues such as getting unusably slow, instead of cleanly dying, are major roadblocks of the network attached storage.

- **XFS filesystem**: http://en.wikipedia.org/wiki/XFS.

- **AWS EBS**: http://aws.amazon.com/ebs/. Instead of using EBS, use ephemeral devices attached to the instance (also known as an instance store). Instance stores are fast and do not suffer any problems as EBS. Instance stores can be configured as RAID 0 to utilize it even further.

RAM

Larger memory boosts Cassandra performance from multiple aspects. More memory can hold larger MemTables, which means that fresh data stays for a longer duration in memory and leads to lesser disk accesses for recent data. This also implies that there will be fewer flushes (less frequent disk I/O) of MemTable to SSTable, and the SSTables will be larger and fewer. This leads to improved read performance as fewer SSTables are needed to scan during a lookup. Larger RAM can accommodate larger row cache, thus decreasing disk access.

For any sort of production setup, a RAM capacity less than 8 GB is not recommended. A memory capacity above 16 GB is preferred.

CPU

Cassandra is a highly-concurrent application. All of the CPU-intesive tasks, such as compaction, writes, and fetching results from multiple SSTables and joining them to create a single view for the client, keep running during the life cycle of Cassandra. It is suggested to use an eight-core CPU, but anything with a higher core will just be better.

For a cloud-based setup, a couple of things need to be kept in mind:

- A provider that gives a CPU-bursting feature should be used. One such provider is **Rackspace**.

- AWS Micro instances should be avoided for any serious work. There are many reasons for this. AWS Micro comes with EBS storage and no option to use an instance store. But the deal-breaker issue is CPU throttling that makes it useless for Cassandra. If one performs a CPU-intensive task for 10 seconds or so, CPU usage gets restricted on micro instances. However, AWS Micro instances may be good (cheap), if one just wants to get started with Cassandra.

Is node a server?

With vnodes from 1.2 onward, it is confusing what we mean by node. This section assumes a node is a machine. Unless you have specifically turned off vnodes by setting initial tokens and commenting out num_tokens in cassandra.yaml, you would have as many vnodes on that machine as the number specified by num_tokens. With the virtualization of nodes making each Cassandra machine behave as multiple small Cassandra nodes that hold a small range of row keys, version 1.2 and onward can hold lot more data than they could before.

The suggested size of data per machine closely depends on an application's read and write load. However, in general, keeping the data size of per machine to 1 TB or below is a good idea, although Cassandra can work decently well up to 5 TB of data per node.

Network

As any other distributed system, Cassandra is highly dependent on the network. Although Cassandra is tolerant to network partitioning, a reliable network with less outages is preferred for the system — less repairs and less inconsistencies.

A congestion-free, high-speed (gigabit or higher), reliable network is pretty important as each read-write, replication, and moving and/or draining node puts heavy load on the network.

System configurations

Operating system configurations play a significant role in enhancing Cassandra performance. On a dedicated Cassandra server, resources must be tweaked to utilize the full potential of the machine.

Cassandra runs on a JVM, so it can be run on any system that has a JVM. It is recommended to use a Linux variant (CentOS, Ubuntu, Fedora, RHEL, and so on) for Cassandra's production deployment. There are many reasons to it. Configuring system-level settings is easier. Most of the production servers rely on Linux-like systems for deployment. As of April 2013, 65 percent of servers use it. The best toolings are available on Linux: SSH and pSSH commands such as top, free, df, and ps to measure system performance and excellent filesystems such as ext4 and XFS. There are built-in mechanisms to watch the rolling log using tail, and there are excellent editors such as Vim and Emacs, and they're all free!

More information on the usage share of operating systems is available at `http://en.wikipedia.org/wiki/Usage_share_of_operating_systems#Summary`.

We will be using a Linux-like system for the rest of the book, unless mentioned otherwise. If you are unfamiliar with Linux, there is an excellent book to cover everything you need to know about it: *Linux Administration Handbook, Nemeth, Snyder,* and *Hein, Addison-Wesley Professional.*

Optimizing user limits

The `limits.conf` file (located at `/etc/security/`) gives a simple mechanism to set resource limits to users. To make Cassandra work without choking, it must be provided with higher resource availability, which can be easily done by this file. Add or update the following values to various resources (you need to have root access to do this):

```
* softnofile 32768
* hard nofile 32768
root soft nofile 32768
root hard nofile 32768
* softmemlock unlimited
* hard memlock unlimited
root soft memlock unlimited
root hard memlock unlimited
* soft as unlimited
* hard as unlimited
root soft as unlimited
root hard as unlimited
```

If you are using a cloud, you may want to set and store the values mentioned in the following list to your machine image file:

- `nofile`: By default, a Linux-based system has an upper cap on the number of open files. This may cause trouble for a moderately large setup. Reading and/or writing may involve a large number of file accesses. Apart from this, node-to-node communication is socket-based, that is, it takes one file descriptor per socket. Thus, having a setting that allows a high number of concurrently open file descriptors is a good idea.

  A file descriptor can be anything below 2^{20} for RHEL and family. 32768 (= 2^{15}) is a good range of values to start with.

- `memlock`: If you are coming from a relational database background, `memlock` is chiefly used for a huge page. The `memlock` parameter specifies how much memory any `* = wild card` user can lock in its address space. It can be set to unlimited or the maximum value of RAM in KB.

The rest of the settings in the preceding configuration are just for hard and soft limits. In actuality, both are set to unlimited. For more information about `limits.conf`, visit `http://linux.die.net/man/5/limits.conf`. This and the other limit configurations can be seen by issuing the `ulimit -a` command.

Swapping memory

Swap is bad for Cassandra, especially in the production setup. It is advisable to disable swap on a production machine (assuming it's a dedicated Cassandra server). Basically, swap space is an area on the secondary storage (hard drive) that works as extended memory. Swap is used when the total memory required by processes is more than the available memory. The operating system moves memory segments (also known as **pages**) from or to the swap area to free up memory. This is called **paging**. Reading from secondary storage to access these pages is painfully slow when compared to access from the main memory. This is a major performance hit. (More information on paging performance is available at `http://en.wikipedia.org/wiki/Paging#Performance`.)

Cassandra is fault tolerant, so we can trade the possibility of a node going down for a speedy response when it is up. That is a quick node death caused by the **Out-Of-Memory (OOM)** killer resulting from memory crunch, which is better than a sluggish system.

To disable swap permanently, you need to edit `/etc/fstab` (requires root access) and comment out all the lines containing the type `swap` by putting # at the beginning of the line, as shown in the following line of code:

```
#/dev/sda3  none  swap  sw  0  0
```

To immediately and/or temporarily switch off `swap`, execute the following command:

```
$ sudo swapoff --all
```

Clock synchronization

In *Chapter 2, Cassandra Architecture*, we've learned that Cassandra uses a timestamp for conflict resolution. It is very important to have clocks on each server and client machines to be synchronized with a reliable central clock to avoid unexpected overwrites.

The most common way to do this is by using the **Network Time Protocol** (**NTP**) daemon. It sets the system time in synchronism with the time server, and can maintain time resolution to within milliseconds. You may check whether your system has NTP installed and running by executing `ntpq -p`.

Here is how you install and configure NTP:

1. Install NTP on Fedora/RHEL/CentOS:

    ```
    $ yum install ntp
    ```

2. Install NTP on Debian/Ubuntu:

    ```
    $ sudo apt-get install ntp
    ```

3. Configure time servers (they are most likely, configured already):

    ```
    $ vi /etc/ntp.conf #open with editor, root access needed
    ```

4. Add server(s) and save:

    ```
    $ server pool.ntp.org
    ```

5. Restart the NTP service:

    ```
    $ /etc/init.d/ntpd restart
    ```

6. Force an immediate update:

    ```
    $ ntpdate pool.ntp.org
    ```

Although we have mentioned that the timestamp for the column is provided by the client, it is not true for CQL. CQL uses the server-side timestamp unless specified by the `USING TIMESTAMP` clause.

Even if you do not use CQL, the importance of synchronization on the server-side expiring columns is retained, and tombstone removal does require time to be correctly set. In general, it is advisable to have your production servers (of any application) to be time synchronized.

With Amazon Web Services or any other cloud service, it is a general perception that depending on a hardware clock is a safe bet. This is not correct. There may be situations when time on these virtual instances gets drifted. In AWS EC2 instances, to be able to set up NTP, you need to disable sync with the clock on the physical machine. You can do that by using the following command:

```
$ echo 1 > /proc/sys/xen/independent_wallclock
```

This is transient, but to make it permanent, you can edit /etc/ sysctl.conf by adding the following line of code:

```
    xen.independent_wallclock=1
```

Disk readahead

Disk readahead boosts sequential access to the disk by reading a little more data than requested ahead of time to mitigate some effects of slow disk reads. This is called **readahead (RA)**. This means less frequent requests to the disk.

But this function has its disadvantages as well. If your system is performing high-frequency random reads and writes, a high RA would translate them into magnified reads and/or writes—much higher I/O operations than actually is. This will slow down the system. (It also piles up memory with the data that you do not actually need.)

To view the current value of RA, execute blockdev -report as shown in the following command line:

```
$ sudo blockdev -report
```

RO	RASSZ	BSZ	StartSec	Size	Device
rw256	512	4096	0	320072933376	/dev/sda
rw256	512	4096	2048	104857600	/dev/sda1
rw256	512	4096	206848	73295462400	/dev/sda2
rw256	512	1024	143362110	1024	/dev/sda3

```
...
```

In the preceding example, RA is 256 blocks of a **sector size (SSZ)** of 512 bytes. Therefore, 512 * 256 bytes = 128 KB.

Unfortunately, the commonly suggested value of RA is 65536, or 32 MB! This is very bad for a Cassandra setup. Do not use this high value for RA. It is recommended to set the readahead to `512`. Here is how to do that:

```
# set RA, may require sudoer permission
$ sudo blockdev --setra 512 /dev/<device>
```

The setting can be made permanent by placing it in a local `run-config` file.

The required software

Cassandra runs over a JVM, and this is all you need to get Cassandra up and running. Any platform that has the JVM can have Cassandra. At the time of writing this, Java's latest version was Java SE 8. However, it is highly recommended to use Oracle Java 7 for Cassandra, to avoid unexplainable bugs due to any inconsistency in the Java version or vendor implementation.

The other thing that one should consider for the production setup is to have the **Java Native Access (JNA)** library. It provides access to the native platform's shared libraries. JNA can be configured to disallow swapping of the JVM and hence improve Cassandra memory usage.

Installing Oracle Java 7

The default installation of Linux systems usually contains the OpenJDK **Java Runtime Environment (JRE)**. This should be removed or, alternatively, OpenJDK should be retained, but the default JRE should be set as Oracle JRE. This guide will use a 64-bit system. To check whether your system has JRE, and what version of it executes, run the `java -version` command in the shell:

```
# Check Java (important fields are highlighted)
$ java -version

java version "1.6.0_24"
OpenJDK Runtime Environment (IcedTea6 1.11.11) (amazon-61.1.11.11.53.
amzn1-x86_64)
OpenJDK 64-Bit Server VM (build 20.0-b12, mixed mode)
```

RHEL and CentOS systems

We are going to follow three basic steps for installing Oracle Java 6 for RHEL and CentOS systems:

- **Downloading the binary file from the Oracle website**: JRE 7 can be downloaded from Oracle's website at `http://www.oracle.com/technetwork/java/javase/downloads/jre7-downloads-1880261.html`. Unfortunately, at the time of writing of this book, we couldn't perform `wget` to download this file from the command line. This is due to the fact that Oracle mandates the users to accept the Oracle Binary Code License before downloading can commence. The easiest way that I find is to accept and download the file on your work desktop and then copy and paste it onto the server using `scp`.

  Choose the **Linux x64-rpm.bin** version to download in order to install it on RHEL-like systems.

- **Installing a JRE**: Set the downloaded file as executable, and execute it as follows:

  ```
  $ chmod a+x jre-7u67-linux-x64-rpm.bin
  $ sudo ./jre-7u67-linux-x64-rpm.bin
  ```

   Note that the `7u67` part of the filename may be different for you. It was the latest version at the time of writing of this book.

- **Configuring Oracle JRE as default**: If you have OpenJDK on your server machine, you will have to set it as an alternative, and use Oracle JRE by default. The RHEL family has a utility called `alternatives` inspired by Debian's `update-dependencies` utility for conflict resolution in cases where there are multiple software applications that perform similar functionalities, but the user will prefer one type of software to be the default for those functions.

 The `alternatives` utility takes four parameters to install software as default: a symbolic link to where the software is to be installed, the generic name of the software, the actual path of where the software is installed, and a priority that determines which type of software is to be chosen by default. The highest-priority software is set to the default.

The following code block will go through the details of the process:

```
# See the details Default: OpenJDK, priority: 16000
$ alternatives --display java
java - status is auto.
link currently points to /usr/lib/jvm/jre-1.6.0-openjdk.x86_64/bin/
java
/usr/lib/jvm/jre-1.6.0-openjdk.x86_64/bin/java - priority 16000


# Install Oracle JRE with HIGHER preference
$ sudo alternatives --install /usr/bin/java java /usr/java/
jre1.7.0_64/bin/java 31415


# See the details
$ alternatives --display java
java - status is auto.
link currently points to /usr/java/jre1.6.0_34/bin/java
/usr/lib/jvm/jre-1.6.0-openjdk.x86_64/bin/java - priority 16000
  [-- snip --]
/usr/java/jre1.7.0_67/bin/java - priority 31415
  [-- snip --]
Current `best' version is /usr/java/jre1.6.0_34/bin/java.


# View the current version
$ java -version

java version "1.7.0_67"
Java(TM) SE Runtime Environment (build 1.7.0_67-b19) Java HotSpot(TM)
64-Bit Server VM (build 24.67-b09, mixed mode)
```

The `sudo alternatives --config java` command can be used to switch the default version.

Once all this is done, the `Bash` profile can be updated to have JAVA_HOME. To do this, you need to append the following line in `~/.bashrc`:

```
export JAVA_HOME=/usr/java/jre1.6.0_34
```

Debian and Ubuntu systems

Fortunately, installing Java on Ubuntu is much easier than on RHEL. It is probably not the official way to install Java, but is certainly the most popular way. It takes away the pain of downloading manually and copying over the server. Here are the steps:

1. Add the `webupd8team` PPA repository to the machine:

   ```
   sudo add-apt-repository ppa:webupd8team/java
   ```

2. Update the package list from the repositories and install Java 7:

   ```
   sudo apt-get update

   sudo apt-get install oracle-java7-installer
   ```

   This will open an interactive shell where you need to accept the Oracle license to be able to complete the installation.

3. Check your Java version:

   ```
   $ java -version


   java version "1.7.0_67"

   Java(TM) SE Runtime Environment (build 1.7.0_67-b01)

   Java HotSpot(TM) 64-Bit Server VM (build 24.65-b04, mixed mode)
   ```

Installing the Java Native Access library

The installer for **Java Native Access (JNA)** is available to all the decently modern operating systems. Cassandra requires JNA 3.4 or higher. JNA can be installed manually; see the details at `https://github.com/twall/jna`.

- To install JNA on RHEL/CentOS, run the following command:

  ```
  $ yum install jna
  ```

- To install JNA on Debian/Ubuntu, run the following command:

  ```
  $ sudo apt-get install libjna-java
  ```

Installing Cassandra

With the JVM ready, installing Cassandra is as easy as downloading the appropriate tarball from the Apache Cassandra's download page (`http://cassandra.apache.org/download`) and untarring it. On Debian or Ubuntu, you may install Cassandra from either a `.tar` file or an Apache Software Foundation repository.

Installing from a tarball

It is assumed that Cassandra is installed in the /opt directory, the data files are installed in the /cassandra-data directory, and the system logs are installed in /var/log/cassandra. These are just some conventions that were chosen by me. You may choose a location that suits you best:

```
# Download. Please select appropriate version and URL from http://
cassandra.apache.org/download
$ wget \
http://mirror.sdunix.com/apache/cassandra/1.1.11/apache-cassandra-1.1.11-
bin.tar.gz
[-- snip --]
Saving to: 'apache-cassandra-1.1.11-bin.tar.gz'


# extract
$ tar xzf apache-cassandra-1.1.11-bin.tar.gz


# (optional) Symbolic link to easily switch versions in future without
having to change dependent scripts
$ ln -s apache-cassandra-1.1.11 cassandra
```

Installing from ASFRepository for Debian or Ubuntu

Apache Software Foundation provides Debian packages for different versions of Cassandra for its direct installation from the repository. To list the packages, run the following command:

```
# Edit sources
$ sudo vi /etc/apt/sources.list
```

Also, append the following three lines:

```
# Cassandra repo
deb http://www.apache.org/dist/cassandra/debian 21x main

deb-src http://www.apache.org/dist/cassandra/debian 21x main
```

Next, execute sudo apt-get update, as follows:

```
$ sudo apt-get update
Ign http://us-east-1.ec2.archive.ubuntu.com trusty InRelease
```

```
[-- snip -- ]


Reading package lists... Done


W: GPG error: http://www.apache.org 21x InRelease: The following
signatures couldn't be verified because the public key is not available:
NO_PUBKEY 749D6EEC0353B12C
```

If you get the preceding error, add the public keys as follows:

```
gpg --keyserver pgp.mit.edu --recv-keys 749D6EEC0353B12C


gpg --export --armor 749D6EEC0353B12C | sudo apt-key add -
```

Now, you can install Cassandra using the following commands:

```
$ sudo apt-get update
$ sudo apt-get install cassandra
```

This installation does most of the system-wide configurations for you. It makes all the executables available to the `$PATH` system path, copies the configuration file to /etc/cassandra, and adds the .init script to set up proper JVM and ulimits. It also sets run-level, so Cassandra starts at boot as cassandra user.

Anatomy of the installation

There are a couple of programs and files that one must know about to work effectively with Cassandra. These programs and files come to use during investigation, maintenance, configuration, and optimization.

Depending on how the installation is done, the file may be available at different locations. For a tarball installation, everything is neatly packaged under the directory where Cassandra is installed: binaries under the bin directory and the configuration file under the conf directory. For repository-based installations, binaries are available in /usr/bin and /usr/sbin directories and configuration files are available under /etc/cassandra and /etc/default/cassandra.

Cassandra binaries

Cassandra binaries contain executables for various tasks. These executables exist in the installation directory under the `bin/` folder or `tools/bin/`. Let's take a quick glance at them:

- `bin/cassandra`: It starts the Cassandra daemon using the default configuration. To start Cassandra in the foreground, use the `-f` option. You can use *Ctrl + C* to kill Cassandra and view logs on the console. One may also use `-p <pid_file>` to have a handle and kill Cassandra running in the background by using `kill `cat <pid_file>``.

  If Cassandra is installed from the repository, it must have created a service for it. Therefore, one should use `sudo service cassandra start`, `sudo service cassandra stop`, and `sudo service cassandra status` to start, stop, and query the status of Cassandra, respectively.

- `bin/cassandra-cli`: Cassandra's **command-line interface** (CLI) gives very basic access to execute simple commands meant for modifying and accessing keyspaces and column families. The typical use of Cassandra looks like this:

  cassandra-cli -h <hostname> -p <port> -k <keyspace>

  A file of statements can be passed to the CLI using the `-f` option.

- `bin/cqlsh`: This is a CLI to execute CQL3 queries. Typically, the `cqlsh-connect` command looks like this:

  cqlsh <hostname> <port> -k <keyspace>

- `tools/bin/json2sstable` and `tools/bin/sstable2json`: As the name suggests, they represent the yin and yang of serializing and deserializing the data in SSTable. They can be vaguely assumed to be similar to the `mysqldump --xml <database>` command, except that it works in the JSON format. The `sstable2json` too provides SSTable as JSON and `json2sstable` takes JSON to materialize a functional SSTable. The `sstable2json` tool may have the following three options:
    - `-k`: The keys to be dumped
    - `-x`: The keys to be excluded
    - `-e`: The option making `sstable2json` to dump just keys, not column family data

      One can use the `-k` or `-x` switches up to 500 times. A general `sstable2json` executable looks like this:

      sstable2json -k <key1> -k <key2><sstable_path>

The `sstable_path` must be the full path to SSTable such as /
cassandra-data/data/mykeyspace/mykeyspace-hc-1.data. Also,
the `key` variable must be a hex string.

- `bin/sstablekeys`: This is essentially `sstable2json` with a -e switch.

- `bin/sstableloader`: This is used to bulk load to Cassandra. One can
  simply copy SSTable data files and load them on to another Cassandra setup
  without much hassle. Essentially, `sstableloader` reads the data files and
  streams to the current Cassandra setup as specified by Cassandra's YAML
  file. We will see this tool in more detail in the *Using Cassandra bulk loader to
  restore the data* section in *Chapter 6, Managing a Cluster – Scaling, Node Repair,
  and Backup*.

Configuration files

Cassandra has a central configuration file named `cassandra.yaml`. It contains cluster
settings, node-to-node communication specifications, performance-related settings,
authentication, security, and backup settings.

Apart from this, there are the `logback.xml` and `cassandra-topology.properties`
files. The `log4j-server.properties` file is used to tweak Cassandra logging
settings. The only thing that one may want to change in this file is the following line
so that we can change the location where logs are located:

```
<fileNamePattern>${cassandra.logdir}/system.log.%i.zip</
fileNamePattern>
```

The `cassandra-topology.properties` file is to be filled with cluster-specific values
if you use `PropertyFileSnich`. We'll discuss more on this in the present chapter,
although we have an idea about it from *Chapter 2, Cassandra Architecture*.

The `cassandra.yaml` file and other files can be accessed from the `conf` directory
under the installation directory for a tarball installation. For repository installation,
the `cassandra.yaml` file and other files can be found under `/etc/cassandra`.

Setting up data and commitlog directories

As discussed earlier, one should configure the `data` and `commitlog` directories onto
separate disk drives to improve performance. The `cassandra.yaml` file holds all
these configurations and more.

AWS EC2 users

Although it is recommended to have data and commit logs on two drives, for EC2 instance store type servers, it is recommended to set up the RAID 0 configuration and use it for both the `data` and `commitlog` directories. It performs better than having one of those on the root device and other on ephemeral. Visit `https://aws.amazon.com/articles/1074` to create the RAID 0 setup on EC2 instances.

EBS-backed instances are a bad choice for Cassandra installation owing to their slow I/O performance and the same goes for any NAS setup.

To update data directories, edit the following lines in `cassandra.yaml`:

```
# directories where Cassandra should store data on disk.
data_file_directories: /var/lib/cassandra/data
```

Change `/var/lib/cassandra/data` to a directory that is suitable for your setup. You may as well add more directories spanning different hard disks. Then change the `commitlog` directory as shown in the following code:

```
# commit log
commitlog_directory: /var/lib/cassandra/commitlog
```

Edit the preceding line to set a desired location.

These directories (`data` and `commitlog`) must be available for write. If it is not a fresh install, one may want to migrate data from the old `data` and `commitlog` directories to new ones.

Configuring a Cassandra cluster

Now that you have a single node setup, you may start Cassandra by executing `<cassandra_installation>/bin/cassandra` for a tarball install or by running `sudo service cassandra start` for a repository install. (We'll see later in this chapter how to write a `.init` script for Cassandra and set it up to start on boot.) However, in order to get a Cassandra cluster working, a couple of configuration tweaks are required.

If you look at `cassandra.yaml`, you will find that it has the following six sections:

- **Cluster setup properties**: These are basically startup properties, file location, ports, replica placement strategies, and internode communication settings.
- **Performance tuning properties**: These help in setting up appropriate values for system and/or network resources on the basis of your setup.
- **Client connection properties**: These help in setting up the behavior of client-to-node connectivity, namely the number of requests per client or maximum number of threads (clients).
- **Internode communication**: This section contains configurations for node-to-node communication within a cluster. These include hinted handoff settings and failure detection settings.
- **Backup settings**: These settings are Cassandra-automated backup items.
- **Authorization and authentication settings**: These provide protected access to the cluster. The default is to allow all.

In most cases, you will never have to bother about client connection properties and internode communication settings. Even, by default, the configuration is very smart and robust for any modern-day computer. The rest of this chapter will discuss the cluster setup properties and various options that Cassandra provides out of the box. Security will be discussed briefly. In *Chapter 5, Performance Tuning*, we will tune Cassandra using various properties in `cassandra.yaml`.

The cluster name

A cluster name is used to logically group nodes that belong to the same cluster. It works as a name space for nodes. In a multiple-cluster environment, it works as a preventive mechanism for nodes of a cluster to join some other clusters when they boot up.

It is always a good idea to give a meaningful name to a cluster, even if you have a single cluster at the time. Here is an example of how `cluster_name` can be assigned via `cassandra.yaml`:

```
cluster_name: 'MyAppMainCluster'
```

It is recommended to change the cluster name before you launch the cluster. Changing the cluster name when the cluster is up and running throws an exception. This is because the cluster name resides in the system keyspace.

If you have to change the cluster name, there is an unofficial trick to do that.
Use `cqlsh` to connect to a node. You need to edit the `system.local` table by running
an UPDATE query as follows:

```
UPDATE system.local SET cluster_name='new_cluster_name' WHERE
key='local'
```

After this, you need to perform two steps in the following order:

1. Execute `bin/nodetool flush`.
2. Change `cluster_name` in `cassandra.yaml` to whatever you have used to
   update `system.local`.

After this, restart the node.

The seed node

A seed node is the one that a newly launched node consults with to learn about the
cluster. Although gossip (refer to *Chapter 2, Cassandra Architecture*) is a means for
nodes to know each other, a seed is the first node that any new node will know and
start a gossip with. Eventually, all other nodes in the cluster will know of the new
node's presence and vice versa.

There must be at least one seed node in a cluster. A seed node should be a rather
stable node. One may configure more than one seed node for added redundancy and
increased availability of seed nodes. In `cassandra.yaml`, seed nodes are a comma-
separated list of seed addresses:

```
seed_provider:
  - class_name: org.apache.cassandra.locator.SimpleSeedProvider
    parameters:
      # Ex: "<ip1>,<ip2>,<ip3>"
      - seeds: "c1.mydomain.com,c2.mydomain.com"
```

Listen, broadcast, and RPC addresses

A listen address is the address that nodes use to connect to each other for
communication and/or gossip. It is important to set this address to the private IP of
the machine. If this is not done, the machine will pick up the hostname value, which
if incorrectly configured can cause problems.

A broadcast address is the public address of the node. If it is not set, it will take
whatever value the listen address bears. This is generally required only if you are
setting up Cassandra at multiple data centers.

EC2 users

For multiple data center installations, you need to use EC2 Snitch. The `listen_address` may be set to blank because AWS assigns a hostname that is based on a private IP, but you may set it to a private IP or private DNS. The `broadcast_address` must be a public IP or a public DNS. Also, remember to open `storage_port` (default is `7000`) in your security group that holds Cassandra instances.

An RPC address is for client connections to the node. It can be anything — the IP address, hostname, or `0.0.0.0`. If not set, the node will take the hostname.

In `cassandra.yaml`, these properties look as follows:

```
# listen_address is not set, so it takes hostname.
listen_address:

# broadcast is commented. So, it is what listen_address is+#
broadcast_address: 1.2.3.4
# rpc_address is not set, so it is hostname.
rpc_address:
```

num_tokens versus initial_token

The `num_tokens` and `initial_token` define the way you want your cluster to be set up. `num_tokens` says that the cluster is a modern one with vnodes, and this is the default setting in Cassandra 1.2 and newer versions. The `initial_token` is the old approach where each node can handle just one token and is responsible for one range of row keys. The `initial_token` is commented by default.

It is recommended to use vnodes and `num_tokens` if you are setting up a new Cassandra cluster. A vnode solves a couple of critical problems; for example one is load balancing, which is needed no more. With `intial_token`, if you added or removed servers, you would need to rebalance the cluster by manually setting `initial_token` and moving records over. This approach is error-prone, complex, and unnecessary. Vnode solves this problem. With a vnode, the data is assigned and distributed in such a way that cluster load is balanced between incoming and outgoing nodes. For a vnode, replacing a node or starting up a dead node is a network-centric activity where data from replicas gets copied to the newly booted server. With vnodes, most of the servers in the ring, if not all, participate in the streaming of the data to a new server. In a no vnode case, only a small percentage of a cluster is involved in data streaming. This makes recovery fragile and slow.

num_tokens

The `num_tokens` are a way of determining the number of vnodes you want on a node. By default, there are 256 vnodes, which is good for most of the cases. The `num_tokens` are the number of row-key ranges a node is responsible for. One side effect of this property is that you can have a heterogeneous mix of machines and yet have them loaded according to their capacity. For example, a weak machine with low CPU and memory availability can have 64 vnodes, while a beefy machine with 128 GB RAM and eight-core CPU can have 1024 vnodes. This is a useful feature whereby you can load the machines as per their handling capacity.

Breaking from manual management of node tokens from the older version and enabling `num_tokens` frees users from the headache of balancing and assigning tokens to the nodes, every time a new machine is added to the ring.

initial_token

An `initial_token` is by default commented out. It is a pre-v1.2 setting when there was no vnode and each machine was responsible for one row-key range. Unless, you have a specific use case where you want each machine to have one range, or you are stuck with pre-1.2 distribution, this is not recommended.

An `initial_token` is a number assigned to a node that decides the range of keys that it will hold. A node holds token $T(n-1) + 1$ to Tn, where $T(n-1)$ is the upper limit of the token number that some nodes in the ring hold. In the ring diagram, we showed nodes with successive ranges next to each other. For example, node $(n-1)$, n, and $(n+1)$ is in an order, but they may physically be far apart; maybe in different data centers. For more information, refer to *Chapter 2, Cassandra Architecture*.

In `cassandra.yaml`, you may insert an `initial_token` as follows:

```
initial_token: 85070591730234615865843651857942052864
```

It is important to choose initial tokens wisely to make sure the data is evenly distributed across the cluster. If you do not assign initial tokens to the nodes at the start of a new cluster, it may get automatically assigned, which may lead to a hotspot. However, adding a new node is a relatively smart option. If you do not mention the `initial_token` to the new node, Cassandra will take a node that is loaded the most number of times and assign the new node a key that splits the token's own loaded node into half. It is possible to load balance a running cluster, and this is fairly easy. We'll learn more about load balancing in *Chapter 6, Managing a Cluster – Scaling, Node Repair, and Backup*. The next logical question is how to determine the `initial_token` for a node. It depends on the partitioner that you are using. Basically, we divide the whole range of keys that the partitioner supports into N equal parts, where N is the total number of nodes in the cluster. Then, we assign each node a number. We will see this in the next section.

Partitioners

By assigning initial tokens, we have created buckets of keys. What factor determines which key goes to what bucket? It is the partitioner. A partitioner generates a hash value of the row key. On the basis of the hash value, Cassandra determines to which bucket (node) this row needs to go. This is a good way in which hash will always generate a unique number for a row key. Therefore, this approach is also used to determine which node to read from.

Like everything else in Cassandra, a partitioner is a pluggable interface. You can implement your own partitioner by implementing `org.apache.cassandra.dht.IPartitioner` and dropping the `.class` or `.jar` file in Cassandra's `lib` directory.

Here is how you insert the preference for a partitioner in `cassandra.yaml`:

```
partitioner: org.apache.cassandra.dht.RandomPartitioner
```

In most cases, the default partitioner is generally good for you. It distributes keys evenly. As of version 2.1.0, the default is `Murmur3Partitioner`, but versions under 1.2 have `RandomPartitioner`. The `Murmur3Partitioner` is faster and slightly more efficient than the other.

Be warned that it is a pretty critical decision to choose a partitioner because this determines what data stays where. It affects the SSTable structure. If you decide to change it, you need to clean the data directory. Thus, the decision made for the partitioner at the start of the cluster is likely to stay for the lifetime of a cluster.

Cassandra provides three partitioners by default.

> Actually, there are five partitioners. But two are deprecated, so we will not be discussing them here. It is not recommended to use them. They are `OrderPreservingPartitioner` and `CollatingOrderPreservingPartitioner`.

The Random partitioner

A Random partitioner is the default partitioner before version 1.2. It uses MD5 hash to generate hash values for row keys. Since hashes are not generated in any orderly manner, it does not guarantee any ordering. This means that two lexicographically close row keys can possibly be thrown into two different nodes. This random assignment of a token to a key is what makes it suitable for the even distribution of keys among nodes. This means it is highly unlikely that a balanced node is ever going to have hotspots.

The number of keys generated by a Random partitioner varies from 0 to 2127 - 1. Therefore, for the ith node in an *N*-node cluster, the initial token can be calculated by *2127 * (i - 1) / N*.

 Remember, `initial_token` is for a non-vnode configuration. It is highly likely that you are using one with vnodes, that is, the `num_tokens` setting, so you need not bother about the calculation below or the calculations in subsequent partitioners done for nodes.

The following is simple Python code to generate the complete sequence of initial tokens for a Random partitioner of a cluster of eight nodes:

```
# running in Python shell
>>> nodes = 8
>>> print ("\n".join(["Node #" + str(i+1) +": " + str((2 ** 127)*i/nodes)
for i in xrange(nodes) ]))


Node #1: 0
Node #2: 21267647932558653966460912964485513216
Node #3: 42535295865117307932921825928971026432
Node #4: 63802943797675961899382738893456539648
Node #5: 85070591730234615865843651857942052864
Node #6: 106338239662793269832304564822427566080
Node #7: 127605887595351923798765477786913079296
Node #8: 148873535527910577765226390751398592512
```

The Byte-ordered partitioner

A Byte-ordered partitioner, as the name suggests, generates tokens for row keys that are in the order of hexadecimal representations of the key. This makes it possible for rows to be ordered by row keys and iterate through rows as iterating through an ordered list. However, this benefit comes with a major drawback: hotspots. The reason why a hotspot is created is due to uneven distribution of data across a cluster. If you have a cluster with 26 nodes, a partitioner such as `ByteOrderedPartitioner` and each node is responsible for one letter. Therefore, the first node is responsible for all the keys starting with A, the second for B, and so on. A column family that uses the usernames as row keys will have uneven data distribution across the ring. The data distribution will be skewed with nodes X, Q, and Z being very light, and nodes A and S being heavily loaded.

This is bad for multiple reasons, with the most important one being the generation of a hotspot. The nodes with more data will be accessed more than the ones with less data. The overall performance of a cluster may be dropped down to the number of requests that a couple of highly loaded nodes can serve.

The best way to assign the initial token to a cluster using `ByteOrderedPartitioner` is to sample data and determine what keys are the best to assign as initial tokens to ensure an equally balanced cluster.

Let's take a hypothetical case where your keys of all keyspaces can be represented by five-character strings from `"00000"` to `"zzzzz"`. Here is how we generate initial tokens in Python:

```
>>> start = int("00000".encode('hex'), 16)
>>> end = int("zzzzz".encode('hex'), 16)
>>> range = end - start
>>> nodes = 8
>>> print "\n".join([ "Node #" + str(i+1) + ": %032x" % (start + range*i/
nodes)  for i in xrange(nodes) ])
```

```
Node #1:  00000000000000000000003030303030
Node #2:  00000000000000000000003979797979
Node #3:  00000000000000000000042c2c2c2c2
Node #4:  0000000000000000000004c0c0c0c0b
Node #5:  00000000000000000000005555555555
Node #6:  0000000000000000000005e9e9e9e9e
Node #7:  0000000000000000000067e7e7e7e7
Node #8:  00000000000000000000007131313130
```

Remember, this is just an example. In a real case, you will decide this only after evaluating the data, or if you probably want to have initial tokens assigned by UUIDs.

The Mumur3 partitioner

The Murmur3 partitioner is the new default for Cassandra Version 1.2 or higher. If you are starting a new cluster, it is recommended to keep the Mumur3 partitioner. It is not order preserving, and it has all the features of a Random partitioner plus it is fast and provides better performance than a Random partitioner. Another difference is that a Random partitioner generates token values between -263 and +263.

If you are migrating from a previous version to 1.2 or higher, please make sure that you are using the same partitioner as the previous one. If you were using a default, it is likely that you were using a Random partitioner. This will cause trouble if you have not edited `cassandra.yaml` to change the new default Murmur3 partitioner back to a Random partitioner.

To generate initial tokens, we'll again apply our familiar formula, but this time the start position is not zero, so the range of tokens is (end to start): $+2^{63} - (-2^{63}) = 2^{64}$. Here is the simple Python script to do this:

```
>>> nodes = 8
>>> print "\n".join(["Node #" + str(i+1) + ": " + str( -(2 ** 63) + (2 ** 64)*i/nodes) for i in xrange(nodes)] )
```

```
Node #1: -9223372036854775808

Node #2: -6917529027641081856

Node #3: -4611686018427387904

Node #4: -2305843009213693952

Node #5: 0

Node #6: 2305843009213693952

Node #7: 4611686018427387904

Node #8: 6917529027641081856
```

Snitches

Snitches are the way to tell Cassandra about the topology of a cluster, and about nodes' locations and their proximities. There are two tasks that snitches help Cassandra with. They are as follows:

- **Replica placement**: As discussed in *Chapter 2, Cassandra Architecture*, depending on the configured replication factor, data gets written to more than one node. Snitches are the decision-making mechanism that determine where the replicas should be sent to. An efficient snitch will send place replicas in a manner that provides the highest availability of data.

- **Efficient read and write routing**: Snitches are all about defining cluster schema, and thus, they help Cassandra in deciding the most efficient path to perform reads and writes.

Similar to partitioners, snitches are pluggable. You can plug in your own custom snitch by extending `org.apache.cassandra.locator.EndPointSnitch`. The `PropertyFileEndPointSnitch` class can be used as a guideline on how to write a snitch. To configure a snitch, you need to alter `endpoint_snitch` in `cassandra.yaml`:

```
endpoint_snitch: SimpleSnitch
```

For custom snitches, mention the fully qualified class name of the snitch, assuming you have dropped the custom snitch `.class`/`.jar` file in Cassandra's `lib` directory.

Out of the box, Cassandra provides the snitches detailed in the upcoming sections.

SimpleSnitch

`SimpleSnitch` is basically a do-nothing snitch. If you see the code, it basically returns `rack1` and `datacenter1` for whatever IP address the endpoint has. Since it discards any information that may be retrieved from the IP address, it is appropriate for installations where data center related information is not available, or all the nodes are in the same data center. This is the default snitch.

PropertyFileSnitch

`PropertyFileSnitch` is a way to explicitly tell Cassandra the relative location of various nodes in the clusters. It gives you a means to handpick the nodes to group under a data center and a rack. The location definition of each node in the cluster is stored in a configuration file, `cassandra-topology.properties`, which can be found under the `conf` directory (for a tarball installation, it is `<installation>/conf`; for repository installations, it is `/etc/cassandra`). Note that if you are using `PropertyFileSnitch`, all the nodes must have an identical topology file.

The `cassandra-topology.properties` file is a standard properties file with keys as the IP address of the node and values expressed as `<data-center-name>:<rack-name>`. It is up to you what data center name and what rack name you give. Two nodes with the same data center name will be treated as nodes within a single data center. Two nodes with the same data center name and rack name combination will be treated as two nodes on the same rack.

Here is an example topology file:

```
# Cassandra Node IP=Data Center:Rack
# Data-center 1
10.110.6.30=DC1:RAC1
10.110.6.11=DC1:RAC1
```

```
10.110.4.30=DC1:RAC2

# Data-center 2
10.120.8.10=DC2:RAC1
10.120.8.11=DC2:RAC1

# Data-center 3
10.130.1.13=DC3:RAC1
10.130.2.10=DC3:RAC2

# default for unknown nodes
default=DC1:RAC0
```

DCX and RACX are commonly used patterns to denote a data center and a rack, respectively. Nevertheless, you are free to choose anything that suits you. The default option is to take care of any node that is not listed in `PropertyFileSnitch`.

GossipingPropertyFileSnitch

Even with all the fancy naming and grouping, one thing that is a nuance in `PropertyFileSnitch` is the manual effort to keep the topology files updated with every addition or removal of the node. `GossipingPropertyFileSnitch` is there to solve this problem. This snitch uses the gossip mechanism to propagate the information about the node's location.

In each node, you put a file named `cassandra-rackdc.properties` under the `conf` directory. This file contains two components, the names of the node's data center and rack expressed as follows:

```
dc=DC3
rack=RAC2
```

RackInferringSnitch

If `SimpleSnitch` is one end of the spectrum, where a snitch does not assume anything, `RackInferringSnitch` is the other extreme of the spectrum. `RackInferringSnitch` uses an IP address to guess the data center and rack of a node. It assumes that the second octet of the IP address uniquely denotes a data center, and the third octet uniquely represents a rack within a data center. Thus, for `10.110.6.30`, `10.110.6.4`, `10.110.2.42`, and `10.108.10.1`, this snitch assumes that the first two nodes reside in the same data center and in the same rack, while the third node lives in the same data center but in a different rack. It assumes that the fourth node exists in a different data center than the rest of the nodes in the example:

```
    +---------> Data center
    |   +------> Rack
```

```
10.110.6.30
```

This can be dangerous to use if your machines do not use this pattern for IP assignment to the machines in data centers.

EC2Snitch

Ec2Snitch is a snitch specially written for Amazon AWS installations. It uses the node's local metadata to get its availability zone and then breaks it into pieces to determine the rack and data center. Note that the rack and data center determined in this way do not correspond to the physical location of hardware in Amazon's cloud facility, but this approach gives a pretty nice abstraction.

Ec2Snitch treats the region name as the data center name and availability zone as the rack name. EC2Snitch does not work across AWS regions. Therefore, effectively, Ec2Snitch is the same as a single data center setup. If one of your nodes is in us-east-1a and another in us-east-1b, it means that you have two nodes in a data center named us-east in two racks, 1a and 1b.

EC2MultiRegionSnitch

Ec2Snitch does not work well if you decide to keep nodes across different EC2 regions. The reason being EC2Snitch uses private IPs, which will not work across regions (but does work across availability zones in a region).

If your cluster spans multiple regions, you should use EC2MultiRegionSnitch.

EC2 users

If you plan to distribute nodes in different regions, there is more than just a proper snitch that is needed to make nodes successfully communicate with each other. You need to change the following configurations:

- broadcast_address: This should be the public IP or DNS of the node.
- listen_address: This should be set to a private IP or DNS. But if not set, the hostname on EC2 is generally derived from the private IP, which is fine.
- endpoint_snitch: This should be set to EC2MultiRegionSnitch.
- storage_port: The default port number 7000 is fine, but remember to open this port in the security group that holds Cassandra instances.

Replica placement strategies

Apart from putting data in various buckets on the basis of nodes' tokens, Cassandra has to replicate the data depending on what replication factor is associated with the keyspace. Replica placement strategies come into action when Cassandra has to decide where a replica should be placed.

There are two strategies that can be used on the basis of the demand and structure of the cluster.

SimpleStrategy

SimpleStrategy places the data on the node that owns it on the basis of the configured partitioner. It then moves to the next node (toward a higher bucket), places a replica, moves to next node and places another, and so on, until the replication factor is met.

SimpleStrategy is blind to cluster topology. It does not check whether the next node to place the replica in is in the same rack or not. Thus, this may not be the most robust strategy to use to store data. What happens if all the three replicas of a key range are physically located in the same rack (assuming RF=3) and there is a power failure on that rack? You lose access to some data until power is restored. This leads us into a rather smarter strategy, NetworkTopologyStrategy.

Although we discussed how bad SimpleStrategy could be, this is the default strategy. In addition, if you do not know the placement or any configuration details of your data center and you decide to stay in a single data center, NetworkTopologyStrategy cannot help you much.

NetworkTopologyStrategy

NetworkTopologyStrategy, as the name suggests, is a data center- and rack-aware replica placement strategy. NetworkTopologyStrategy tries to avoid the pitfalls of SimpleStrategy by considering the rack name and data center names that it figures out from the configured snitch. With the appropriate strategy_option, stating how many replicas go to which data centers makes NetworkTopologyStrategy a very powerful and robust mirrored database system.

NetworkTopologyStrategy requires the system admin to put a little extra thought when deciding appropriate values for initial tokens for multiple data center installations. For a single data center setup, initial tokens make up an evenly divided token range assigned to various nodes.

Multiple data center setups

Here is the issue with multiple data center setups. Suppose you have two data centers with each having three nodes in it; then, here is how the keyspace looks:

```
CREATE KEYSPACE my_keyspace
WITH REPLICATION = {
  'class' : 'NetworkTopologyStrategy',
  'DC1' : 3,
  'DC2' : 2
};
```

It says that there are at least six nodes in the ring. Keep three copies of each row in DC1 and three more copies in DC2. In Cassandra 1.2 and later versions, Cassandra will distribute the data almost evenly and make sure the specified number of replicas live in a given data center. If you are using the pre-1.2 version of Cassandra or have decided not to use the vnode cluster, you should know how to assign tokens to make sure both the data centers are equally loaded. (If you are using vnodes, you can safely skip to the next section.)

Assume the system actually has four nodes in each data center, and you calculated the initial token by dividing the possible token range into eight equidistant values. If you assign the first four tokens to four nodes in DC1 and the rest to the nodes in DC2, you will end up having a lopsided data distribution.

Let's take an example. Say, we have a partitioner that generates tokens from 0 to 200. If token distribution is carried out in the way previously mentioned, the resulting ring will look like what is shown in the following figure. Since the replication factor is bound by the data center, all the data from 25 to 150 will go to one single node in Data Center 1, while other nodes in the data center will owe relatively smaller number of keys. The same happens to Data Center 2, which has one overloaded node.

This creates a need for a mechanism that balances nodes within each data center. The first option is to divide the partitioner range by the number of nodes in each data center and assign the values to nodes in data centers. However, it wouldn't work because no two nodes can have the same token. The following figure shows multiple data centers—even key distribution causing lopsided nodes:

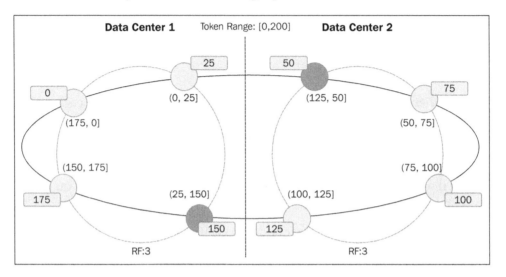

There are two ways to avoid this imbalance in key distribution:

- **Offsetting tokens slightly**: This mechanism is the same as the one that we just discussed. The algorithm for offsetting tokens is as follows:

  1. Calculate the token range as if each data center is a ring.
  2. Offset the values that are duplicated by a small amount, say by 1 or 10 or 100.

     Here is an example. Let's say we have a cluster spanning three data centers. `Data-center 1` and `Data-center 2` have three nodes each, and `Data-center 3` has two nodes. We use `RandomPartitioner`. Here is the split (the final value is used, the duplicates are offset):

     ```
     # Duplicates are offset, final are assigned

     Data-center 1:
     node1:
     0 (final)

     node2:
     56713727820156410577229101238628035242 (final)
     ```

```
node3:
113427455640312821154458202477256070485 (final)


Data-center 2:
node1:
0 (duplicate, offset to avoid collision)
1 (final)


node2:
567137278201564105772291012386280352242 (duplicate, offset)
567137278201564105772291012386280352243 (final)


node3:
113427455640312821154458202477256070485 (duplicate, offset)
113427455640312821154458202477256070486 (final)


Data-center 3:
node1:
0 (duplicate, offset)
2 (final)


node2:
850705917302346158658436518579420528864 (final)
```

If you draw the ring and re-evaluate the token ownership, you will find that all the data centers have balanced nodes.

- **Alternating token assignment**: This is a much simpler technique than the previous one, but it works when all the data centers have an equal number of nodes, which is a pretty common setup.

In this methodology, we divide the token range by the total number of nodes across all the clusters. Then we take the first token value, assign it to a node in `Data-center 1`, take a second token and assign it to a node in the second data center, and so on. Keep revolving through the data centers and assigning the next initial token to nodes until all the nodes are done (and all the tokens are exhausted).

For a setup with three data centers, with each having two nodes, here are the details:

```
$ python -c 'print "\n".join([str((2 ** 127)*i/6) for i in xrange(6) ])'

0
28356863910078205288614550619314017621
567137278201564105772291012386280352242
850705917302346158658436518579420528864
113427455640312821154458202477256070485
141784319550391026443072753096570088106
```

```
Data-center1: node1
0


Data-center2: node1
28356863910078205288614550619314017621


Data-center3: node1
56713727820156410577229101238628035242


Data-center1: node2
85070591730234615865843651857942052864


Data-center2: node2
113427455640312821154458202477256070485


Data-center3: node2
141784319550391026443072753096570088106
```

Launching a cluster with a script

Now that we have configured the machines and we know the cluster settings to carry
out, what snitch to use, and what the initial tokens should be, we'll download the
latest Cassandra installation on multiple machines, set it up, and start it. But it is too
much work to do this manually.

We will see a custom script that does all this for us—after all we are dealing with a
large amount of data and a large number of machines, so doing all of this manually
can lead to errors and can be exhausting (and more importantly, there's no fun!).
This script is available on GitHub at https://github.com/naishe/mastering-
cassandra-v2. You may tweak it as per your needs and work with it.

There are two scripts: install_cassandra.sh and upload_and_execute.sh. The
former is the one that is supposed to be executed on the to-be Cassandra nodes, and
the latter is the one that uploads the former to all the nodes, passes the appropriate
initial token, and executes it. It is the latter that you need to execute on your local
machine and make sure both scripts are in the same directory from where you are
executing. If you are planning to use this script, you may need to change a couple of
variables at the top.

Here is the script configured to set up a three-node cluster on Amazon EC2 machines. Note that it uses `EC2Snitch`, so it does not need to set up a snitch configuration file as it would have if it was using `PropertyFileSnitch` or `GossippingPropertyFileSnitch`. If you are using those snitches, you may need to upload those files to appropriate locations in remote machines too:

```
#install_cassandra.sh

#!/bin/bash

set -e

# This script does the following:

# 1. download cassandra

# 2. create directories

# 3. update cassandra.yaml with

#      cluster_name

#      seeds

#      listen_address

#      rpc_address

#      initial_token

#      endpoint_snitch

#      data dir, commit log dir and logging dir

# 4. start Cassandra

# YOU MUST CHANGE THE VARIABLES TO ADAPT YOUR

# CONFIGURATION OF THE NODE


#SYNOPSYS
```

```
function printHelp(){

  cat << EOF

Synopsis:

  $0



  Downloads, installs, configures and starts Cassandra.

EOF

}



#if [ $# -lt 1 ] ; then

#  printHelp

#  exit 1

#fi



# VARIABLES !!! EDIT AS YOUR CONFIG

# --------------------------------



# DOWNLOAD URL, GET ONE CLOSEST TO YOUR LOCATION FROM http://
cassandra.apache.org/download

download_url='http://www.us.apache.org/dist/cassandra/2.1.0/apache-
cassandra-2.1.0-bin.tar.gz'

file_name="cassandra.tar.gz"
```

```
# NAME OF THE FOLDER THAT GETS CREATED WHEN UNZIPPED
name='cassandra'


# DIRECTORY WHERE CASSANDRA WILL BE INSTALLED TO

install_dir='/opt'


# DATA DIRECTORY

data_dir='/mnt/cassandra-data'


# LOGGING DIRECTORY, YOU NEED NOT SUMP EVERYTHING IN /MNT

logging_dir='/mnt/cassandra-logs'


# CASSANDRA CONFIG !!! EDIT AS YOUR CONFIG

# WATCH FOR DOUBLE QUOTES WITHIN SINGLE QUOTES, THEY ARE INTENTIONAL!


cluster_name='"My Cluster"'

seeds='"c1.mydomain.com"'

listen_address=''

rpc_address=''

endpoint_snitch="Ec2Snitch"


echo "--- DOWNLOADING CASSANDRA"
```

```
wget -O /tmp/${file_name} ${download_url}


echo "--- EXTRACTING..."

sudo mkdir ${install_dir}/${name}

sudo tar xzf /tmp/${file_name} -C ${install_dir}/${name} --strip-
components 1


#echo "--- SETTING UP SYM-LINK"

#sudo ln -s ${install_dir}/${name} ${install_dir}/cassandra


echo "--- CREATE DIRECTORIES"

sudo mkdir -p ${data_dir}/data ${data_dir}/commitlog ${logging_dir}

sudo chown -R ${USER} ${data_dir} ${logging_dir}


echo "--- UPDATING CASSANRA YAML (in place)"

sudo cp ${install_dir}/cassandra/conf/cassandra.yaml ${install_dir}/
cassandra/conf/cassandra.yaml.BKP


sudo sed -i \

  -e "s/^cluster_name.*/cluster_name: ${cluster_name}/g" \

  -e "s/\(\-\s*seeds:\).*/\1 ${seeds}/g" \

  -e "s/^listen_address.*/listen_address: ${listen_address}/g" \

  -e "s/^rpc_address.*/rpc_address: ${rpc_address}/g" \
```

```
 -e "s/^endpoint_snitch.*/endpoint_snitch: ${endpoint_snitch}/g" \

 -e "s|^#\s\+data_file_directories:|data_file_directories:\n  -
${data_dir}/data|g" \

 -e "s|^#\s\+commitlog_directory:.*|commitlog_directory: ${data_dir}/
commitlog|g" \

 -e "s|^#\s\+saved_caches_directory:.*|saved_caches_directory:
${data_dir}/saved_caches|g" \

 ${install_dir}/cassandra/conf/cassandra.yaml


sudo sed -i \

 -e "s|\${cassandra.logdir}|${logging_dir}|g" \

 ${install_dir}/cassandra/conf/logback.xml


echo "--- STARTING CASSANDRA"

# NOHUP, ignore SIGHUP signal to kill Cassandra Daemon

nohup ${install_dir}/cassandra/bin/cassandra > ${logging_dir}/startup.
log &

sleep 5


echo "--- INSTALLATION FINISHED"

exit 0


#upload_and_execute.sh
set -e


# THIS IS THE FILE THAT YOU EXECUTE LOCALLY
```

```
# YOU MUST FILL UP THE APPROPRIATE VARIABLES

# YOU MAY NEED TO CHANGE THIS SCRIPT UPLOAD

# SNITCH FILES, IF ANY


# LOCATION TO USE IDENTITY FILE FROM

identity_file="/LOCATION/OF/IDENTITY_FILE.pem"


# REMOTE USER TO LOG IN AS

remote_user="root"


#YOU MAY CHANGE LOCATION LIKE: "${HOME}/Desktop/install_cassandra.sh"

install_script="install_cassandra.sh"


# YOUR SERVERS WHERE CASSANDRA IS TO BE INSTALLED

servers=( 'c1.mydomain.com' 'c2.mydomain.com' 'c2.mydomain.com' )


for server in ${servers[@]} ; do

  echo ">> Uploading script to ${server} to remote user's home"

  scp -i ${identity_file} ${install_script} ${remote_
user}@${server}:~/install_cassandra.sh

  echo ">> Executing script..."

  ssh -t -i ${identity_file} ${remote_user}@${server} "sudo chmod a+x
~/install_cassandra.sh && ~/install_cassandra.sh"
```

```
    echo ">> Installation finished for server: ${server}"

    echo "-------------------------------------------"

  done

  echo ">> Cluster initialization is finished."

  exit 0;
```

Let's discuss a couple of things before we move forward. If you decide to use this script, and you have an Internet connection, it is recommended to take the code from either my GitHub repository (`https://github.com/naishe/mastering-cassandra-v2`) or you can download the code bundle from the book's website.

When I execute the following script for the demonstration of a three-node cluster, it takes less than two minutes to get up and running. Since I ran it on a set of machines in AWS EC2, I have tuned the settings that way. The script thus created is as follows:

```
$ ./upload_and_execute.sh


>> Uploading script to c1.mydomain.com to remote user's home
install_cassandra.sh    100% 2484      2.4KB/s    00:00
>> Executing script with initial_key=0
--- DOWNLOADING CASSANDRA
[-- snip --]
Saving to: '/tmp/cassandra.tar.gz'
100%[=========>] 1,29,73,061  598KB/s    in 22s


--- EXTRACTING...
--- CREATE DIRECTORIES
--- UPDATING CASSANRA YAML (in place)
--- STARTING CASSANDRA
--- INSTALLATION FINISHED
>> Installation finished for server: c1.mydomain.com
-------------------------------------------


>> Uploading script to c2.mydomain.com to remote user's home
```

```
[-- snip --]
>> Executing script with initial_key=56713727820156410577229101238628035
242
--- DOWNLOADING CASSANDRA
[-- snip --]


 --- EXTRACTING...
--- SETTING UP SYM-LINK
--- CREATE DIRECTORIES
--- UPDATING CASSANRA YAML (in place)
--- STARTING CASSANDRA
--- INSTALLATION FINISHED
[-- snip --]
-----------------------------------------------

>> Uploading script to c3.mydomain.com to remote user's home
[-- snip -]
--- DOWNLOADING CASSANDRA
[-- snip --]

--- EXTRACTING...
--- SETTING UP SYM-LINK
--- CREATE DIRECTORIES
--- UPDATING CASSANRA YAML (in place)
--- STARTING CASSANDRA
--- INSTALLATION FINISHED
-----------------------------------------------


>> Cluster initialization is Finished.
```

Let's see how our newly launched cluster looks:

```
[root@es05 ~]# /opt/cassandra/bin/nodetool -h localhost status
Datacenter: us-east
===================
Status=Up/Down
|/ State=Normal/Leaving/Joining/Moving
--  Address       Load       Tokens  Owns (effective)  Host ID                                Rack
UN  10.10.21.228  54.84 KB   256     66.0%             d3de1bfd-52e7-4230-b591-a5da8ba1f501   1a
UN  10.10.21.206  69.28 KB   256     67.5%             7dcedec8-046c-41ef-9658-8cae04212e3d   1a
UN  10.10.21.169  85.88 KB   256     66.6%             55ac5356-7f05-48b1-af24-6d619914fabf   1a
```

The preceding screenshot shows the ring query with all three nodes up and running with tokens equally distributed among them.

Creating a keyspace

You might wonder why creating a keyspace is discussed in a chapter that is oriented more toward system administration tasks. The reason we do this is that keyspace creation is hard linked with the way you have set the snitch.

Unless you are using `SimpleSnitch`, you should use `NetworkTopologyStrategy` as the replica placement strategy. It needs to know the replication factor for the keyspace for each data center.

Therefore, if you have `PropertyFileSnitch` or `GossipingPropertyFileSnitch`, your keyspace creation looks like the following code snippet:

```
CREATE KEYSPACE myks
WITH REPLICATION = {
  'class' : 'NetworkTopologyStrategy',
  'DC1' : 2
};
```

Here, `DC1` is the data center name as defined in snitch configuration files and the value is the replication factor in each data center.

In EC2-related snitches, such as `EC2MultiRegionSnitch` or `Ec2Snitch`, the data center name is nothing but the name of the region as it appears in the availability zone. Therefore, for us-east-1a, the data center is `us-east`. The code to create a keyspace (for `EC2MultiRegionSnitch`) is as follows:

```
CREATE KEYSPACE myks
WITH REPLICATION = {
  'class' : 'NetworkTopologyStrategy',
  'us-east':2,
  'us-west': 1
};
```

Thus, if you have set the replication factor smartly, and your queries make use of the right consistency level, your request will never have to travel beyond the one data center (if all the replicas in that data center are up).

For `SimpleSnitch`, you just specify `replication_factor` as the replication option as it is oblivious to the data center or the rack:

```
CREATE KEYSPACE my_simple_ks
WITH REPLICATION = {
  'class' : 'SimpleStrategy',
  'replication_factor' : 2
};
```

Authorization and authentication

By default, Cassandra is open to everyone who has access to Cassandra's node address and ports. Since most of the time it's just your applications that access Cassandra and generally the whole application ecosystem is heavily guarded (by VPN, VPC, and firewall), it may not bother you that Cassandra has no security.

Cassandra 1.2.2 and higher provide an RDBMS-like security authorization and authentication mechanism that is a notable departure from the text file-based security before this version. To enable security, all you need to do is change two things in the `cassandra.yaml` file: authenticator and authorizer. By default, they are set to `AllowAllAuthenticator` and `AllowAllAuthorizer`, respectively. They work exactly in ways their names suggest. Cassandra ships with `PasswordAuthenticator` as authenticator and `CassandraAuthorizer` as authorizer. This will enable a MySQL-like authorization and authentication system in Cassandra. For more details on working with Cassandra `authn` and `authz`, refer to *Chapter 3, Effective CQL*. But if you want to implement one of your own or want to hook it up with your existing security mechanism, you can implement `Iauthenticator` for authentication and/or `Iauthorizer` for authorization.

The default username and password for Cassandra is `cassandra/cassandra`. It is advised that when you first log in, you create a new superuser and remove any permission from the default user and change the default password, for obvious reasons. The details on how to do that are described in *Chapter 3, Effective CQL*.

Summary

We have performed a complete cluster installation. It is not as difficult as it seems. Once we have fixed the variables and decided what hardware requirement is needed, it is just a matter of running a shell script that does everything. Multiple data center setups are equally simple. Many variables depend on your particular use case, but if you do not have a particular specification in mind, go with the suggested ones or the default one. They are generally good.

Setting up a cluster is probably a one-time task for an organization. It is likely that your first cluster will be just a couple of nodes. It is equally likely that you will stick with that cluster for first production, or at least till you plan to make the first release with Cassandra in your system. In production, the first couple of things that come to everyone's mind are questions such as the software is tuned to perform its best? What happens when things start to break? What if we needed to ramp up the servers? How safe is our data? Chances are that you will be expected to answer these questions. Therefore, you should know the answers before these questions are directed to you. The next few chapters are about all these questions.

5
Performance Tuning

Cassandra is all about speed—quick installation, fast reads, and fast writes. You got your application optimized, minimized the network trips by batching, and denormalized the data to get maximum information in one request. However, the performance is not what you read over the Web and in various blogs. You start to doubt whether the claims actually measure. Hold on! You may need to tune things up.

This chapter will discuss how to get a sense of a Cassandra cluster's capacity and have a performance number handy to back up our claims. It then dives into the various settings that affect read and write throughput, a couple of JVM tuning parameters, and finally, a short discussion on how scaling systems horizontally and vertically can improve the performance.

Stress testing

Before you start to claim the performance numbers of your Cassandra backend, based on numbers that you have read elsewhere, it is important to perform your own stress testing. It is very easy to do that in Cassandra, as it provides special tools for stress testing. It is a good idea to customize the parameters of the stress test, which represents a use case that is closer to what your application is going to do. This will save a lot of heated discussion later, due to discrepancies in the load testing and the actual throughput that the software is able to pull out of the setting.

Cassandra 2.1 ships with very sophisticated stress test tools that can be fine-tuned to simulate the expected load on the system and can help to measure Cassandra's performance under stress conditions. To create a load scenario, you need to set up a YAML file that specifies the four things: database schema, data distribution, write pattern, and read queries.

Database schema

You need to provide the keyspace name, the keyspace creation query, the table name that is to be stressed, and the table creation query.

Data distribution

You can provide the pattern of the data you are expecting in your application, and their spread across a partition key. So, basically, you choose the following:

- **Size**: This shows the statistical distribution of the size of data in a column. For example, for the e-mail address, I would like a 3 to 15 character column with normal distribution. So, the mean e-mail address length would be 9–10 characters, which seems reasonable. The default value is UNIFORM(4..8).

- **Population**: This shows the unique column values, and how they are distributed. For example, for a city column, I would opt for 20,000 unique values. Also assuming that most of the records belong to just a few cities, for example 20 percent of cities account for 80 percent of records, we want some sort of diminishing distribution. Therefore, we would like to choose exponential distribution across rows for the city column. The default value is UNIFORM(1..100B).

- **Cluster**: If you are using a composite key, there are probable chances that you have more than one record for a given row-key partition key. The clustering attribute defines how the cluster size varies. For example, whether you wanted to fix the number of rows for a given partition key or you wanted to have some kind of variation. The default value is FIXED(1).

The stress tool provides six types of statistical distributions. They are as follows:

- FIXED(value): This distribution always returns the same value as specified by the argument

- GAUSSIAN(min..max, mean, standard_deviation): Normal distribution over [min, max] with mean as mean and standard_deviation

- GAUSSIAN(min..max, standard_deviation_range): Gaussian distribution over [min, max] with mean at (min+max)/2 and standard_deviation as (mean-min)/standard_deviation_range

- UNIFORM(min..max): Uniform distribution over [min, max]

- EXP(min..max): Exponential distribution over the range [min, max]

- EXTREME(min..max, shape): Weibull distribution over the range [min, max]

Write pattern

When writing data, you can specify how it should be distributed across the rows and clusters. There are four things that may be specified as follows:

- **Partitions**: This attribute specifies the distribution of the INSERT queries in each batch across all partitions (clusters). The default is FIXED(1), which means one value per partition per batch.

- **Pervisit**: This shows the ratio of rows that goes into a partition; this ratio is proportional to the total number of rows for the partition. If you have a secondary key column distribution as FIXED(20000), then FIXED(1)/2000 will denote that each batch will insert 10 rows. If not specified, it defaults to FIXED(1)/1.

- **Perbatch**: This shows the ratio of rows each partition should update in a single batch, as a proportion of the number of rows picked by the pervisit ratio and partition count. The default is FIXED(1).

- **Batchtype**: By default, the stress test uses the LOGGED batches. One may set it as UNLOGGED for better performance.

Read queries

A map (JSON) of queries with the key being its name, and the value is the query itself. The query may have parameters to be filled later by the stress tool.

An example YAML looks like the following (taken from `https://gist.github.com/tjake/fb166a659e8fe4c8d4a3`; you can find the gist on my GitHub account `https://gist.github.com/naishe/f7c7090173f4ea6afc28`):

```
#1: Database Schema
# Keyspace Name
keyspace: stresscql

keyspace_definition: |
  CREATE KEYSPACE stresscql WITH replication = {'class':
'SimpleStrategy', 'replication_factor': 1};

# Table name
table: blogposts

# The CQL for creating a table you wish to stress (optional if it
already exists)
table_definition: |
  CREATE TABLE blogposts (
```

```
            domain text,
            published_date timeuuid,
            url text,
            author text,
            title text,
            body text,
            PRIMARY KEY(domain, published_date)
    ) WITH CLUSTERING ORDER BY (published_date DESC)
      AND compaction = { 'class':'LeveledCompactionStrategy' }
      AND comment='A table to hold blog posts';


#2: Data Distribution
columnspec:
  - name: domain
    size: gaussian(5..100)
    population: uniform(1..10M)

  - name: published_date
    cluster: fixed(1000)

  - name: url
    size: uniform(30..300)

  - name: title
    size: gaussian(10..200)

  - name: author
    size: uniform(5..20)

  - name: body
    size: gaussian(100..5000)


#3: Write pattern

insert:
  partitions: fixed(1)
  pervisit:  fixed(1)/1000
  perbatch:  fixed(1)/1
  batchtype: UNLOGGED

#4: Read pattern
queries:
    singlepost:  select * from blogposts where domain = ? LIMIT 1
    timeline: select url, title, published_date from blogposts where
domain = ? LIMIT 10
```

This stress test was executed on an all default Cassandra 2.1.0 clusters, with the following specifications (AWS i2.xlarge instances):

```
Number of machines: 3 (3*256 Virtual nodes)
RAM: 30GB
Storage: 800GB SSD
CPU cores: 4 (virtualized)
```

To find the test result, run the following command:

```
$ CASSANDRA_HOME/tools/bin/cassandra-stress user profile=blogpost.yaml
ops\(insert=1\)
```

```
[ -- snip -- ]
```

```
Results:
```

op rate	: 9397
partition rate	: 9397
row rate	: 9393
latency mean	: 28.7
latency median	: 17.2
latency 95th percentile	: 94.8
latency 99th percentile	: 173.9
latency 99.9th percentile	: 572.1
latency max	: 791.6
Total operation time	: 00:00:37

The following screenshot shows the test results:

id, partitions,	op/s,	pk/s,	row/s,	mean,	med,	.95,	.99,	.999,	max,	time,	stderr
4 threadCount, 123150 ,	4078,	4078,	4069,	1.0,	0.8,	2.1,	3.0,	7.6,	85.7,	30.2,	0.01162
8 threadCount, 176600 ,	5799,	5799,	5789,	1.4,	1.0,	2.9,	4.5,	14.4,	82.0,	30.5,	0.02023
16 threadCount, 221850 ,	7248,	7248,	7250,	2.2,	1.8,	4.5,	7.5,	39.3,	111.2,	30.6,	0.00993
24 threadCount, 241300 ,	7824,	7824,	7806,	3.0,	2.5,	6.4,	11.9,	48.8,	93.9,	30.8,	0.01173
36 threadCount, 271450 ,	8704,	8704,	8707,	4.1,	2.9,	10.7,	20.8,	64.5,	137.1,	31.2,	0.01072
54 threadCount, 295300 ,	9352,	9352,	9363,	5.8,	4.3,	14.0,	25.6,	75.9,	134.9,	31.6,	0.01239
81 threadCount, 308450 ,	9327,	9327,	9321,	8.6,	4.9,	29.1,	57.0,	97.9,	272.6,	33.1,	0.01266
121 threadCount, 334050 ,	9735,	9735,	9740,	12.4,	6.2,	45.8,	88.9,	144.8,	386.8,	34.3,	0.00762
181 threadCount, 350650 ,	9698,	9698,	9711,	18.6,	9.4,	67.8,	129.0,	243.8,	617.7,	36.2,	0.00897
271 threadCount, 350800 ,	9397,	9397,	9393,	28.7,	17.2,	94.8,	173.9,	572.1,	791.6,	37.3,	0.01095
END											

Although 9,000 writes per second is not the most terrible thing from three expensive machines, it may need a bit tweaking to try to perform better. The rest of this chapter will talk about various settings within Cassandra and JVM to boost the performance for the given use case.

Performance tuning

With stress tests completed, you might have identified the key areas for improvement. The broadest areas that you can categorize performance tuning into is the read and write performance area. Alternatively, there may be worries such as the I/O contention (compaction tuning) on servers. Apart from these, there may be several external factors to it, for example, slow disk, shared resources (such as shared CPU), and connectivity issues. We are not going to discuss external factors here. The assumption is that you will have sufficient resources allocated to the Cassandra servers. This section will discuss various tweaks to get Cassandra to start performing the best that it can within the given resources.

Write performance

Cassandra writes are sequential; all it needs to do is append it to the commit log and put it in memory. There is not much that can be done internally to Cassandra's setting to tweak writes. However, if disk writes are fast, and somehow I/O contentions can be lowered due to multiple things that happen in the Cassandra life cycle, such as flushing MemTable to disk, compactions, and writes to commit logs, it can boost the write performance.

So, having fast disks, commit logs, and data files in separate dedicated hard disks directly attached to the system, will improve write throughput.

Read performance

Reading in Cassandra is rather complicated; it may need to read from the memory or from the hard drive; it may need to aggregate multiple fragments of data from different SSTables; it may require to get data across multiple nodes, take care of tombstones, and validate digest and get it back to the client. Alternatively, the common pattern of increasing the read performance in Cassandra is the same as any other data system's caching—to keep the most frequent data in memory, minimize disk access, and keep search path/hops small on disk. Also, fast network and fewer communication over the network, and low read consistency level may help.

Choosing the right compaction strategy

With each flush of a MemTable, an immutable SSTable gets created. So, with time, there will be numerous SSTables, if their numbers are not limited by an external process (for example, a process that merges them, deletes unused ones, or compresses them). The main problem with lots of SSTables is slow read speed. A search may need to hop through multiple SSTables to fetch the requested data. The compaction process repeatedly executes merging these SSTables into one larger SSTable, which has a cleaned-up version of the data that was scattered in fragments into different smaller SSTables, littered with tombstones. This also means that compaction is pretty disk I/O intensive; so the longer and more frequently it runs, the more contention it will it produce for other Cassandra processes that require to read from or write to the disc.

Cassandra provides two compaction strategies as of version 2.1.0. The compaction strategy is a table-level setting; so you can set an appropriate compaction strategy for a table, based on its behavior.

Size-tiered compaction strategy

The size-tiered compaction strategy is the default strategy. The way it works is as follows: as soon as the count of equal-sized SSTables reaches to `min_threshold` (default 4), they get compacted into one bigger SSTable. As the compacted SSTables get bigger and bigger, it is rare that large SSTables gets compacted further. This leaves some very large SSTables and many smaller SSTables. This also means that row updates will be scattered in multiple SSTables, and will require longer time to process multiple SSTables to get the fragments of a row.

With the occasional burst of the I/O load during compaction, `SizeTieredCompactionStrategy` is a good fit where rows are inserted and never mutated. This will ensure that all the bits of rows are in one SSTable. This is a write and I/O friendly strategy.

Leveled compaction

`LeveledCompactionStrategy` is a relatively new introduction to Cassandra, and the concepts are taken from Google's LevelDB project. Unlike size-tiered compaction, this has many small and fixed size SSTables, grouped into levels. Within a level, the SSTables do not have any overlap. Leveled compaction works in such a way that, for most of the cases, a row will need to access just one SSTable. This is a big advantage over the size-tiered version. It makes `LeveledCompactionStrategy` a better choice for reading heavy tables. Updates are favored in level compaction, since it tries to spread rows as low as possible.

The downside of leveled compaction is high I/O. There is no apparent benefit if the data is write-once type. In this case, even with the size-tiered strategy, the data is going to stay in one SSTable.

Anyone, coming from the traditional database world who has worked on scaling up read requests and speeding up data retrievals, knows that caching is the most effective way to speed up the reads. It prevents database hits for the data that has been fetched (in the recent past) for the price of extra RAM that caching mechanism uses to store the data temporarily. So, you have a third-party memory caching mechanism, such as Memcached, which manages it for you. The nasty side of a third-party caching mechanism is the managing the distributed cache. The cache management logic may intrude into application code.

Cassandra provides an inbuilt caching mechanism that can be really helpful if your application requires heavy read capability. There are two types of caches in Cassandra, row cache and key cache. The following figure shows how caching works:

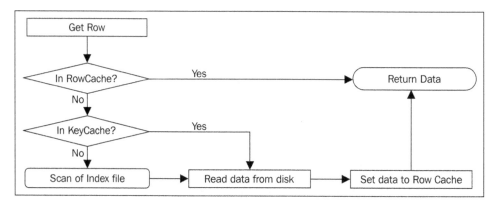

Row cache

Row cache is true caching. It caches a complete row of data and returns immediately without touching the hard drive. It is fast and complete. Row cache stores data off-heap (if JNA is available), which means that it will be unaffected by the garbage collector.

Cassandra is capable of storing really large rows of data with about 2 billion columns in it. This means that the cache is going to take up much space, which may not be what you wanted. While row cache is generally good to boost the read speed, it is best suited for not-so-large rows. However, you can cache the users table in row cache, but it will be a bad idea to have the users_browsing_history or users_click_pattern table, in a row cache.

Key cache

Key cache is to store the row keys in memory. Key caches are default for a table. It does not take much space, but it boosts performance to a large extent (but less than the row cache). As of Cassandra Version 2.1.0, the key cache is assigned to 100 MB or 5 percent of the JVM heap memory, whichever is low.

Key caches contain information about the location of the row in SSTables, so it's just one disk seek to retrieve the data. This short-circuits the process of looking through the sampled index and then scanning the index file for the key range. Since it does not take large space as row cache, one can have large number of keys cached in relatively small memory.

Cache settings

The general rule of thumb is, for all normal purposes, key cache is good enough. You can tweak key cache to stretch its limits. You'd get a lot of performance gain for just a little increase in key cache size in key cache settings. Row caching, on the other hand, needs a little thinking to do. A good fit data for row cache is the same as a good fit data for a third-party caching mechanism. The data should be read mostly, and mutated occasionally. Rows with smaller number of columns are better suited. Before you go ahead with cache tweaking, you may want to check the current cache usage. You can use JConsole to see cache hit. We will learn more about JConsole in *Chapter 7, Monitoring*. In JConsole, the cache statistics can be obtained by expanding the `org.apache.cassandra.db` menu. It shows cache hit rate and the number of hits and cache size for a particular node and table.

Cache settings are mostly global as of Version 2.1.0. The settings can be altered in `cassandra.yaml`. At table level, the only choices that you have are the cache type to use with or if you should use any cache at all. The options are: keys only, rows only, both and none. The following is an example (for more discussion, refer to the *Creating a table* section in *Chapter 3, Effective CQL*):

```
CREATE TABLE users (
user_id uuid,
email text,
password text,
PRIMARY KEY (user_id)
)
WITH
caching = {
'keys' : 'ALL',
'rows_per_partition' : '314'
};
```

The following are the caching-specific settings in `cassandra.yaml`:

- `key_cache_size_in_mb`: By default, it is set to 100 MB or five percent of the heap size. To disable it globally, set it to zero.

- `key_cache_save_period`: This is the time after which the cache is saved to the disk to avoid a cold start. A cold start is when a node starts afresh and gets marred by lots of requests; with no caching at the time of start, it will take some time to get cache loaded with the most requested keys. During this time, the responses may be sluggish.

The caches are saved under the directory that is described by the `saved_caches_directory` setting in the `.yaml` file. We configured it during the cluster deployment in *Chapter 4, Deploying a Cluster*. The default value for this setting is 14,400 seconds.

- `key_cache_keys_to_save`: This is the number of keys to save. It is commented to store all the keys. In general, it is okay to let it be commented.

- `row_cache_size_in_mb`: Row caching is disabled by default, by setting this attribute to zero. Set it to an appropriate positive integer. It may be worth taking a look at `nodetool -h <hostname> cfstats` and taking the row mean size and the number of keys into account.

- `row_cache_save_period`: Similar to `key_cache_save_period`, this saves the cache to saved caches directory after the prescribed time. Unlike key caches, row caches are bigger and saving it to the disk is an I/O expensive task to do. Compared to the fuss for saving row cache, it does not give proportional benefit. It is okay to leave it to zero, that is, disabled.

- `row_cache_keys_to_save`: This is the same as `key_cache_keys_to_save`.

- `memory_allocator`: Out of the box, Cassandra provides two mechanisms to enable row cache:

  - `NativeAllocator`: This uses the native GCC allocator to store off heap data. This is by default, and good for most of the use cases.

  - `JEMallocAllocator`: This is a slightly better alternative to `NativeAllocator`. The main feature of this allocator is that it is fragmentation-resistant. To be able to use this, you will need to install `jemalloc` (`http://www.canonware.com/jemalloc/`) and then edit `conf/cassandra-env.sh`. Here is the part that you need to change; uncomment the last two lines with `JEMALLOC_HOME` set as the location, where `jemalloc` is installed as follows:

```
# Configure the following for JEMallocAllocator and if jemalloc is
not available in the system
# library path (Example: /usr/local/lib/). Usually "make install"
will do the right thing.

# export LD_LIBRARY_PATH=<JEMALLOC_HOME>/lib/
# JVM_OPTS="$JVM_OPTS -Djava.library.path=<JEMALLOC_HOME>/lib/"
```

Enabling compression

Table (or column family) compression is a very effective mechanism to improve read and write throughput. As one can expect, compression (any) leads to compact representation of data at the cost of some CPU cycles. Enabling compression on a table makes the disk representation of the data (SSTables) terse. This means efficient disk utilization, lesser I/O, and a little extra burden to the CPU. In the case of Cassandra, the trade-off between I/O and the CPU, due to compression, almost always yields favorable results. The cost of CPU performing compression and decompression is less than what it takes to read more data from the disk.

Compression setting is table-wise; if you do not mention any compression mechanism, LZ4Compressor is applied to the table by default. This is how you alter compression type (see details about assigning compression setting when the table is created in *Chapter 3, Effective CQL*):

```
ALTER TABLE users
WITH
COMPRESSION = {
  'sstable_compression': 'DeflateCompressor'
};
```

Let's see the compression options we have.

The sstable_compression parameter specifies which compressor is used to compress disk representation of SSTable, when MemTable is flushed (compression takes place at the time of flush). Cassandra Version 2.1.0 provides three compressors out of the box: LZ4Compressor, SnappyCompressor, and DeflateCompressor.

The LZ4Compressor is 50 percent faster than SnappyCompressor, which is faster than DeflateCompressor. In general, this means, when you move from DeflateCompressor to LZ4Compressor, the compression will take a little extra space, but it will have higher read speed.

Like everything else in Cassandra, compressors are pluggable. You can write your own compressor by implementing `org.apache.cassandra.io.compress.ICompressor`, compiling the compressor, and putting the `.class` or `.jar` files in the `lib` directory. Provide the fully-qualified class name of the compression as the `sstable_compression` value.

The chunk length (`chunk_length_kb`) is the smallest slice of the row that gets decompressed during reads. Depending on the query pattern and median size of the rows, this parameter can be tweaked in such a way that it is big enough to not have to deflate multiple chunks, but small enough to not have to decompress excessive unnecessary data. Practically, it is hard to guess this. The most common suggestion is to keep it 64 KB, if you do not have any idea.

Compression can be added, removed, or altered anytime during the lifetime of a table. In general, compression always boosts performance and it is a great way to maximize the utilization of disk space. Compression gives double to quadruple reduction in data size when compared to an uncompressed version. So, one should always set a compression to start with, and it can be disabled pretty easily as follows:

```
# Disable Compression
ALTER TABLE users
WITH
COMPRESSION = {
  'sstable_compression': ''
};
```

It must be noted that enabling compression may not immediately halve the space used by SSTables. The compression is applied to the SSTables that get created after the compression is enabled. With time, as compaction merges SSTables, older SSTables get compressed.

Tuning the bloom filter

Accessing a disk is the most expensive task. Cassandra thinks twice before needing to read from a disk. The bloom filter helps to identify which SSTables may contain the row that the client has requested. Alternatively, the bloom filter being a probabilistic data structure, yields a false positive ratio (refer to *Chapter 2, Cassandra Architecture*). The more the false-positives, the more the SSTables needed to be read before realizing whether the row actually exists in the SSTable or not.

The false-positive ratio is basically the probability of getting a true value from the bloom filter of an SSTable for a key that does not exist in it. In simpler words, if the false-positive ratio is 0.5, chances are that 50 percent of the times you end up looking into the index file for the key but it is not there. So, why not set the false-positive ratio to zero; never make a disk touch without being 100 percent sure. Well, it comes with a cost—memory consumption. If you remember from *Chapter 2, Cassandra Architecture*, the smaller the size of the bloom filter, the smaller the memory consumption. A smaller bloom filter increases the likelihood of the collision of hashes, which means a higher false positive. So, as you decrease the false-positive value, your memory consumption shoots up. Therefore, we need a balance here.

In the bloom filter, the default value of the false-positive ratio is set to 0.000744. To disable the bloom filter, that is, to allow all the queries to SSTable—all false positive—this ratio needs to be set to 1.0. One may need to bypass the bloom filter by setting the false-positive ratio to 1, if one has to scan all SSTables for data mining or other analytical applications.

You can create a table with the false-positive chance as 0.001 as follows:

```
# Create column family with false positive chance = 0.001
CREATE TABLE toomanyrows (id int PRIMARY KEY, name text)
WITH
bloom_filter_fp_chance = 0.001;
```

One may alter the false-positive chance on an up-and-running cluster without any need to reboot. Alternatively, the false-positive chance is applied only to the newer SSTables—created by means of flush or via compaction.

One can always see the bloom filter chance by running the `describe` command in `cqlsh` or `cassandra-cli` or by running a `nodetool` request for `cfstats`. The node tool displays the current ratio too. The following is an example using the `DESC` command:

```
# Incassandra-cli
 DESC TABLE toomanyrows;
CREATE TABLE demo_cql.toomanyrows (
    id int PRIMARY KEY,
    name text
) WITH bloom_filter_fp_chance = 0.001
    [-- snip --]
    AND speculative_retry = '99.0PERCENTILE';
```

The current ratio is displayed via `nodetool` (all the statistics are zero because the table is unused, but as soon as you start reading and writing out of it statistics like this are pretty helpful to make decisions):

```
bin/nodetool cfstats demo_cql.toomanyrows
Keyspace: demo_cql
  Read Count: 0
  Read Latency: NaN ms.
  Write Count: 0
  Write Latency: NaN ms.
  Pending Flushes: 0
Table: toomanyrows
  SSTable count: 0
      [-- snip -- ]
  Bloom filter false positives: 0
  Bloom filter false ratio: 0.00000
  Bloom filter space used, bytes: 0
  [-- snip --]
    Compacted partition mean bytes: 0
    Average live cells per slice (last five minutes): 0.0
    Average tombstones per slice (last five minutes): 0.0
```

More tuning via cassandra.yaml

The `cassandra.yaml` file is the hub of almost all the global settings for the node or the cluster. It is well-documented, and one can understand very easily by reading it. Listed in the following sections are some of the properties from Cassandra Version 2.1.0, and short descriptions of it. You should refer to the `cassandra.yaml` file of your version of Cassandra and read the details.

commitlog_sync

Durability — as we know from *Chapter 2, Cassandra Architecture* — provides durable writes by the virtue of appending the new writes to the commit logs. This is not entirely true. To guarantee that each write is made in such a manner that a hard reboot/crash does not wash off any data, it must be fsync'd to the disk. Flushing commit logs after each write is detrimental to write performance due to slow disk seeks. Instead of doing that, Cassandra periodically (by default, `commitlog_sync: periodic`) flushes the data to the disk after an interval described by `commitlog_sync_period_in_ms` in milliseconds. However, Cassandra does not wait for commit log to synchronize; it immediately acknowledges the write.

This means that if a heavy write is going on and the machine crashes, at the most, you will lose the data written in the `commitlog_sync_period_in_ms` window. You should not really worry. We have a replication factor and consistency level to help recover this loss; unless you are unlucky enough that all the replicas die in the same instant.

> The `fsync` function transfers (flushes) all modified in-core data of (that is, modified buffer cache pages for) the file referred to by the **file descriptor** (**fd**) to the disk device (or other permanent storage device) so that all changed information can be retrieved even after the system was crashed or rebooted. For more information, visit `http://linux.die.net/man/2/fsync`.

The `commitlog_sync` setting gives high performance at some risk. To someone who is paranoid about data loss, Cassandra provides a guarantee write option. Set `commitlog_sync` to batch mode. In batch mode, Cassandra accrues all the writes to go to the commit log, and then fsyncs after `commitlog_sync_batch_window_in_ms`, which is usually set smaller such as 50 milliseconds. This prevents the problem of flushing to the disk after every write, but the durability guarantee forces the acknowledgement (that the data is persisted) to be done only after the flush is done or the batch window is over, whichever is sooner. This means the batch modes will always be slower than the periodic modes.

For most practical cases, the default periodic value and default `fsync()` period of ten seconds will do just fine.

column_index_size_in_kb

The `column_index_size_in kb` property tells Cassandra to add a column index if the size of a row (serialized size) grows beyond the KBs mentioned by this property. In other words, if row size is 314 KB and `column_index_size_in_kb` is set to 64 (KB), there will be a column index with at least five entries, each containing the start and the finish column name in the chunk and its offset and width.

If the row contains many columns (wide rows) or you have columns with really large-sized values, you may want to increase the default. It has a con; for a large column index in KB, Cassandra will need to read at least this much amount of data, even a single column of a small row with small values needs to be read. On the other hand, a small value for this property, large index data will need to be read at each access. The default is okay for most of the cases.

commitlog_total_space_in_mb

The commit log file is **memory mapped** (**mmap**). This means that the file takes the virtual address space. Cassandra flushes any unflushed MemTables that exist in the oldest memory mapped commit log segment to the disk. Thinking from the I/O point of view, it does not make sense to keep this property small because the total space of smaller commit logs will be filled up quickly, requiring frequent write to the disk and higher disk I/O. On the other hand, we do not want commit logs to hog all the memory. Note that the data that was not flushed to the disk. In the event of a shutdown, it is replayed from the commit log. So, the larger the commit log, the more the replay time it will take to restart.

The default for the 32-bit JVM is 32 MB and for 64-bit JVM is 1024 MB. You may tune it based on the memory availability on the node.

Tweaking JVM

Cassandra runs in **Java Virtual Machine** (**JVM**): all the threading, memory management, processes, and the interaction with the underlying OS is done by Java. Investing time to optimize the JVM settings to speed up Cassandra's operation pays off. We will see that the general assumptions, such as setting Java, heap too high to eat up most of the system's memory. This may not be a good idea.

Java heap

If you look at `conf/cassandra-env.sh`, you will see nicely written logic that does the following: `max(min(1/2 ram, 1024MB)` and `min(1/4 ram, 8GB)`. This means that the max heap depends on the system's memory as Cassandra chooses a decent default, which is as follows:

- Max heap = 50 percent for a system with less than 2 GB of RAM
- Max heap = 1 GB for 2 GB to 4 GB RAM
- Max heap = 25 percent for a system with 4 GB to 32 GB of RAM
- Max heap = 8 GB for 32 GB onwards RAM

The reason to not go down with a large heap is that garbage collection does not do well for more than 8 GB of RAM. A high heap may also lead to poor page cache of the underlying operating system. In general, the default serves good enough. If you choose to alter the heap size, you need to edit `cassandra-env.sh` and set `MAX_HEAP_SIZE` to the appropriate value.

Garbage collection

Further down the `cassandra-env.sh` file, you may find the garbage collection setting as follows:

```
# GC tuning options
JVM_OPTS="$JVM_OPTS -XX:+UseParNewGC"
JVM_OPTS="$JVM_OPTS -XX:+UseConcMarkSweepGC"
JVM_OPTS="$JVM_OPTS -XX:+CMSParallelRemarkEnabled"
JVM_OPTS="$JVM_OPTS -XX:SurvivorRatio=8"
JVM_OPTS="$JVM_OPTS -XX:MaxTenuringThreshold=1"
JVM_OPTS="$JVM_OPTS -XX:CMSInitiatingOccupancyFraction=75"
JVM_OPTS="$JVM_OPTS -XX:+UseCMSInitiatingOccupancyOnly"
JVM_OPTS="$JVM_OPTS -XX:+UseTLAB"
```

Cassandra, by default, uses **concurrent mark and sweep garbage collector (CMS GC)**. It performs garbage collection concurrently with the execution of Cassandra and pauses for a very short while. This is a good candidate for high-performance applications such as Cassandra. With the concurrent collector, a parallel version of the young generation copying collector is used. Thus, we have `UseParNewGC`, which is a parallel copy collector that copies surviving objects in young generation from Eden to Survivor spaces and from there to old generation. It is written to work with concurrent collectors such as CMS GC.

Further, `CMSParallelRemarkEnabled` reduces the pauses during the remark phase.

The other garbage settings do not impact garbage collection significantly. However, low values for `CMSInitiatingOccupancyFraction` may lead to frequent garbage collection because concurrent collection starts if the occupancy of the tenured generation grows above the initial occupancy. The `CMSInitiatingOccupancyFraction` option sets the percentage of current tenured generation size.

If you decide to debug the garbage collection, it is a good idea to use tools such as JConsole, in order to look into how frequent garbage collection takes place, CPU usage, and so on. You may also want to uncomment the GC logging options in `cassandra-env.sh` to see what's going on beneath the Cassandra process.

If you decide to increase the Java heap size over 6 GB, it may be interesting to switch the garbage collection settings too. **Garbage First Garbage Collector (G1 GC)** is shipped with Oracle Java 7 update 4+. It is claimed to work reliably on larger heap sizes and it's claimed that applications currently running on CMS GC will be benefited by G1 GC in more ways than one. (Read more about G1 GC on `http://www.oracle.com/technetwork/java/javase/tech/g1-intro-jsp-135488.html`.)

Other JVM options

The other JVM options are as follows:

- **Compressed Ordinary Object Pointers**: In the 64-bit JVM, **ordinary object pointers** (**OOPs**) normally have the same size as machine pointer, and that is 64 bit. This causes larger heap size requirement on a 64-bit machine for the same application when compared to the heap size requirement on a 32-bit machine. Compressed OOP options help to keep the heap size smaller on 64-bit machines. (Read more about compressed OOPs on http://docs. oracle.com/javase/7/docs/technotes/guides/vm/performance- enhancements-7.html#compressedOop.)

  It is generally suggested to run Cassandra on Oracle Java 6. Compressed OOPs are supported and activated by default from Java SE Version 6u23+. For earlier releases, you need to explicitly activate this by passing the -XX:+UseCompressedOops flag.

- **Enable JNA**: Refer to *Chapter 4, Deploying a Cluster*, for the specifics of installing the JNA library for your operating system. JNA gives Cassandra access to native OS libraries (shared libraries and DLLs). Cassandra uses JNA for off-heap row cache that does not get swapped and in general gives favorable performance results on reads and writes. If no JNA exists, Cassandra falls back to on-heap row caching, which has a negative impact on performance. JNA also helps while taking backups; snapshots are created with help of JNA, which would have taken much longer with fork and Java exec.

Scaling horizontally and vertically

We will see scaling in more detail in *Chapter 6, Managing Cluster – Scaling, Node Repair, and Backup*, but let's discuss scaling in the context of performance tuning. As we know, Cassandra is linearly and horizontally scalable. So, adding more nodes of Cassandra will result in proportional gain in performance. This is called **horizontal scaling**.

The other thing that we have observed is that Cassandra reads are memory and disk speed bound. So, having larger memory, allocating more memory to caches, and dedicated and fast spinning hard disks (or SSDs) will boost the performance. Having high processing power with multicore processors will help compression, decompression, and garbage collection to run more smoothly. So, having a beefy server will help in overall performance improvement. In today's cloud age, it is economical to use a lot of cheap and low-end machines than use a couple of expensive but high I/O, high CPU, and high memory machines.

Network

Cassandra, like any other distributed system, has network as one of the important aspects that can vary performance. Cassandra needs to make calls across networks for both read and write. A slow network, thus, can be a bottleneck for the performance. It is suggested to use a gigabit network and redundant network interfaces. In a system with more than one network interface, it is recommended to bind `listen_address` for clients (Thrift) to one network interface card and `rpc_address` to another.

Summary

Starting with the stress test, we got a sense of how good a given Cassandra setup will do under an artificially standardized load. This may or may not reflect the particular use case that you are planning to use Cassandra for. You may tweak the stress test parameters to get closer to your test case. If needed, you should simulate a load that represents the load condition that you are expecting on Cassandra. This will give you a baseline for what to tune. It will be helpful to keep some profiling running at the OS level to gauge what resource is getting depleted—things such as JConsole, `nodetool cfstats`, and `tpstats`. Linux commands such as `iostats`, `vmstats`, `top`, `df`, and `free` can help to look through what's getting heated up or whether everything is okay. We will see these tools in more detail in *Chapter 6, Managing a Cluster – Scaling, Node Repair, and Backup*, and *Chapter 7, Monitoring*.

With the performance tuned, the next step is the maintenance of a cluster. In the next chapter, we will see different ways to tackle everyday DevOps problems such as how to scale up when traffic is high, how to replace a dead node, and other issues. In later chapters, we will see how to keep tabs on various performance statistics. We will see that what you have learned in this and the next couple of chapters will help when troubleshooting an issue.

6
Managing a Cluster – Scaling, Node Repair, and Backup

As a system grows, an application matures, the cloud infrastructure starts to warn us about the failure of underlying hardware, or if you get hit by the TechCrunch effect, you may need to do one of these things: repair, backup, or scale up/down. Alternatively, the management might decide to have another data center setup just for the analysis of data (maybe using Hadoop) without affecting the user's experience for which the data is served from the existing data center. These tasks are an integral part of a system administrator's day job. Fortunately, all these tasks are fairly easy in Cassandra, and there is a lot of documentation available for it.

In this chapter, we will go through Cassandra's built-in DevOps tool and discuss how to scale a cluster up and shrink it down. We will also see how one can replace a dead node or just remove it, and let other nodes bear the extra load. Further, we will briefly see backup and restoration of Cassandra data. We will also observe how a virtual node takes away the burden of manually rebalancing the cluster, which used to be a source of headache in the versions before Cassandra Version 1.2. You will still have to balance nodes if you decide to not use virtual node.

Most of the tasks are mechanical and really simple to automate. It may be a burden to maintain a large cluster of nodes if you have to do everything by hand and you will make a mistake.

Note that the default installation of Cassandra Version 1.2 onwards uses virtual nodes, but as of Cassandra 2.1.x, one may opt out of vnode (which is not a good idea). A major part of this chapter deals with initial_token, load balancing, token distribution, and token generation. All of these things are *not* required if you are using vnodes.

Scaling

Adding more nodes to Cassandra (scaling out) or shrinking the number of nodes (scaling in) is a pretty straightforward task. In a smaller and moderate-sized Cassandra cluster setup (say, less than 25 nodes), adding or shrinking nodes can be easily managed by doing the tasks manually. Alternatively, in larger clusters, the whole process can be automated by writing an appropriate shell script to perform the task.

Adding nodes to a cluster

Cassandra is one of the purest distributed systems, where the nodes are the same. Adding a new node is just a matter of launching a Cassandra service with almost the same parameters as any other machine in the ring. In a cloud environment, such as AWS, it is a pretty common practice to have a machine image of Cassandra that contains the blueprint of a Cassandra node. Each time you have to add a node to the cluster, you launch the Amazon Machine Image, tweak a couple of parameters that are specific to the node, and done. It is as simple as that.

To add a new node to the cluster, you need to have a Cassandra setup that has the following:

- **Set up the node's identity**: Edit `cassandra.yaml` to set the following appropriately:
    - `cluster_name`: This is the same as the other nodes in the cluster, where this node is joining in.
    - `listen_address`: Set it to the IP or the hostname, where other nodes connect the Cassandra service on this node. Be warned that leaving this field empty may not be a good idea. It will assume `listen_address` is the same as the hostname, which may or may not be correct. In Amazon EC2, it is usually just right.
    - `broadcast_address`: This may be needed to be set for a multi data center Cassandra installation.

- **Seed node**: Each node must know the seed node to be able to initialize the gossip (refer to *Chapter 2, Cassandra Architecture*, for the gossip protocol), learn about the topology, and let other nodes know about itself.

- **Initial token**: This is not needed for default/vnode enabled setup. If you use a single token per node setup, this step matters. It is the data range this node is going to be responsible for. One can just leave the initial token, and Cassandra will assign the token by choosing the middle of a token range of the most loaded node. This is the fastest way to make a lopsided cluster. The nodes should be well balanced.

Apart from these settings, for any customization in other nodes, `cassandra.yaml` should also be incorporate into new nodes configuration.

Now that the node is ready, here are the steps to add new nodes:

- **Initial tokens**: This step is not needed if you are using a vnode. Depending on the type of partitioner that you are using for key distribution, you will need to recalculate the initial tokens for each node in the system (refer to *Chapter 4, Deploying a Cluster* for initial token calculation). This means older nodes are going to have different datasets than they originally owned. However, there are a couple of smart tricks in the initial token assignment.

    - **N-folding the capacity**: If you are doubling, triplicating, or increasing the capacity N times, you'd find that the initial token generated, includes older initial tokens. Say, for example, you had a three-node cluster with initial tokens as 0, $t/3$, and $2t/3$. If you decide to triple the capacity by adding six more nodes, the new tokens should be 0, $t/9$, ... $t/3$, ... $2t/3$, and ... $8t/9$. The trick here is to leave the tokens that are already in use in the existing cluster and assign the rest of the nodes with remaining tokens. This saves extra move commands to adjust the tokens. You just launch the new nodes and wait till data streams out to all the nodes.

    - **Rebalance later**: This is the most common technique among those who have started with Cassandra. The idea is not to bother about imbalance. You can just launch new nodes. Cassandra will assign it with a token value, that is, the middle value of the highest loaded node. This, as expected, does a pretty decent job in removing hotspots from the cluster (and this is often what you want when you are adding a new node). Once the data streaming between the nodes is done, the cluster may or may not be perfectly balanced. You may want to load balance now. (Refer to the *Load balancing* section.)

       ° **Right token to the right node**: This is the most complex but the most common case. Usually, you do not go for doubling or quadrupling the cluster. It is more likely that you are asked to add two new nodes. In this case, you calculate the tokens for the new configuration, edit new nodes in `cassandra.yaml`, and set initial tokens to them (no specific choice). You start them and move the data around the nodes so that the nodes comply with the new initial tokens that we calculated. (We'll see how to do this later in this chapter.)

- **Start a new node**: With the initial token assigned or not assigned to the new nodes, we should start the nodes one by one. It is recommended to have a pause of at least 2 minutes between two nodes to start. These two minutes are to make sure that the other nodes know about this new node via gossip.

- **Move data**: This step is not needed if you are using a vnode. If adding a new node has skewed the data distributed in the cluster, we may need to move the data around in such a way that each node has equal share of the token range. This can be done using `nodetool`. You need to run `nodetool move NEW_INITIAL_TOKEN` on each node.

- **Cleanup**: Cassandra does not really move the data from one machine to another; it copies the data instead. This leaves nodes with unused old data. To clean this data, execute `nodetool cleanup` on each node.

There is a demonstration of the addition of a node into a three-node cluster, that is, the expansion of a three-node cluster into a four-node cluster in the following section.

Adding new nodes in vnode-enabled clusters

It is simple to add new node to vnode-enabled clusters because Cassandra takes care of distributing data (almost) evenly across the nodes without any manual intervention.

Use `nodetool -h HOSTNAME status` to see the cluster status:

```
$ bin/nodetool status
Note: Ownership information does not include topology; for complete
information, specify a keyspace
Datacenter: us-east
===================
Status=Up/Down
|/ State=Normal/Leaving/Joining/Moving
--  Address        Load        Tokens  Owns    Host ID        Rack
```

```
UN   10.10.21.228   1.88 GB   256   35.2%   d3de1...   1a
UN   10.10.21.206   1.86 GB   256   33.1%   7dced...   1a
UN   10.10.21.169   1.55 GB   256   31.7%   55ac5...   1a
```

So, our cluster is more or less balanced. Let's start a new node, and check the status:

```
$ bin/nodetool status
Note: Ownership information does not include topology; for complete
information, specify a keyspace
Datacenter: us-east
===================
Status=Up/Down
|/ State=Normal/Leaving/Joining/Moving
--   Address        Load      Tokens  Owns    Host ID        Rack
UN   10.10.21.228   2.05 GB   256     26.1%   d3de1...   1a
UN   10.10.21.206   1.92 GB   256     24.2%   7dced...   1a
UN   10.10.21.169   1.84 GB   256     24.7%   55ac5...   1a
UN   10.10.21.7     1.42 GB   256     25.0%   97c2f...   1a
```

We are done here. A new node is added, and the cluster is all up and balanced. You can monitor the data transfer using nodetool -h HOSTNAME netstats with HOSTNAME as the newly added node's address. Once that is done, one may want to run nodetool -h HOSTNAME cleanup on each node when all the transfers are done.

Adding a new node to a cluster without vnodes

Clusters without vnodes require some extra work to be done to add a new node. They need to add a node and make sure the cluster is balanced. The steps are as follows:

- **Ring status**: Use nodetool -h HOSTNAME ring to see the current ring distribution:

```
$ /opt/cassandra/bin/nodetool status
Datacenter: us-east
==================
Status=Up/Down
|/ State=Normal/Leaving/Joining/Moving
--   Address        Load      Tokens  Owns (effective)   Host ID
Rack
UN   10.10.21.228   4.55 GB   1       66.7%              5589b...
1a
```

```
UN   10.10.21.206   4.54 GB    1        66.7%              a3cfc...
1a

UN   10.10.21.169   4.58 GB    1        66.7%              089b2...
1a
```

The previous sample looks pretty balanced with three nodes and replication factor of 2

- **New tokens**: Adding additional nodes is going to split the token range into four. Let's see what they are:

```
$ python -c 'print [str(((2**64 / 4) * i) - 2**63) for i in
range(4)]'


['-9223372036854775808', '-4611686018427387904', '0',
'4611686018427387904']
```

Note that the preceding calculation assumes that you are using `Murmur3Partitioner`, which ships as default with Cassandra Version 1.2 onwards. If you have `RandomPartitioner`, instead of calculating the tokens manually, let the tooling provided by Cassandra do it for us. We will see it in the *Load balancing* section.

> Be aware that token numbers are partitioner-dependent and in this case it is `RandomPartitioner`. The other thing is if you see the old and new tokens, you will realize that the first node is not going to be touched. It is already set to the correct value. Also, it will be profitable in the old node, 2. The old node 3 gets assigned to the token values of node 2 and node 3 in the new configuration. This way, we'll minimize data movement across the nodes (streaming). The new node will have the initial token as described by node 4 in the previous results.

- **Start the new node**: Edit `cassandra.yaml` of the new node to set the appropriate value of the cluster name, initial token, seed node, listen address, and any other customization as per the environment (such as broadcast address, snitch, security, data file, and so on). Now, start the node by issuing the `cassandra` command or starting the Cassandra service. Wait for a couple of minutes as the new node gets introduced with the cluster. The cluster now looks pretty lopsided:

```
$ # /opt/cassandra/bin/nodetool ring


Note: Ownership information does not include topology; for
complete information, specify a keyspace
```

```
Datacenter: us-east

==========

Address        Rack      Status State  Load        Owns
Token


4611686018427387904
10.10.21.228  1a         Up     Normal 4.7 GB      25.00%
-9223372036854775808
10.10.21.169  1a         Up     Normal 4.71 GB     33.33%
-3074457345618258603
10.10.21.206  1a         Up     Normal 4.54 GB     33.33%
3074457345618258602
10.10.21.7    1a         Up     Normal 2.89 GB     8.33%
4611686018427387904
```

• **Move tokens**: Let's balance the nodes by moving data around. We need not touch Node #1 and Node #4. We need to move data from Node #2 and Node #3. They are the ones with wrong tokens. One of them should have the token as 0, and another should have token as 4611686018427387904. This is how we make this happen:

```
# Move data on Node #2
$ /opt/cassandra/bin/nodetool -h 10.10.21.169   move
-4611686018427387904


# Cassandra is still unbalanced.
# Move data on Node #3
$ /opt/cassandra/bin/nodetool -h 10.10.21.206   move 0
```

This is a blocking operation, which means you will need to wait until the process finishes. In a really large cluster with huge data, it may take some time to move the data. Be patient; this operation moves data. It heavily burdens the network, and the data size on disks may change. Therefore, it is not ideal to do this task when your site is running under heavy load. Perform this task at a relatively slow traffic time. It may be useful to watch streaming statistics on the node using nodetool netstats. Here is an example of how it looks (sampled every 1 second):

```
$ for i in {1..300} ; do  /opt/cassandra/bin/nodetool -h
10.10.21.169 netstats; sleep 1; done


Mode: NORMAL
Not sending any streams.
```

```
Not receiving any streams.
Pool Name         Active   Pending      Completed
Commands          n/a      0            1371882
Responses         n/a      0            7871820
Mode: MOVING
Not sending any streams.
Not receiving any streams.


Pool Name         Active   Pending      Completed
Commands          n/a      0            1371882
Responses         n/a      0            7871823
[-- snip --]
Mode: MOVING
Streaming to: /10.10.21.169
/mnt/cassandra-data/data/Keyspace1/Standard1/Keyspace1-Standard1-
hf-1-Data.db sections=1 progress=8126464/20112794 - 40%

/mnt/cassandra-data/data/Keyspace1/Standard1/Keyspace1-Standard1-
hf-2-Data.db sections=1 progress=0/15600228 - 0%


Not receiving any streams.


Pool Name         Active   Pending      Completed
Commands          n/a      0            1371882
Responses         n/a      0            7871925
Mode: NORMAL
Not sending any streams.
Not receiving any streams.


Pool Name         Active   Pending      Completed
Commands          n/a      0            1371882
Responses         n/a      0            7871934
```

After the move is done, the balancing is done. The latest cluster now looks much better:

```
$ /opt/cassandra/bin/nodetool ring


Note: Ownership information does not include topology; for
complete information, specify a keyspace
```

```
Datacenter: us-east

==========

Address          Rack        Status State   Load        Owns
Token

4611686018427387904

10.10.21.228  1a            Up      Normal  5.86 GB     25.00%
-9223372036854775808

10.10.21.169  1a            Up      Normal  4.71 GB     25.00%
-4611686018427387904

10.10.21.206  1a            Up      Normal  4.72 GB     25.00%
0

10.10.21.7    1a            Up      Normal  2.89 GB     25.00%
4611686018427387904
```

• **Cleanup**: Now that everything is done and there is relatively low traffic on the database, it is a good time to clean the useless data from each node as follows:

```
$ /opt/cassandra/bin/nodetool -h 10.10.21.228 cleanup

$ /opt/cassandra/bin/nodetool -h 10.10.21.169 cleanup

$ /opt/cassandra/bin/nodetool -h 10.10.21.206 cleanup

$ /opt/cassandra/bin/nodetool -h 10.10.21.7 cleanup
```

Now, we are done with adding a new node to the system.

Removing nodes from a cluster

It may not always be desired to have a high number of nodes up all the time. It adds to the cost and maintenance overhead. In many situations where one has scaled out to cope with a sudden surge in the traffic (for high I/O) or to avoid a hotspot for a while, it may be required to retire some machines and come back to the normal operation mode. Another reason to remove a node is due to hardware or communication failure, like a dead node that needs to be ejected out of the ring.

Removing a live node

Removing a live node is to stream the data out of the node to its neighbors. The command to remove a live node is `nodetool decommission`. That's all. You are done with removing a live node. It will take some time to stream the data, and you may need to rebalance the cluster.

We will see what decommissioning a node looks like. Assume that the ring is the same as when we added a node to a three-node cluster. The following command will show the process of decommissioning a live node:

```
$ /opt/cassandra/bin/nodetool -h 10.10.21.206 decommission
```

This will decommission the node at `10.10.21.206`. It is a blocking process, which means the CLI will wait till the decommissioning gets done. Here is how `netstats` on the node looks:

```
$ for i in {1..300} ; do  /opt/cassandra/bin/nodetool -h 10.10.21.206
netstats; sleep 1; done
```

```
Mode: NORMAL
Not sending any streams.
Read Repair Statistics:

Attempted: 0
Mismatch (Blocking): 0
Mismatch (Background): 0
```

Pool Name	Active	Pending	Completed
Commands	n/a	1	2
Responses	n/a	0	3485751

```
- - - - -
```

```
Mode: LEAVING
Not sending any streams.
Read Repair Statistics:

Attempted: 0
Mismatch (Blocking): 0
Mismatch (Background): 0
```

Pool Name	Active	Pending	Completed
Commands	n/a	1	2
Responses	n/a	0	3485760

```
- - - -
```

```
Mode: LEAVING
```

```
Unbootstrap e5d4bba0-61b0-11e4-b2ce-87642b1a7033
    /10.10.21.228
    /10.10.21.7
        Sending 18 files, 1055936170 bytes total
            /mnt/cassandra-data/stresscql-blogposts-ka-70-Data.db
97202078/97202078 bytes(100%) sent to idx:0/10.10.21.7
            /mnt/cassandra-data/stresscql-blogposts-ka-80-Data.db
83266856/83266856 bytes(100%) sent to idx:0/10.10.21.7
            /mnt/cassandra-data/system_auth-users-ka-1-Data.db 55/55
bytes(100%) sent to idx:0/10.10.21.7
            [-- snip -]


Read Repair Statistics:
Attempted: 0
Mismatch (Blocking): 0
Mismatch (Background): 0


Pool Name                       Active      Pending      Completed
Commands                         n/a           1              2
Responses                        n/a           0          3486151


----

Mode: DECOMMISSIONED
Not sending any streams.
Read Repair Statistics:

Attempted: 0
Mismatch (Blocking): 0
Mismatch (Background): 0

Pool Name                       Active      Pending      Completed
Commands                         n/a           1              2
Responses                        n/a           0          3486231
```

Here is how the ring looks after we decommissioned two of the nodes:

```
$   /opt/cassandra/bin/nodetool status
```

```
Note: Ownership information does not include topology; for complete
information, specify a keyspace
```

```
Datacenter: us-east
==================
Status=Up/Down
|/ State=Normal/Leaving/Joining/Moving
--  Address         Load        Tokens  Owns    Host ID         Rack
UN  10.10.21.228    3.44 GB     256     50.4%   d3de1...    1a
UN  10.10.21.7      2.82 GB     256     49.6%   97c2f...    1a
```

If you look carefully, you will see the ring is still balanced. This is because virtual nodes take care of balancing. If we do not have virtual nodes like the versions before Cassandra Version 1.2, you would find that this leads the cluster imbalance and you have to rebalance it manually.

Removing a dead node

Removing a dead node is closely similar to decommissioning, except for the fact that data is streamed from replica nodes to other nodes instead of streaming from the node that is being replaced. Take a look at a cluster with a dead server:

```
[root@es06 cassandra]# bin/nodetool status
Note: Ownership information does not include topology; for complete information, specify a keyspace
Datacenter: us-east
==================
Status=Up/Down
|/ State=Normal/Leaving/Joining/Moving
--  Address         Load      Tokens  Owns    Host ID                                  Rack
UN  10.10.21.228    3.44 GB   256     33.2%   d3de1bfd-52e7-4230-b591-a5da8ba1f501     1a
UN  10.10.21.169    1.95 GB   256     34.3%   6dc00dd6-4311-4b03-b840-3108563cca6d     1a
DN  10.10.21.7      2.82 GB   256     32.5%   97c2f5f0-9d71-4d50-9100-74f2b3611359     1a
```

As you can see from preceding status, the node `10.10.21.7` is down. The command to remove a dead node from the cluster is as follows:

```
$ nodetool -h HOSTNAME removenode NODE_HOST_ID
$ bin/nodetool removenode 97c2f5f0-9d71-4d50-9100-74f2b3611359
$ bin/nodetool status
```

```
Datacenter: us-east
===================
Status=Up/Down
|/ State=Normal/Leaving/Joining/Moving
--  Address         Load        Tokens  Owns    Host ID         Rack
```

```
UN   10.10.21.228  3.44 GB   256   50.9%   d3de1...  1a
UN   10.10.21.169  1.95 GB   256   49.1%   6dc00...  1a
```

It has a similar effect on the ring as `nodetool decommission`. Alternatively, `decommission` or `disablegossip` cannot be used with a dead node. You might need to move/rebalance the cluster tokens after this, if you are not using virtual node.

 It must be noted that decommissioning or removing a token does not remove the data from the node that is being removed from the system. If you plan to reuse the node, you must clean the data directories manually.

Replacing a node

More often than not, you find yourself in a less than situation where you do not really want to remove a dead node; instead, you want to replace it. The reasons can be many, your cloud service provider finds that a node is sitting on degraded hardware and kills the nodes with a notification mail to you.

All versions after Cassandra Version 1.2 have simplified replacing a node to merely running one command. Here are the steps to replace a node:

1. Install Cassandra on the new node. Make sure `conf/cassandra.yaml` has all the custom changes that exist in other nodes. (The best way to do this is to copy `cassandra.yaml` from a live node, and change the node-specific setting.)

2. Make sure you have got the following variables right: `cluster_name`, `endpoint_snitch`, `listen_address`, `broadcast_address`, and `seeds`.

3. Make sure the data directories are clean. If you are reusing a node that used to be a part of Cassandra cluster, it can possibly lead to a startup failure if the data directory has old data.

4. Start Cassandra with the `cassandra.replace_address` environment variable set as the address of the dead node that this node is replacing. This can be done either by editing `cassandra-env.sh` or by adding a line like this:

   ```
   JVM_OPTS="$JVM_OPTS -Dcassandra.replace_address=DEAD_NODE_ADDRESS"
   ```

   You can also start Cassandra with this variable:

   ```
   $ bin/cassandra -Dcassandra.replace_address=DEAD_NODE_ADDRESS
   ```

This is how it looks before the removal of the dead node:

```
[root@es06 cassandra]# bin/nodetool status
Note: Ownership information does not include topology; for complete information, specify a keyspace
Datacenter: us-east
===================
Status=Up/Down
|/ State=Normal/Leaving/Joining/Moving
--  Address        Load       Tokens  Owns    Host ID                               Rack
UN  10.10.21.228   3.44 GB    256     33.2%   d3de1bfd-52e7-4230-b591-a5da8ba1f501  1a
UN  10.10.21.169   1.95 GB    256     34.3%   6dc00dd6-4311-4b03-b840-3108563cca6d  1a
DN  10.10.21.7     2.82 GB    256     32.5%   97c2f5f0-9d71-4d50-9100-74f2b3611359  1a
```

You can replace the node by running the following command:

```
$ bin/cassandra -Dcassandra.replace_address=10.10.21.7
```

If you watch the log, it states that this node is replacing the dead node mentioned in the startup variable as follows:

INFO   09:31:03 Node es07.nishantlabs.internal/10.10.21.206 state jump to normal

WARN   09:31:03 Not updating token metadata for es07.nishantlabs. internal/10.10.21.206 because I am replacing it

INFO   09:31:03 Waiting for gossip to settle before accepting client requests...

After the replacement, we get the following output:

```
[root@es07 cassandra]# bin/nodetool status
Note: Ownership information does not include topology; for complete information, specify a keyspace
Datacenter: us-east
===================
Status=Up/Down
|/ State=Normal/Leaving/Joining/Moving
--  Address        Load       Tokens  Owns    Host ID                               Rack
UN  10.10.21.228   3.44 GB    256     33.2%   d3de1bfd-52e7-4230-b591-a5da8ba1f501  1a
UN  10.10.21.206   111.4 KB   256     32.5%   97c2f5f0-9d71-4d50-9100-74f2b3611359  1a
UN  10.10.21.169   1.95 GB    256     34.3%   6dc00dd6-4311-4b03-b840-3108563cca6d  1a
```

As you can see in the preceding screenshot, the host ID of the replacing node is the same as the replaced node.

Backup and restoration

Cassandra provides a simple backup tool called `nodetool snapshot` to take incremental snapshots and back up of data. The `snapshot` command flushes MemTables to the disk and creates a backup by creating a hard link to SSTables (SSTables are immutable).

Hard link is a directory entry associated with file data on a filesystem. It can roughly be assumed as an alias to a file that refers to the location where data is stored. It is unlike a soft link that just aliases filenames, not the actual underlying data.

These hard links stay under the `data` directory, which is placed under `<keyspace>/<column_family>/snapshots`.

The general plan to back up a cluster roughly follows these steps:

1. Take a snapshot of each node one by one. The `snapshot` command provides an option to specify whether to back up the entire keyspace or just the selected column families.

2. Taking a snapshot is just half of the story. To be able to restore the database at a later point, you need to move these snapshots to a location that cannot be affected by the node's hardware failure or the node's unavailability. One of the easiest things to do is to move the data to a network-attached storage. To AWS users, it is fairly common to back up the snapshots in the S3 bucket.

3. Once you are done with backing up the snapshots, you need to clean them. The `nodetool clearsnapshot` command cleans all the snapshots on a node.

It is important to understand that creating snapshots creates hard links to the data files. These data files do not get deleted when they become obsolete because they are saved for backup. This unnecessary disk space usage can be avoided by `clearsnapshot` after the snapshots are copied to a different location.

For really large datasets, it may be hard to back up the entire keyspace on a daily basis. Plus, it is expensive to transfer large data over a network to move the snapshots to a safe location. You can take a snapshot at first and copy it to a safe location. Once this is done, all we need to do is move the incremental data. This is called **incremental backup**. To enable incremental backup to a node, you need to edit `cassandra.yaml` and set `incremental_backups: true`. This will result in the creation of hard links in the backup's directory under the `data` directory.

Therefore, you have snapshots with incremental backup. You also have a backup of all the SSTables created after the snapshot is taken. Incremental backups have the same problem as snapshots. They are hard links; they delete obsolete data files that are not to be deleted. It is recommended to run `clearsnapshot` before a new snapshot is created, and make sure that the backup's directory has no incremental backup.

Backing up the data is just half the story. Backups are meaningful when they are restored in the case of node replacement or to launch a whole new cluster from the backup data of another cluster. There is more than one way to restore a node. We will see two approaches here. The first step is to just paste the appropriate files to the appropriate location. Perform the following steps:

1. Shut down the node that is going to be restored. Clean the `.db` files for the column family from the `data` directory. It is located under `<data_directoy>/<keyspace>/<column_family>`. Do not delete anything other than the `.db` files. Also, delete the commit logs from the `commitlog` directory.

2. From the backup, take the `snapshot` directory that you wanted to replace. Paste the content of everything in that snapshot directory to the `data` directory mentioned in the previous step.

    If you have enabled incremental backup, you may want to take them into account too. You need to paste all the incremental backup taken from your backup (it is situated under `<data_directory>/<keyspace>/<column_family>/backups`) to the `data` directory, the same as we did with snapshots in the previous step.

3. Restart the node.

Here are a couple of things to note:

*   If you are restoring the complete cluster, shut down the cluster while restoring and restore the nodes one by one.

*   Once the restoration process is done, execute `nodetool repair`.

*   If you are trying to restore on a completely new machine that has no idea about the keyspace that is being restored, it may be worth checking the schema for the keyspace and the column family that you wanted to restore. The schema can be queried by executing `desc schema` in the `cqlsh` console. You may need to create a schema to be able to get the restoration working.

Using the Cassandra bulk loader to restore the data

An alternative technique to load the data to Cassandra is using the `sstableloader` utility. It can be found under the `bin` directory of the Cassandra installation. This tool is especially useful when the number of nodes and the replication strategy is changed, because unlike the copy method, it streams appropriate data to appropriate nodes, based on the configuration.

Assuming that you have the -Index.db and -Data.db files with you, here are the steps to use sstableloader:

1. Check the node's schema. If it does not have the keyspaces and the column families that are being restored, create the appropriate keyspaces and the column families.

2. Create a directory with the same name as the keyspace that is being loaded. Inside this directory, all the column families' data (the .db files) that is being restored should be kept in a directory with the same name as the column family name. For example, if you are restoring a myCF column family in keyspace, mykeyspace, all mykeyspace-myCF-hf-x-Data.db and mykeyspace-myCF-hf-x-Index.db (where x is an integer) files should be placed within the directory structure: mykeyspace/myCF/.

3. Finally, execute bin/sstableloadermykeyspace.

Cassandra's bulk loader simplified the task to an extent that one can just store the backup in the exact same directory structure as required by sstableloader, and whenever a restoration is required just download the backup directory and execute sstableloader.

It can be observed that the backup step is very mechanical and can easily be automated to perform a daily backup using the cron job and the shell script. It may be a good idea to clear the snapshot once in a while, and take a snapshot then on.

Backup

Coming from the traditional database, one thinks that data backup is an essential part of data management. Data must be backed up daily, stored in a hard disk, and stored in a safe place. This is a good idea. It gets harder and inefficient to achieve this as the data size grows to terabytes. With Cassandra, you may set up a configuration that makes it really hard to lose data. For example, a setup with three data centers in Virginia (US East), California (US West), and Tokyo (Japan), where data is replicated across all the three data centers, you will seldom need to worry about data. If you are nervous, you may have a cron job backing up the data from one of the data centers, at every time interval up to which you may take a risk. With this setup, in the rare event of the two US data centers going down, you can serve the users without any repercussions. Things will catch up as soon as the data centers come back up.

Load balancing

A balanced Cassandra cluster is the one where each node owns an equal number of keys. This means when you query `nodetool status`, a balanced cluster will show the same percentage for all the nodes under the `Owns` or `Effective Ownership` columns. If the data is not uniformly distributed between the keys, even with equal ownership you will see some nodes are more occupied by the data than others. We use `RandomPartitioner` or `Murmur3Partitioner` to avoid this sort of lopsided cluster.

> Note that this section is valid for a setup that does *not* use vnodes. If you are using Cassandra Version 1.2 or a version after it with default settings, you can skip this section.
>
> This section is specifically for a cluster that uses one token per Cassandra instance.

Anytime a new node is added or a node is decommissioned, the token distribution gets skewed. Normally, one always wants Cassandra to be fairly load balanced to avoid hotspots. Fortunately, it is very easy to load balance. The two-step load balancing process is as follows:

1. Calculate the initial tokens based on the partitioner that you are using. It can be manually generated by equally dividing token range for a given partitioner among the number of nodes.

   If you are using `RandomPartitioner`, you can use `tools/bin/token-generator` to generate tokens for you. For example, the following command generates the tokens for two data centers; each has three nodes:

   ```
   $ tools/bin/token-generator 3 3
   DC #1:
     Node #1:  0
     Node #2:  56713727820156410577229101238628035242
     Node #3:  113427455640312821154458202477256070484

   DC #2:
     Node #1:  169417178424467235000914166253263322299
     Node #2:  55989722784154413846455963776007251813
     Node #3:  112703450604310824423685065014635287055
   ```

   For, `Murmur3Partitioner` (default type of partitioner, since Cassandra Version 1.2), you can use this Python script:

   ```
   python -c 'print [str(((2**64 / nodes_count) * i) - 2**63) for i
   in range(nodes_count)]'
   ```

For example, if you have six nodes, run the following command:

```
python -c 'print [str(((2**64 / 6) * i) - 2**63) for i in
range(6)]'
```

```
['-9223372036854775808', '-6148914691236517206',
'-3074457345618258604', '-2', '3074457345618258600',
'6148914691236517202']
```

If you have nodes distributed across two data centers, you may want to assign alternate tokens to each data center:

```
DC #1:
  -9223372036854775808
  -3074457345618258604
  3074457345618258600
DC #2:
  -6148914691236517206
  -2
  6148914691236517202
```

2. Now that we have tokens, we need to call the following command:

```
bin/nodetool -h <node_to_move> move <token_number>
```

The trick here is to assign a new token to a node that is closest to it. This will allow faster balancing as there will be less data to move. A live example of how load balancing is done is covered in the *Adding nodes to a cluster* section, where we add a node to the cluster, which makes the cluster lopsided. We finally balance it by moving tokens around.

It is actually very easy to write a shell or Python script that takes the ring and then balances it automatically. For someone using `RandomPartitioner`, there is a GitHub project, Cassandra-Balancer (`https://github.com/tivv/cassandra-balancer`), which calculates the tokens for a node and moves the data. So, instead of writing one of your own you can just use this Groovy script. Execute it on each node, one by one, and you are done.

DataStax OpsCenter – managing large clusters

Managing a large Cassandra cluster can be a pain in the neck with installations over hundreds of machines and across multiple data centers comprising test, staging, prod, and other environments with multiple keyspaces running on virtual machines with a cloud providers' hardware getting compromised more often than you would expect. Fortunately, people at DataStax have built OpsCenter.

OpsCenter is a web application that takes care of all operation-related tasks from a user-friendly user interface. It smartly uses Cassandra's JMX calls and operations commands to perform the task. On top of this, you can use it to monitor alerts, performance reviews, and diagnosis. We will see OpsCenter in more detail in the next chapter.

For a small cluster setup (say, under 25 nodes), it is may be simpler to stick with simple automation based on `nodetool` and perhaps shell or Python script. It will keep the administration simple.

Summary

We know how to move data around and manage Cassandra instances to handle the production situations. Cassandra provides simple one-liner commands to perform various complicated maintenance tasks to make life easy. Scaling out, scaling in, removing live or dead nodes, and load balancing are pleasantly simple and can be automated based on your configuration using scripts. Backups fall in the same category, but restoration can be a bit tricky. With the Cassandra data model, built-in replication, and support for multiple data center setups, one can configure Cassandra such that it may never need to be backed up. Also, for really large databases, it may be impractical to siphon out data instead of using replication. It may make sense to back up in a case where the database is not very large and one uses a replication factor of 1. In such a case, even a single malfunctioning server can cause loss of data. However, RF=1 is a bad idea in production setup and backup can just restore the data until the latest backup is made.

OpsCenter gives a decent option to move on from the nodetool-based mechanism to more sophisticated tooling. If you are just starting out or have a small cluster, it may not be worth the effort it takes to configure OpsCenter. It is a good suggestion for large cluster owners. Also, if you are just starting to look into Cassandra, it is more fun to play with CLI tools such as `nodetools` and to check `netstat`, `top`, memory usage, and so on to see what is actually happening underneath.

There is another Cassandra project for DevOps from NetFlix called Priam (`https://github.com/Netflix/Priam/wiki`). The reason why Priam wasn't discussed in the chapter is that it seems a bit outdated and confusing. Moreover, Priam is built to support the AWS infrastructure and tied to the AWS configuration. So, it might not be useful to everyone. If you decide to explore Priam, make sure you read this wiki entry first: `https://github.com/Netflix/Priam/wiki/Compatibility`.

This chapter gives you enough knowledge to tackle an infrastructure issue. Now, as an operations person, you need to keep a watch on how things are going without losing your sleep and waking up from nightmares. The next chapter will walk you through the various ways to monitor and recognize problems and troubleshoot the Cassandra infrastructure in detail.

7
Monitoring

Monitoring is the key to provide reliable service. For distributed software, monitoring becomes more important and more complex. Fortunately, Cassandra has an excellent tool built in for monitoring. It is called `nodetool`. Apart from this, there are third-party tools to monitor Cassandra.

The purpose of monitoring is to be able to catch a problem before or as soon as it happens and resolve it. Therefore, this chapter will be a mix of monitoring, management (it comes with monitoring tools), and very quick troubleshooting tips. It familiarizes you with the **Java Management Extension (JMX)** interface that Cassandra provides and then moves on to accessing it via JConsole. Cassandra's `nodetool` — the application to monitor and administer Cassandra — is discussed in detail. Further, DataStax OpsCenter (the community version), which is an excellent web-based tool that stores performance history, is discussed. Nagios is another tool that can be used to monitor not only Cassandra but also the complete infrastructure with heterogeneous components. Nagios is a veteran monitoring tool. It is a pretty simple, intuitive, extendable, and robust tool. It provides monitoring along with e-mail notifications.

Cassandra's JMX interface

Cassandra has a powerful JMX interface to monitor almost all of its aspects. JMX is a standard part of Java **standard edition (SE)** 5.0 and onward. It provides a standard interface to manage and monitor resources such as applications, devices, JVM settings, and services. The way JMX technology manages and monitors a resource is called **Managed Beans (MBeans)**. JMX defines standard connectors that enable us to access JMX agents remotely. With this introductory JMX knowledge, let's see what Cassandra offers us to control or monitor almost all of its aspects using JMX.

This discussion is sufficient to get you to work with JMX in the context of Cassandra. Learn more about it at `http://docs.oracle.com/javase/tutorial/jmx/TOC.html`.

Cassandra exposes JMX MBeans in different packages. These are as follows:

- `org.apache.cassandra.internal`: This package includes MBeans that inform us about internal operations. Therefore, you can view the status of AntiEntropy, FlushWriter, gossip, hinted handoff, response stage, migration and stream stages, pending range calculation, and commit log archival. Other than getting internal status statistics, there is not much that can be done with these MBeans.

- `org.apache.cassandra.db`: This is probably the most interesting MBean package. It includes vital metrics and actionable operational items. MBeans give statistics and commands for database components such as cache management, table, commit log, compaction control, hinted handoff management, storage service (general ring statistics and operations), and storage proxy (client read/write statistics).

- `org.apache.cassandra.net`: This package contains statistics on network communication within the cluster. It has some interesting Mbeans, such as FailureDetector, gossip, internode messaging, and data stream status.

- `org.apache.cassandra.request`: One can view pending and completed tasks at different stages. The stages listed under this package are mutation, read repair, read, replicate on write, and read response.

  Cassandra is designed around **Staged Event Driven Architecture (SEDA)**. At very high levels, it chunks a task into multiple stages, with each having its own thread pool and event queue. To read more about SEDA, visit `http://www.eecs.harvard.edu/~mdw/proj/seda`.

- `org.apache.cassandra.metrics`: This package includes statistics about client read and write; specifically, the number of requests that are timed out and those that have thrown `UnavailableException`. That is, not enough replicas are available to satisfy the operation with the given consistency level or, maybe, many replicas are down.

Accessing MBeans using JConsole

JConsole is a built-in utility in JDK 5+. You can access it from `$JAVA_HOME/bin/jconsole`. It is a JVM monitoring tool and allows you to access MBeans in the Java application to which JConsole is connected. It allows you to monitor the CPU, memory, thread pools, heap information, and other important JVM-related things.

To peek into the insides of Cassandra, launch JConsole. The GUI shows two options to connect to—**Local Process** and **Remote Process**. If you are running JConsole on the same machine as Cassandra, you will see the option to connect to Cassandra in the drop-down under the **Local Process** radio button. However, it is not recommended to run JConsole on the same machine as Cassandra. This is because JConsole takes a large amount of system resources and can hamper Cassandra's performance. Thus, unless you just want to test Cassandra on your local machine, it may not be a good idea to have Cassandra and JConsole running on the same machine.

The **Overview** tab of JConsole is shown in the following screenshot:

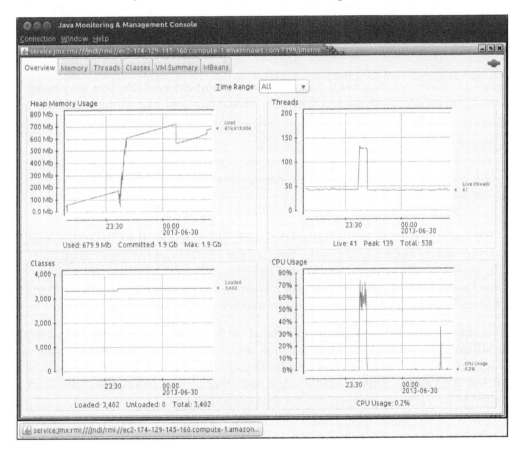

To connect to a remote machine, you need to select the **Remote process** radio button and fill in the URL of the Cassandra node. The format is as follows:

```
# CASSANDRAHOST is address of remote Cassandra node
  service:jmx:rmi:///jndi/rmi://CASSANDRAHOST:7199/jmxrmi
```

If you have a firewall or port blocking the Cassandra node, you may face some issues in connection.

It requires some work to get JConsole connected to your Cassandra instance running within EC2 from outside the security group without compromising its security. The suggested way is to connect via a **Secure Shell (SSH)** tunnel. Setting up an SSH tunnel is beyond the scope of this book. You may refer to articles online. Refer to the online article at `http://simplygenius.com/2010/08/jconsole-via-socks-ssh-tunnel.html` for information on using an SSH tunnel to connect to JConsole.

> You may want to add your local machine's external IP to Cassandra's security group and open all the TCP ports (0 to 65535) to it. By doing this, you are compromising the security of the server. It is not a recommended way to get around this problem. Remember to remove this entry once you are done with the JConsole task.

If you have a server set up with different internal and external IPs, you may need to configure an RMI host name. Open `config/cassandra-env.sh` and add the hostname parameter for JMX as part of `JVM_OPTS` in the following manner:

```
JVM_OPTS="$JVM_OPTS -Djava.rmi.server.hostname=174.129.145.160"
JVM_OPTS="$JVM_OPTS -Dcom.sun.management.jmxremote.port=$JMX_PORT"
JVM_OPTS="$JVM_OPTS -Dcom.sun.management.jmxremote.ssl=false"
JVM_OPTS="$JVM_OPTS -
  Dcom.sun.management.jmxremote.authenticate=false"
```

AWS users may need to put a public DNS name provided for the Cassandra node. Once you are connected to the node, you can see an overview of the JVM on that node (refer to the previous screenshot). Look through the tabs and analyze them more closely. Interestingly, you can see a spike in the memory usage, CPU usage, and thread counts. This is the duration in which a sample stress was running.

To execute various JMX operations provided via JConsole, you will need to switch to the **MBeans** tab. Expand the various menu items in the bar on the left-hand side of the screen. The interesting ones are under **org.apache.cassandra.***. For example, you can clear the value of hinted handoff for a node that is dead before the configured timeout (`max_hint_window_in_ms`) for that node arrives.

As a matter of taste, some people prefer VisualVM to JConsole. VisualVM does not provide JMX support out of the box. However, it is fairly easy to add a VisualVM-MBeans plugin to enable such functionality. VisualVM combines JConsole, jstat, jinfo, jstack, and jmap. This is available in versions starting from JDK 6 and can be accessed at `$JDK_HOME/bin/jvisualvm`.

Details on VisualVM are beyond the scope of this book, but you can learn about them at `https://visualvm.java.net/jmx_connections.html`.

Cassandra's nodetool utility

The `nodetool` utility is a command-line utility that comes out of the box with Cassandra. You can access it from `$CASSANDRA_HOME/bin/nodetool`. It communicates with JMX to perform operational and monitoring tasks exposed by MBeans. It is much easier to use than JConsole. We have already seen a bit of `nodetool` in the previous chapter. The `nodetool` utility is a great tool for administration and monitoring. The following section will discuss some of its useful functionalities. Most of the nodetool commands are obvious and can be easily learned by reading the help text. Unfortunately, there is no help option, but it prints help messages anyway.

The following screenshot shows how to invoke methods via JConsole:

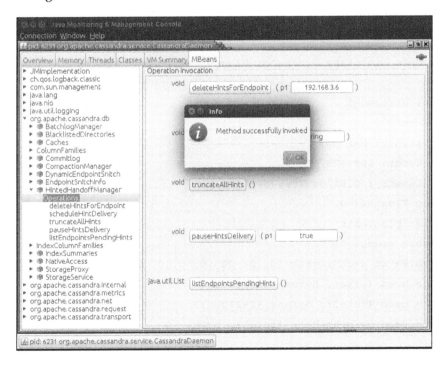

The standard way to execute any command on a Cassandra node using `nodetool` is as follows:

```
nodetool -h CASSANDRA_HOST [-p JMX_PORT -u JMX_USERNAME -pw JMX_PASSWORD]
COMMAND
```

In general, you need not provide `JMX_PORT`, `JMX_USERNAME`, and `JMX_PASSWORD` unless you've explicitly configured them. The following sections discuss the `COMMAND` keyword in the previous command.

Monitoring with nodetool

The `nodetool` utility provides some basic, yet very informative, statistics on Cassandra. This is often used to take a quick glance at how Cassandra is doing and to monitor it. This section will introduce you to some of the interesting commands that `nodetool` offers to monitor Cassandra.

cfstats

The term `cfstats` stands for "column family statistics". It comprises details about every significant statistic regarding all the tables in the ring and across all the keyspaces. The command is as follows:

```
$ bin/nodetool cfstats [keyspace_name[.table_name]]
```

Executing `cfstats` looks as follows (this statistic is per node):

```
$ bin/nodetool cfstats stresscql.blogposts
```

```
Keyspace: stresscql
  Read Count: 0
  Read Latency: NaN ms.
  Write Count: 2291978
  Write Latency: 0.017063794678657474 ms.
  Pending Flushes: 0
    Table: blogposts
    SSTable count: 30
    SSTables in each level: [0, 8, 22, 0, 0, 0, 0, 0, 0]
    Space used (live), bytes: 6292666026
    Space used (total), bytes: 6292735112
    Space used by snapshots (total), bytes: 0
```

```
SSTable Compression Ratio: 0.9719074538796416
Memtable cell count: 0
Memtable data size, bytes: 0
Memtable switch count: 15
Local read count: 0
Local read latency: NaN ms
Local write count: 2291978
Local write latency: 0.018 ms
Pending flushes: 0
Bloom filter false positives: 0
Bloom filter false ratio: 0.00000
Bloom filter space used, bytes: 296864
Compacted partition minimum bytes: 373
Compacted partition maximum bytes: 3379391
Compacted partition mean bytes: 12046
Average live cells per slice (last five minutes): 0.0
Average tombstones per slice (last five minutes): 0.0
```

A few important statistics are as follows:

- **Read Latency and Write Latency**: These provide the average time elapsed in performing these operations. Look at these if you see that the throughput is slow.

- **Read Count and Write Count**: These can provide a general idea of how frequently a table is accessed. It may be an indicator of how busy a table is.

- **Pending Tasks**: Lots of pending tasks are an indication of an overloaded node. Maybe you should look into adding more machines or improving the node's hardware.

- **Space Used (live and total)**: The live statistic represents the space used by the SSTables in use. The total statistic is the total space used by the SSTable. The total statistic is always greater than or equal to the live statistic owing to the existence of deleted, but yet-to-be-removed, data. All these data are in bytes (just bytes, not kilobytes or megabytes).

netstats

The netstats command is used to view the network statistics (streaming information) of the node within the ring. This is a very useful tool, especially during maintenance work, such as moving, repairing, removing the node (decommission), or starting up a new one.

The following commands show various stages of the node as provided by netstats while a node is being added:

```
$ bin/nodetool -h cassandra01.naishe.in netstats


Mode: JOINING
Bootstrap 3cb55a90-7798-11e4-8b2e-d74579598740
    /10.10.21.228
        Receiving 33 files, 1612364017 bytes total
            bin/../data/data/stresscql/blogposts-946f4e60761911e4a6ea
7d86f73d83eb/stresscql-blogposts-tmp-ka-35-Data.db 27898542/27898542
bytes(100%) received from idx:0/10.10.21.228
            bin/../data/data/stresscql/blogposts-946f4e60761911e4a6ea
7d86f73d83eb/stresscql-blogposts-tmp-ka-50-Data.db 36126372/36126372
bytes(100%) received from idx:0/10.10.21.228
[ -- snip -- ]


$ bin/nodetool -h cassandra01.naishe.in netstats
Mode: NORMAL
Not sending any streams.
Read Repair Statistics:
Attempted: 0
Mismatch (Blocking): 0
Mismatch (Background): 0
```

Pool Name	Active	Pending	Completed
Commands	n/a	0	1154
Responses	n/a	0	554

status

The status command is the most frequently used command. Whenever you want to investigate the ring, this is likely to be the first command you will want to run. The status command is a general ring health check and it gives a human-readable summary of the cluster. Here is an example of this command, wherein the command was run twice, once while adding a new node and then after the node joined the ring:

```
# A new node is joining the cluster
$ bin/nodetool status


Datacenter: us-east
===================
Status=Up/Down
|/ State=Normal/Leaving/Joining/Moving
--   Address         Load      Tokens  Owns (effective)  Host ID        Rack
UN   10.10.21.228    54.9 KB   256     100.0%            fcc...    1a
UJ   10.10.21.206    61.62 KB  256     ?                 a81...    1a
UN   10.10.21.169    85.83 KB  256     100.0%            6ae...    1a


#After the node has joined the ring
$ bin/nodetool status


Datacenter: us-east
===================
Status=Up/Down
|/ State=Normal/Leaving/Joining/Moving
--   Address         Load      Tokens  Owns (effective)  Host ID        Rack
UN   10.10.21.228    54.9 KB   256     68.9%             fcc...    1a
UN   10.10.21.206    85.7 KB   256     64.0%             a81...    1a
UN   10.10.21.169    85.83 KB  256     67.1%             6ae...    1a
```

ring and describering

The `ring` and `describering` commands are more fine-grained versions of `status`.
They provide information at the virtual node level. These commands make more
sense when you have one node per machine, not so much for the modern incarnation
of Cassandra. Here is a truncated version of these commands:

```
$ bin/nodetool ring


Datacenter: us-east

==========

Address          Rack          Status State    Load          Owns
Token

9195361415106703489

10.10.21.206   1a            Up      Normal   4.85 GB       63.99%
-9215028159696936540

10.10.21.228   1a            Up      Normal   5.24 GB       68.91%
-9198474146250837999

10.10.21.206   1a            Up      Normal   4.85 GB       63.99%
-9190603604318268109

10.10.21.228   1a            Up      Normal   5.24 GB       68.91%
-9187967111064408216

10.10.21.206   1a            Up      Normal   4.85 GB       63.99%
-9174944753936214859

10.10.21.206   1a            Up      Normal   4.85 GB       63.99%
-9215028159696936540

10.10.21.228   1a            Up      Normal   5.24 GB       68.91%
-9198474146250837999

10.10.21.206   1a            Up      Normal   4.85 GB       63.99%
-9190603604318268109

10.10.21.228   1a            Up      Normal   5.24 GB       68.91%
-9187967111064408216

10.10.21.206   1a            Up      Normal   4.85 GB       63.99%
-9174944753936214859


# describe ring, you may need to provide keyspace name
$ bin/nodetool describering stresscql


Schema Version:ee46e5a9-7ed5-34a0-a297-d15a86107a49
```

```
TokenRange:


  TokenRange(start_token:6311173006280019255, end_
token:6312578980665460017, endpoints:[10.10.21.206, 10.10.21.169], rpc_
endpoints:[10.10.21.206, 10.10.21.169], endpoint_details:[EndpointDeta
ils(host:10.10.21.206, datacenter:us-east, rack:1a), EndpointDetails(ho
st:10.10.21.169, datacenter:us-east, rack:1a)])


  TokenRange(start_token:-2983242081861042081, end_
token:-2960989697188644852, endpoints:[10.10.21.228, 10.10.21.206], rpc_
endpoints:[10.10.21.228, 10.10.21.206], endpoint_details:[EndpointDeta
ils(host:10.10.21.228, datacenter:us-east, rack:1a), EndpointDetails(ho
st:10.10.21.206, datacenter:us-east, rack:1a)])


  TokenRange(start_token:2795178789021647703, end_
token:2799131500537456455, endpoints:[10.10.21.228, 10.10.21.206], rpc_
endpoints:[10.10.21.228, 10.10.21.206], endpoint_details:[EndpointDeta
ils(host:10.10.21.228, datacenter:us-east, rack:1a), EndpointDetails(ho
st:10.10.21.206, datacenter:us-east, rack:1a)])
[-- snip -- ]
```

tpstats

The term `tpstats` stands for "thread pool statistics". This is an important measure of how much pressure the node is bearing at a given instant. You can see task counts that are running, pending, completed, and blocked in various stages. The rule of thumb is that more pending tasks indicate a performance bottleneck. The following command-line output shows the result of the usage of `tpstats`:

```
$ bin/nodetool tpstats
```

Pool Name All time blocked	Active	Pending	Completed	Blocked
CounterMutationStage 0	0	0	0	0
ReadStage 0	0	0	13	0
RequestResponseStage 0	0	0	1298937	0
MutationStage 0	0	0	2542081	0
ReadRepairStage 0	0	0	0	0

GossipStage	0	0	7715	0
0				
CacheCleanupExecutor	0	0	0	0
0				
AntiEntropyStage	0	0	0	0
0				
MigrationStage	0	0	6	0
0				
ValidationExecutor	0	0	0	0
0				
CommitLogArchiver	0	0	0	0
0				
MiscStage	0	0	0	0
0				
MemtableFlushWriter	0	0	90	0
0				
MemtableReclaimMemory	0	0	90	0
0				
PendingRangeCalculator	0	0	5	0
0				
MemtablePostFlush	0	0	144	0
0				
CompactionExecutor	0	0	175	0
0				
InternalResponseStage	0	0	2	0
0				
HintedHandoff	0	0	0	0
0				

Message type	Dropped
RANGE_SLICE	0
READ_REPAIR	0
PAGED_RANGE	0
BINARY	0
READ	0
MUTATION	0
_TRACE	0
REQUEST_RESPONSE	0
COUNTER_MUTATION	0

It also displays various types of message drop that happen for various reasons. These message drops may or may not be significant to you. A message to a node that does not get processed within the limits of `rpc_timeout_in_ms` (`cassandra.yaml`) is dropped so that the coordinator node does not go on waiting. This means the coordinator node will get a timeout response for executing a request made to the node. For example, a read request may get a couple of timeouts, but the user will get the data as long as there are sufficient replicas that return valid responses for the request such that the consistency level of the query is satisfied. For a write or mutate request, this means the node that has timed out is in an inconsistent state. It will get fixed either during a read repair or an anti-entropy repair operation. If you get lots of dropped messages, it may be worth investigating what is going on in the node.

One may relate thread pools getting backed up to dropping messages in `tpstats`. There are more tasks that can be processed by the threads within timeout limits.

compactionstats

The `compactionstats` command shows the compaction process running in the instant. Compaction is a CPU- and I/O-intensive task. It may temporarily increase used disk space. Thus, it may be a good idea to check whether any compaction is running, if there is no obvious indication from other monitoring statistics but you suddenly see high I/O, CPU, or space consumption. Let's take a look at the following example:

```
$ bin/nodetool -h 10.147.171.159 compactionstats
pending tasks: 0
Active compaction remaining time :        n/a
```

info

The `info` command prints an overall bird's-eye view of the node's health. This command can be used to get a quick summary of the node. Some of the labels, such as heap size and recent cache hit rate, may give you some sense of how the node is doing. Let's take a look at the following example:

```
$ bin/nodetool -h cassandra02.naishe.in info

ID               : a8168502-1f0b-4537-984f-3d4e74a5ed9b

Gossip active    : true
Thrift active    : true
Native Transport active: true
Load             : 4.85 GB
```

```
Generation No     : 1417080773

Uptime (seconds) : 2490

Heap Memory (MB) : 4692.12 / 7568.00

Data Center       : us-east

Rack              : 1a

Exceptions        : 0

Key Cache         : entries 528, size 63232 (bytes), capacity 104857600
(bytes), 28 hits, 1189 requests, 0.024 recent hit rate, 14400 save period
in seconds

Row Cache         : entries 0, size 0 (bytes), capacity 0 (bytes), 0 hits,
0 requests, NaN recent hit rate, 0 save period in seconds

Counter Cache     : entries 0, size 0 (bytes), capacity 52428800 (bytes),
0 hits, 0 requests, NaN recent hit rate, 7200 save period in seconds

Token             : (invoke with -T/--tokens to see all 256 tokens)
```

Managing administration with nodetool

We have seen some usage of `nodetool` while setting up the Cassandra cluster in
Chapter 4, Deploying a Cluster, and during various maintenance tasks in *Chapter 6,
Managing a Cluster – Scaling, Node Repair, and Backup.* We will see more on the use of
administrative tools in this section.

drain

The `drain` command forces the node to stop listening to other nodes and clients. It
flushes all the data to SSTables. No more write commands are processed. This is a
handy tool if you want to safely shutdown Cassandra to upgrade it. The following
is an example where we'll check the status of a cluster, drain a node, and recheck
the status:

```
# Drain the data to SSTables
$ bin/nodetool status


Datacenter: us-east

===================

Status=Up/Down
|/ State=Normal/Leaving/Joining/Moving
```

```
--  Address          Load          Tokens    Owns      Host ID
Rack
UN  10.10.21.228     5.36 GB       256       23.8%     fcc...    1a
UN  10.10.21.206     4.98 GB       256       28.6%     a81...    1a
UN  10.10.21.169     5.24 GB       256       23.7%     6ae...    1a
UN  10.10.21.7       3.81 GB       256       23.9%     354...    1a


$ bin/nodetool -h cassandra01.naishe.in drain


$ bin/nodetool status
Datacenter: us-east

===================

Status=Up/Down
|/ State=Normal/Leaving/Joining/Moving
--  Address          Load          Tokens    Owns      Host ID
Rack
UN  10.10.21.228     5.36 GB       256       23.8%     fcc...    1a
UN  10.10.21.206     4.98 GB       256       28.6%     a81...    1a
UN  10.10.21.169     5.24 GB       256       23.7%     6ae...    1a
DN  10.10.21.7       3.8 GB        256       23.9%     354...    1a


$ bin/cqlsh cassandra01.naishe.in
Connection error: ('Unable to connect to any servers', {'cassandra01.
naishe.in': error(111, 'ECONNREFUSED')})
```

decommission

We have seen `decommission` during node removal in the *Removing nodes from a cluster* section in *Chapter 6, Managing a Cluster – Scaling, Node Repair, and Backup*, earlier. Decommissioning is a way to remove a live node from the cluster. It streams all the data that it has to a replica node or a node that will be responsible for the data after the node that is being decommissioned dies.

removenode

To remove a dead node from the ring, use `removenode`. The `removenode` command has three options:

```
nodetool -h <hostname> removenode <node_UUID>
nodetool -h <hostname> removenode status
nodetool -h <hostname> removenode force
```

The first removes the mentioned node (one can obtain the node `uuid` from the `nodetool` status command), the second checks the status of the removal process, and the third command forces finalization of any pending node removal.

The `removenode` command works on a dead node where decommissioning cannot function but, if the node is alive, decommissioning is the right technique.

move

The `move` command makes more sense for a cluster that does not use a vnode and you need to balance the cluster manually. In a single-node-per-machine setup, decommissioning or adding a new node usually causes imbalance in the cluster. To reassign a different token ID to a node, you need to execute the following command:

```
$ bin/nodetool -h NODE_IP_TO_CHANGE_TOKEN move NEW_TOKEN
```

Like `decommission`, the `move` command streams data off the node. These may create a lot of network traffic and affect performance temporarily. These tasks should be done during the time the application is relatively free. Refer to *Chapter 6, Managing a Cluster – Scaling, Node Repair, and Backup*, for more information on the `move` command.

repair

The `repair` command performs pretty useful maintenance tasks. It helps the cluster avoid returning unwanted data from the dead node (the re-appearance of deleted data). It is highly recommended to run repair periodically on the whole cluster to avoid forgotten deletes. The time period between two consecutive repairs should be less than the value assigned to `gc_grace_seconds` (configured per table, the default is 10 days).

Hinted handoff is useful only as long as there is no hardware failure that lasts more than the value assigned to `max_hint_window_in_ms`. Therefore, it is generally a good idea to set up a cron job for your production machines that executes `nodetool` repair for all the nodes.

The way forgotten deletes come back can be explained with an example. Let's say you have two nodes A and B with the data X replicated between them. If you issue a delete action with `CL.ONE` when node B is down, the client will get success, and hinted handoff will make a note to resend the request to B when it comes back. If, unfortunately, node B does not come back before hinted handoff is cleared, `gc_grace_seconds` wipes the data from node A. Now, if node B comes back to life, Cassandra will treat the deleted row as a new row that is not replicated to node A (it will be copied to node A during read repair). Running a node repair does not fix the problem, now that `gc_grace_seconds` has been exceeded.

The `nodetool repair` command has the following format:

```
nodetool -h HOSTNAME repair [Keyspace] [cfnames] [-pr]
```

Therefore, `repair` can be executed for a node, a given keyspace, or a list of tables. There is an interesting option called **primary range**, denoted by `-pr`. The primary range option just repairs the range that the node owns. Without the primary range option, however, the command forces Cassandra to repair the node as well as all the replicas. Thus, if you are planning to repair an entire cluster, you should use the `-pr` switch. Otherwise, you are duplicating the task RF times. The following are the scenarios for the `repair` command:

- **Periodic repair**: Periodic repair should be executed on every node periodically within `gc_grace_seconds`, normally within 10 days. Running the repair weekly, timed at a relatively low-traffic zone, is a good idea. It is suggested that periodic repair should be executed with the `-pr` option.

- **Outage**: When a node goes down long enough to get hinted handoff, since the node may have been deleted, `repair` should be executed. Note that you should not use the `-pr` option in this case.

A typical complete node repair looks as follows:

```
$bin/nodetool -h cassandra01.naishe.in repair

[2014-11-29 15:07:49,923] Nothing to repair for keyspace 'system'

[ -- snip -- ]
[2014-11-29 15:24:39,178] Repair command #1 finished

[2014-11-29 15:24:39,264] Nothing to repair for keyspace 'system_auth'

[2014-11-29 15:24:39,270] Starting repair command #2, repairing 507
ranges for keyspace system_traces (seq=true, full=true)
```

```
[2014-11-29 15:25:03,035] Repair session d6152290-77db-11e4-
b488-d74579598740 for range (38800545708018974,96096257197984437]
finished


[2014-11-29 15:25:03,035] Repair session d61c9ca0-77db-11e4-
b488-d74579598740 for range (-6999654802673786063,-6991737081345190369]
finished


[2014-11-29 15:25:03,035] Repair session d6261280-77db-11e4-
b488-d74579598740 for range (8899547794114173830,8919386680314068240]
finished


[ -- snip -- ]
```

upgradesstable

This `upgradesstable` command rebuilds SSTables. It is generally used during upgrades or during compression ratio changes.

snapshot

The `nodetool snapshot` command we have seen earlier while taking a backup (refer to *Chapter 6, Managing a Cluster – Scaling, Node Repair, and Backup*) basically creates hard links for SSTables in the `snapshots` folder; these are used to restore the node. There is a command called `clearsnapshot` to remove the snapshot. The command has the following options:

```
# Create snapshot
nodetool -h CASSANDRA_HOST snapshot [Keyspaces...] -cf [columnfamilyName]
-t [snapshotName]


# Remove snapshots
nodetool -h CASSANDRA_HOST clearsnapshot [Keyspaces...] -t [snapshotName]
```

There are more commands that `nodetool` provides that we have not discussed here. In general, we have discussed the commands that you will find frequently. The rest of the commands can be learned from the help text provided by `nodetool`.

The nodetool documentation (this is probably outdated) can be found at
http://wiki.apache.org/cassandra/NodeTool.

Relatively newer documentation on nodetool is available at
http://www.datastax.com/documentation/cassandra/2.1/
cassandra/tools/toolsNodetool_r.html.

DataStax OpsCenter

DataStax (http://www.datastax.com) is the leading company that provides
commercial support for Cassandra. At the time of writing, DataStax claimed to
employ more than 90 percent of Cassandra committers. DataStax provides an easy-
to-use, web-based utility—OpsCenter—that is a little more than a GUI wrapper over
Cassandra's JMX instrumentation. OpsCenter provides a clean, simple, and intuitive
interface to manage and monitor a Cassandra cluster. This section will briefly go
over OpsCenter. The following screenshot shows DataStax OpsCenter's cluster view
and actionable items:

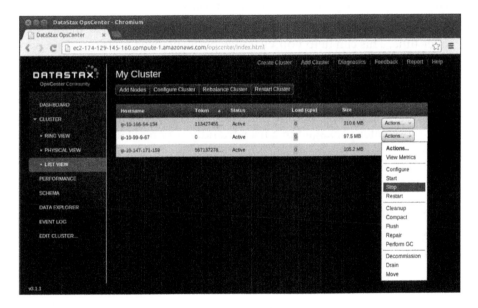

DataStax provides two versions of OpsCenter: an enterprise version and a community version. The enterprise version has more features and official support, and it is paid for. The community version can be downloaded and used for free in a production environment. You may download and evaluate the enterprise version for free for development purposes. In this section, we will briefly go over installing, configuring, monitoring, and administrating a single data center, three-node cluster using OpsCenter's community version.

The OpsCenter features

OpsCenter is a superset of `nodetool`. It provides all the functionality of `nodetool`, displays metrics in an intuitive way, and provides administrative tooling beyond the default toolset that comes with Cassandra. The following is a short list of features:

- **Centralized view of all the clusters**: A centralized view provides options to visualize clusters in different modes: ring view, list view, and view by data centers.

- **Manage cluster configuration**: OpsCenter enables one to edit and update cluster-wide configuration from the web console.

- **Visualize performance**: OpsCenter actually stores the performance history over time. This can help you visualize performance in various time windows: 20 minutes, hourly, daily, weekly, and monthly.

- **Add a new node**: On your local cluster, you can ask OpsCenter to add another node by providing the node address and credentials (of a sudoer), and choosing the appropriate DataStax package, which is basically Cassandra and OpsCenter packaged in a user-friendly way by DataStax.

OpsCenter's enterprise edition has the following features that are more advanced:

- New cluster addition from GUI
- Downloadable diagnostic information
- Single-click cluster rebalancing
- Multiple cluster management
- Alerts and e-mail notifications

 If you are on AWS EC2, OpsCenter allows you to automatically add a new node to your existing cluster. This node is basically an instance of DataStax AMI with the appropriate Cassandra version that you have chosen.

Installing OpsCenter and an agent

OpsCenter installation comprises two parts: installing the OpsCenter web interface on one machine and installing agents on each Cassandra node. The web interface and nodes communicate with each other to be able to display information.

Prerequisites

The following are the prerequisites needed to install OpsCenter and an agent:

- **Python 2.6+**: The web interface is Python-based and utilizes the `Twisted` package. Python's recommended version is 2.6+. It may or may not work with Python 3. Use the following command to find out the version of Python installed on your computer:

```
# yes, UPPERCASE V
$ python -V
Python 2.6.8
```

- **sysstat**: This is a bundle of system monitoring utilities. It provides statistics about CPU usage, memory usage, space monitoring, I/O activity information, and network statistics, and some other data about system resources. The presence of `sysstat` can be checked by executing the following command:

```
# iostat is one the utilities in sysstat. V is uppercase.
$ iostat -V
sysstat version 9.0.4
(C) Sebastien Godard (sysstat <at> orange.fr)
```

If it is not already installed, use the following commands depending on your Linux distribution:

```
# CentOS or RHEL like systems
sudo apt-get install sysstat
# Ubuntu or Debian like systems
yum install sysstat
```

- **OpenSSL**: This is an optional component. OpsCenter uses a secure connection to communicate within the OpsCenter web interface and agents by default. If you are just testing OpsCenter, you are running within a secure internal network; alternatively, if there is no appropriate OpenSSL implementation for the platform, you may just avoid this step by adding the following lines in `$OPSCENTER_HOME/conf/opscenterd.conf`:

```
[agents]
use_ssl = false
You will also need to update the agent's conf/address.yaml file
using:
use_ssl: 0
```

If you want SSL to be enabled, make sure you have the correct OpenSSL version installed for your platform with the following command:

```
$ openssl version

OpenSSL 1.0.1e-fips 11 Feb 2013
```

DataStax provides the following compatibility list for OpenSSL with OpsCenter:

Version	Operating system
0.9.8	CentOS 5.x, Debian, Mac OS X, Oracle Linux 5.5, RHEL 5.x, SuSe Enterprise 11.x, Ubuntu, and Windows
1.0.0	CentOS 6.x, Oracle Linux 6.1, and RHEL 6.x

If you have the 1.0.0 version on an operating system that requires version 0.9.8 for OpsCenter to work, installing a 0.9.8 version may solve the problem. It may not be ideal to have two versions of OpenSSL. The following commands shows how a server with CentOS 5.x with the 1.0.0 version was fixed (OpsCenter requires version 0.9.8). Note that this may not be an ideal solution, and it could potentially break another functionality:

```
$ yum install openssl098e


# Bad practice!
$ sudo ln -s /usr/lib64/libssl.so.0.9.8e \
  /usr/lib64/libssl.so.0.9.8
$ sudo ln -s /usr/lib64/libcrypto.so.0.9.8e \
  /usr/lib64/libcrypto.so.0.9.8
```

A better way to get around the OpenSSL version issue is to install pyOpenSSL 0.10 or onward. Check the version of the existing pyOpenSSL by executing the following command:

```
$ python -c "import OpenSSL; print OpenSSL.__version__"
```

Install the latest version of pyOpenSSL as follows:

```
$ easy_install pyOpenSSL
```

Running a Cassandra cluster

You need to have a running Cassandra cluster that can communicate with OpsCenter's web interface machine.

Installing OpsCenter from tarball

DataStax provides different binaries packaged specifically for different operating systems. One may download an RPM package, a Deb package, or an MSI (Windows) package based on which operating system one is using. In this section, we will use the tarball archive because it works across several platforms (Linux, Mac OS X).

 View all the download options for OpsCenter Community Edition at http://planetcassandra.org/Download/DataStaxCommunityEdition.

To download and install OpsCenter, perform the following steps:

1. Download and untar OpsCenter as follows:

   ```
   # Download latest OpsCenter
   $ wget \
    http://downloads.datastax.com/community/opscenter.tar.gz
   # Untar
   $ tar -xzf opscenter.tar.gz
   ```

2. Edit conf/opscenterd.conf and insert the appropriate hostname, OpsCenter's port number, and SSL setting (if required):

   ```
   # vi conf/opscenterd.conf
   [webserver]
   port = 80
   interface = 10.147.171.159 #IP of OpsCenter machine
   ```

```
[agents]
use_ssl = false
```

3. Start the OpsCenter web server as follows:

```
# Use -f to start in foreground
$OPSCENTER_HOME/bin/opscenter


# In the preceding command, $OPSCENTER_HOME is just a reference to
the OpsCenter installation location
```

If the web server starts without any error, you should be able to access OpsCenter from your browser. Make sure the security settings allow the port mentioned in opscenterd.conf. When no agent is added, it will ask you to create a new cluster or join an existing cluster. This is the time to set up agents on each Cassandra node.

Setting up an OpsCenter agent

OpsCenter works in such a way that there are agents that the web interface of OpsCenter talks to. These agents collect data points and send commands to the nodes as shown in the following screenshot:

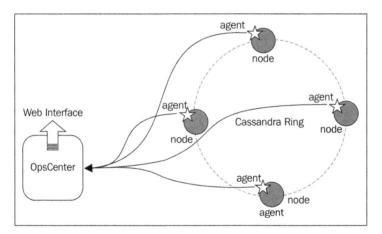

OpsCenter in action

An agent is available within the `OpsCenter` directory under the `agent` directory. You need to set up the agent and then copy the `agent` directory to all other nodes. Then, start the agents. The following are the steps to set up the agent:

1. Go to the agent directory:

   ```
   cd $OPSCENTER_HOME/agent
   ```

2. Set up the agent:

   ```
   bin/setup OPSCENTER_IP
   ```

   Here, `OPSCENTER_IP` is the address of the machine hosting OpsCenter. This updates the `$AGENT_HOME/conf/address.yaml` file.

3. If you have SSL disabled, add `use_ssl: 0`:

   ```
   # address.yaml
   stomp_interface: "10.147.171.159"
   use_ssl: 0
   ```

4. Once this is done and the `agent` directory is copied across all nodes. Start the agents on each node by executing the following command:

   ```
   # Execute this from agent directory, user -f for foreground
   $ bin/opscenter-agent
   ```

5. After OpsCenter and the agents are up, open OpsCenter in the browser, click on **Join existing cluster**, and provide the node IPs (data of a single node should be sufficient).

Monitoring and administrating with OpsCenter

OpsCenter exposes all the functionality of JMX via a web console. This means everything that we were able to do using `nodetool` we can now do with OpsCenter. Most of the node-level administrative options are available by clicking on the node (under the **Cluster View** menu) and then clicking on the **Action** button.

For cluster-wide operations, there are menus under the cluster view page. You can add a node, change the configuration file cluster-wide, and perform a rolling restart of the cluster. In the paid version, you can create a cluster, add more than one cluster to OpsCenter, download information to diagnose a problem, and generate reports. The following screenshot shows a subset of monitoring options by OpsCenter:

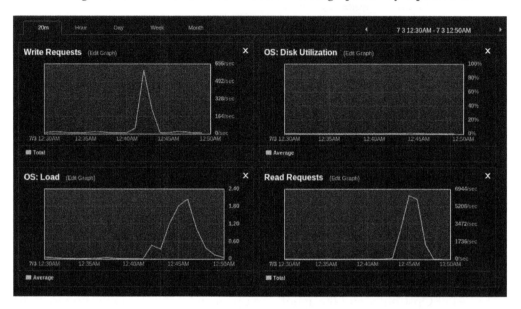

OpsCenter provides a plethora of attributes to keep a tab on. It covers Cassandra-specific attributes such as read/write requests; pending tasks in different stages; the row and key cache hit rate; table-specific statistics such as pending read and writes and SSTables size and count; and operating system resource-specific statistics such as CPU, memory, disk usage, and network. Basically, a superset of monitoring options is provided by `nodetool`. To add more plots to the **Performance** screen, you need to click on the **Add Graph** button and select the appropriate graph. To make this setting permanent, save this plot setting by choosing **Save as...** from the drop-down menu next to the **Performance Metrics** heading.

Other features of OpsCenter

Apart from operational tasks, OpsCenter can be pretty useful to add, remove, or modify keyspaces. The **Schema** screen provides options to play with keyspaces and tables.

Another interesting feature is the **Data Explorer** screen. This provides a visually pleasing interface to browse keyspaces and tables. You can also search within a table with the row key.

OpsCenter provides security features. It allows us to enable SSL for the OpsCenter web console, a simple authentication mechanism for OpsCenter. Advanced configuration and setup are beyond the scope of this book. Refer to the official DataStax documentation for this at `http://www.datastax.com/docs/opscenter/index`.

Nagios – monitoring and notification

Nagios (`http://www.nagios.org`) is an open source monitoring and notification utility. It enables users to monitor various resources, such as CPU, memory, disk usage, network status, reachability, HTTP status, testing of web page rendering, and various checks using Nagios-compatible sensors. There is a giant list of Nagios plugins that covers the monitoring of almost all popular services and software. The best thing with Nagios is its plugin architecture. You can write a simple plugin for custom resource monitoring. Thus, effectively, if you can measure a state, you can monitor its source in Nagios. This section will discuss, very briefly, Nagios setup and how it can be enabled to monitor system resources and Cassandra.

Installing Nagios

Nagios ships in different packages, such as DIY, student, professional, and business, based on a number of features and support. One may visit the Nagios website and choose one on the basis of one's needs. With the number of free plugins, the Nagios free version is generally a good option. In this section, we will see how to install and configure the Nagios free version (from the source) on a CentOS machine. These instructions should work on any RHEL variant. For Ubuntu- or Debian-like environments, you may need to look for an `apt-get` equivalent of the `yum` commands in the script. On the basis of your Linux distribution, the Nagios distribution can be installed from additional repositories. It may or may not be the latest and greatest among Nagios, but it eases a lot of installation hassles. We use tarball installation for this book to keep things generic.

Prerequisites

The Nagios server (PHP-based) has some dependencies to be fulfilled before you can start installing it:

- **PHP**: You will need to have a PHP processor to run Nagios. Check its availability using the following command:

```
$ php -v
PHP 5.3.26 (cli) (built: Jun 24 2013 18:08:10)
Copyright (c) 1997-2013 The PHP Group
```

```
Zend Engine v2.3.0, Copyright (c) 1998-2013 Zend Technologies
```

If PHP does not exist, install it as follows:

```
$ sudo yum install php
```

- **httpd**: The Apache httpd web server serves as the front end to a PHP-based Nagios web application. To check whether you have httpd or not, execute the following command:

```
$ httpd -v
Server version: Apache/2.2.24 (Unix)
Server built:   May 20 2013 21:12:45
```

If httpd does not exist, install it as follows:

```
$ sudo yum install httpd
```

- **GCC compiler**: Check for the installed version of GCC compiler using the following command:

```
$ gcc -v
Using built-in specs.
COLLECT_GCC=gcc
COLLECT_LTO_WRAPPER=/usr/libexec/gcc/x86_64-amazon-linux/4.6.3/
lto-wrapper
Target: x86_64-amazon-linux
Configured with: ../configure --prefix=/usr --mandir=/usr/
share/man --infodir=/usr/share/info --with-bugurl=http://
bugzilla.redhat.com/bugzilla --enable-bootstrap --enable-shared
--enable-threads=posix --enable-checking=release --with-system-
zlib --enable-__cxa_atexit --disable-libunwind-exceptions
--enable-gnu-unique-object --enable-linker-build-id --enable-
languages=c,c++,objc,obj-c++,,fortran,ada,go,lto --enable-
plugin --disable-libgcj --with-tune=generic --with-arch_32=i686
--build=x86_64-amazon-linux
Thread model: posix
gcc version 4.6.3 20120306 (Red Hat 4.6.3-2) (GCC)
```

If it does not exist, install it as follows:

```
$ sudo yum install gcc glibc glibc-common
```

- **GD graphics library**: GD is a dynamic graphics development library to generate various formats of dynamically generated images. Unfortunately, there is no quick way to see GD installation. To install the GD library, execute the following command:

```
$ yum install gd gd-devel
```

Preparation

Before we jump into installing Nagios, we need to set up a user account and a group for Nagios as follows:

```
$ sudo -i
$ useradd -m nagios
$ passwd nagios
$ groupadd nagcmd
$ usermod -a -G nagcmd nagios
$ usermod -a -G nagcmd apache
```

Installation

Nagios installation can be divided into four parts: installing Nagios, configuring Apache httpd, installing plugins, and setting up Nagios as a service.

Installing Nagios

The following are the steps to install Nagios from tarball:

1. Download tarball from the Nagios download page and untar it:

    ```
    $ wget http://prdownloads.sourceforge.net/sourceforge/nagios/
    nagios-3.5.0.tar.gz
    ```

    ```
    $ tar xzf nagios-3.5.0.tar.gz
    ```

2. Install Nagios from the source:

    ```
    $ cd nagios
    $ ./configure -with-command-group=nagcmd
    $ make all
    $ sudo make install \
        install-base \
        install-cgis \
        install-html \
        install-exfoliation \
    ```

```
install-config \
install-init \
install-commandmode \
fullinstall
```

3. Nagios is installed now. Update the contact details before you move to the next step:

```
$ sudo vi /usr/local/nagios/etc/objects/contacts.cfg
define contact{
 contact_name nagiosadmin      ; Short name of user
 use          generic-contact ; Inherit default values
 alias        Nagios Admin     ; Full name of user
 email        YOUR_EMAIL_ID    ; *SET EMAIL ADDRESS*
 }
```

Configuring Apache httpd

Perform the following steps to configure Apache httpd:

1. Set Apache httpd with the appropriate Nagios configuration:

```
$ sudo make install-webconf
/usr/bin/install -c -m 644 sample-config/httpd.conf /etc/httpd/
conf.d/nagios.conf
*** Nagios/Apache conf file installed ***
```

2. Set the password for the Nagios web console for the nagiosadmin user:

```
$ sudo htpasswd -c /usr/local/nagios/etc/htpasswd.users
nagiosadmin
```

3. Restart Apache httpd:

```
$ sudo service httpd restart
```

Installing Nagios plugins

Perform the following steps to install Nagios plugins:

1. Download and untar Nagios plugins from the Nagios website's plugins page (http://www.nagios.org/download/plugins/) using the following commands:

```
$ wget http://prdownloads.sourceforge.net/sourceforge/nagiosplug/
nagios-plugins-1.4.16.tar.gz
$ tar xzf nagios-plugins-1.4.16.tar.gz
```

2. Install the plugin:

```
$ cd nagios-plugins-1.4.16
$ ./configure --with-nagios-user=nagios -with-nagios-group=nagios
$ make
$ make install
```

> **Warning**
>
> If you get an error such as check_http.c:312:9: error: 'ssl_
> version' undeclared (first use in this function) while
> trying to execute ./configure or make, your system probably lacks the
> libssl library. To resolve this issue, execute the following commands:
>
> On RHEL- or CentOS-like systems, run the following command:
>
> **yum install openssl-devel -y**
>
> On Debian- or Ubuntu-like systems, run the following command:
>
> **sudo apt-get install libssl-dev**

3. Rerun ./configure, then make clean, and finally make.

Setting up Nagios as a service

Everything is set. Now, let's set Nagios as a service, as follows:

```
$ sudo chkconfig --add nagios
$ sudo chkconfig nagios on
```

Check whether the default configuration is good to go and start the Nagios service:

```
# Check configuration file
$ sudo /usr/local/nagios/bin/nagios -v /usr/local/nagios/etc/nagios.cfg
[-- snip --]
Website: http://www.nagios.org
Reading configuration data...
   Read main config file okay...
Processing object config file '/usr/local/nagios/etc/objects/commands.
cfg'...
[-- snip --]
Processing object config file '/usr/local/nagios/etc/objects/localhost.
cfg'...
   Read object config files okay...
Running pre-flight check on configuration data...
[-- snip --]
```

```
Total Warnings: 0

Total Errors:   0

Things look okay - No serious problems were detected during the pre-
flight check


# Start Nagios as a service
$ sudo service nagios start
```

Now you are ready to see the Nagios web console. Open `http://NAGIOS_HOST_` `ADDRESS/nagios` URL in your browser. You should be able to see the Nagios home page with a couple of default checks on the Nagios host.

Nagios plugins

Nagios's power comes from the plethora of plugin libraries available for it. There are sufficient default plugins provided as a part of the base package to perform decent resource monitoring. For advanced or non-standard monitoring, you will have to either download the plugin from somewhere, such as the Nagios plugin directory or GitHub, or you will have to write a plugin of your own. Writing a custom plugin is very simple. There are only two requirements: the plugin should be executable via the command prompt, and the plugin should return with the following exit values:

- 0: This implies the ok state
- 1: This implies the warning state
- 2: This implies the critical state
- 3: This implies the unknown state

This means you are free to choose your programming language and tooling. As long as you follow these two specifications, your plugin can be used in Nagios.

For the Nagios plugin directory, visit `http://exchange.nagios.` `org/directory/Plugins`.

For Nagios plugin projects on GitHub, visit `https://github.com/` `search?q=nagios+plugin&type=Repositories&ref=search` `results`.

Nagios plugins for Cassandra

There are a few Cassandra-specific plugins in the Nagios plugins directory. There is a promising project on GitHub, namely Nagios Cassandra Monitor (`https://github.com/dmcnelis/NagiosCassandraMonitor`). It seems a little immature but worth evaluating. In this section, we will use a JMX-based plugin that is not Cassandra-specific. We will use this plugin to connect to Cassandra nodes and query heap usage. This will tell us about two things: whether or not it can connect to Cassandra (which can be treated as an indication of whether or not the Cassandra process is up) and what the heap usage is.

The following are the steps to get the JMX plugin installed (all these operations take place on the Nagios machine and not on Cassandra nodes):

1. Download the plugins from `http://exchange.nagios.org/directory/Plugins/Java-Applications-and-Servers/check_jmx/details`.

2. Untar the downloaded plugin and navigate to the `libexec` directory:

   ```
   $ tar xvzf check_jmx.tgz
   $ cd check_jmx/nagios/plugin/
   $ sudo cp check_jmx jmxquery.jar /usr/local/nagios/libexec/
   ```

3. Assign proper ownership and run a test:

   ```
   $ cd /usr/local/nagios/libexec/
   $ sudo chown nagios:nagios check_jmx jmxquery.jar
   ```

4. Replace `10.99.9.67` with your Cassandra node:

   ```
   $ ./check_jmx -U
   service:jmx:rmi:///jndi/rmi://10.99.9.67:7199/jmxrmi -O java.
   lang:type=Memory -A HeapMemoryUsage -K used -I HeapMemoryUsage -J
   used -vvvv -w 4248302272 -c 5498760192

   JMX OK HeapMemoryUsage.used=1217368912{committed=1932525568;init=1
   953497088;max=1933574144;used=1217368912}
   ```

Executing remote plugins via the NRPE plugin

NRPE is a plugin to execute plugins on remote hosts. One may think of it as OpsCenter and its agents (see the following figure). With NRPE, Nagios can monitor remote host resources (such as memory, CPU, disk, and network) and can execute any plugin on a remote machine. The following figure shows Nagios with the NRPE plugin in action:

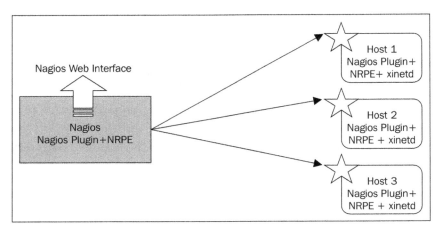

NRPE installation has to be done on the Nagios machine as well as on all the other machines where we want to execute a Nagios plugin locally (for example, to monitor CPU usage).

Installing NRPE on host machines

First, you need to create a nagios user and a nagios group and set the user with a password, as discussed in the *Preparation* section. After that, you need install the Nagios plugin as mentioned in the *Installing Nagios plugins* section. Now, you can install NRPE. Perform the following steps:

1. Install xinetd if it does not already exist:

    ```
    $ sudo yum install xinetd
    ```

2. Download the NRPE daemon and plugin from the NRPE Nagios page at http://exchange.nagios.org/directory/Addons/Monitoring-Agents/ NRPE--2D-Nagios-Remote-Plugin-Executor/details and install them:

    ```
    # Download and untar NRPE
    ```
    ```
    $ wget http://downloads.sourceforge.net/project/nagios/nrpe-2.x/ nrpe-2.14/nrpe-2.14.tar.gz
    ```
    ```
    $ tar xvzf nrpe-2.14.tar.gz
    ```

```
# make and install daemon and plugin, configure xinetd
$ cd nrpe-2.14
$ ./configure
$ make all
$ sudo make install-plugin
$ sudo make install-daemon
$ sudo make install-daemon-config
$ make install-xinetd
```

3. After this, you need to make sure each host machine accepts requests coming from Nagios. For this, you need to edit /etc/xinetd.d/nrpe to add the Nagios host address to it. In the following code snippet, you need to replace NAGIOS_HOST_ADDRESS with the actual Nagios host address:

```
# edit /etc/xinetd.d/nrpe
only_from = 127.0.0.1 NAGIOS_HOST_ADDRESS

# edit /etc/services and append this
nrpe      5666/tcp              # NRPE
```

4. Restart and test whether xinet is functional:

```
# Restart xinetd
$ sudo service xinetd restart
Stopping xinetd:     [FAILED]
Starting xinetd:     [  OK  ]

# Check if it's listening
$ netstat -at | grep nrpe
tcp   0   0 *:nrpe    *:*      LISTEN
# Check NRPE plugin
$ /usr/local/nagios/libexec/check_nrpe -H localhost
NRPE v2.14

# Try to invoke a plugin via NRPE
$ /usr/local/nagios/libexec/check_nrpe -H localhost -c check_load

OK - load average: 0.01, 0.04, 0.06|load1=0.010;15.000;30.000;0;
load5=0.040;10.000;25.000;0; load15=0.060;5.000;20.000;0;
```

Now, we have the machine ready to be monitored via NRPE.

Installing the NRPE plugin on a Nagios machine

Installing an NRPE plugin on a Nagios machine is a subset of the task that we did for the remote host machine. All you need to do is install the NRPE plugin and nothing else. The following are the steps to be performed to install a Nagios plugin:

```
$ wget http://downloads.sourceforge.net/project/nagios/nrpe-2.x/nrpe-
2.14/nrpe-2.14.tar.gz
$ tar xvzf nrpe-2.14.tar.gz
$ cd nrpe-2.14
$ ./configure
$ make all
$ sudo make install-plugin


# Test if plugin is working, you should replace 10.99.9.67
# with one of the machine's address with NRPE + xinetd
$ /usr/local/nagios/libexec/check_nrpe -H 10.99.9.67
NRPE v2.14
```

Setting up things to monitor

In this section, we will talk about how to set up CPU, disk, and Cassandra monitoring. However, the detail is enough to enable you to set up any Nagios plugin and configure monitoring.

- **Monitoring CPU and disk space**: These are the tests that need to be executed on remote machines. Thus, we may need to configure NRPE configuration to allow those plugins to be executed remotely. This configuration is stored in /usr/local/nagios/etc/nrpe.cfg. If you do not find the plugin that you want to execute or you want to change the parameters to be passed to the plugin, this is the place to achieve that. Use the following set of commands:

  ```
  # edit /usr/local/nagios/etc/nrpe.cfg
  command[check_users]=/usr/local/nagios/libexec/check_users -w 5 -c
  10


  command[check_load]=/usr/local/nagios/libexec/check_load -w
  15,10,5 -c 30,25,20


  command[check_hda1]=/usr/local/nagios/libexec/check_disk -w 20% -c
  10% -p /dev/hda1
  [-- snip --]
  ```

```
#custom commands *add your commands here*


# EC2 ephemeral storage root disk
command[check_sda1]=/usr/local/nagios/libexec/check_disk -w 20% -c
10% -p /dev/sda1
```

The following screenshot shows the Nagios interface monitoring local and remote resources:

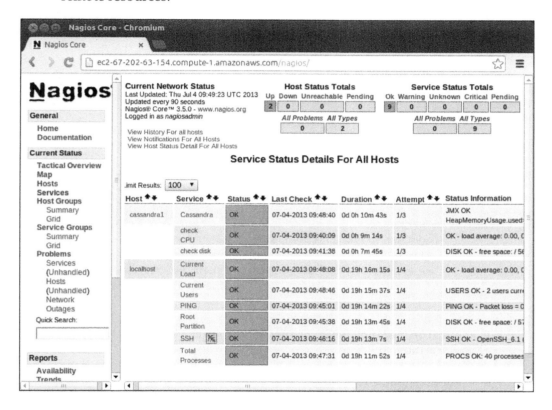

As you can see, we have a CPU check (`check_load`) and a disk check already provided by the default configuration. However, if I wanted to monitor the / dev/sda1 device for space availability, I would add a new check `check_sda1` for this.

- **Setting up a JMX monitor**: For Cassandra, we want to check the JVM heap usage via JMX. Since this executes on the local machine (Nagios) to connect to the JMX service on the remote machine, we do not need to use NRPE for this. Thus, we have nothing to do here.

- **Updating configuration**: The best part of Nagios is its configuration. With a little ingenuity and grouping, you can make a fine configuration that can scale to hundreds of machines. All configurations in Nagios are text-based with a JSON-ish syntax. You can have files organized in whichever way you want and let Nagios know where the files are. For this particular case, the /usr/local/nagios/etc/objects/cassandrahosts.cfg file is created. This file houses all the information related to monitoring. The following code snippet is what it looks like (see the comments in bold):

```
# A machine to be monitored
# DEFINE ALL CASSANDRA HOSTS HERE

define host{
        use                     linux-server
        host_name               cassandra1
        alias                   Cassandra Machine
        address                 10.99.9.67
        }


# create logical groupings, manageable, saves typing
# HOST GROUP TO COLLECTIVELY CALL ALL CASSANDRA HOSTS

define hostgroup{
        hostgroup_name  cassandra_grp
        alias           Cassandra Group
        members         cassandra1   ;this is CSV of
                                     ;hosts defined above
        }


# A service defines what command to execute on what hosts
# MONITORING SERVICES

# A service that executes locally
#Check Cassandra on remote machines

define service{
        use                     generic-service
        hostgroup_name          cassandra_grp
        service_description     Cassandra
        check_command           check_cas ;defined below
        }


# A service that gets executed remotely via NRPE
# check disk space status
```

```
define service{
    use                generic-service
    hostgroup_name     cassandra_grp
    service_description check disk
    check_command      check_nrpe!check_sda1
    }

# check CPU status
define service{
    use                generic-service
    hostgroup_name     cassandra_grp
    service_description check CPU
    check_command      check_nrpe!check_load
    }
```

 # A command is a template of a command line call, here:
```
#    $USER1$ is plugin directory, nagios/libexec
#    $HOSTADRRESS$ resolves to the address defined in
#    the preceding host block; hosts are chosen from the service
that calls this command


# define custom commands
# check JVM heap usage using JMX,
# warn if > 3.7G, mark critical if > 3.85G

define command {
        command_name check_cas
        command_line $USER1$/check_jmx -U service:jmx:rmi:///
jndi/rmi://$HOSTADDRESS$:7199/jmxrmi -O java.lang:type=Memory
-A HeapMemoryUsage -K used -I HeapMemoryUsage -J used -vvvv -w
3700000000 -c 3850000000
        }
```

- **Letting Nagios know about the new configuration**: We have created a new configuration file that Nagios does not know about. We need to register it in /usr/local/nagios/etc/nagios.cfg. Now, append the following lines to the file:

```
#custom file *ADD YOUR FILES HERE*
cfg_file=/usr/local/nagios/etc/objects/cassandrahosts.cfg
Test the configuration and you are done.
$ sudo /usr/local/nagios/bin/nagios -v /usr/local/nagios/etc/
nagios.cfg
Nagios Core 3.5.0
[-- snip --]
```

```
Reading configuration data...
   Read main config file okay...
Processing object config file '/usr/local/nagios/etc/objects/
commands.cfg'...
Processing object config file '/usr/local/nagios/etc/objects/
contacts.cfg'...
Processing object config file '/usr/local/nagios/etc/objects/
timeperiods.cfg'...
Processing object config file '/usr/local/nagios/etc/objects/
templates.cfg'...
Processing object config file '/usr/local/nagios/etc/objects/
cassandrahosts.cfg'...
Processing object config file '/usr/local/nagios/etc/objects/
localhost.cfg'...
   Read object config files okay...
Running pre-flight check on configuration data...
[-- snip --]
 Total Warnings: 0
Total Errors:   0
Things look okay - No serious problems were detected during the
pre-flight check
```

Restart Nagios by executing `sudo service nagios restart`.

Monitoring and notification using Nagios

Nagios has built-in support to send mail whenever an interesting event (such as a warning, an error, or a service coming back to the ok state) occurs. By default, it uses the `mail` command, so if your mail is configured correctly, you should see mails when you execute the following command:

```
# substitute YOUR_EMAIL_ADDRESS with your email id.
/usr/bin/printf "%b" "Hi Nishant, \nthis is Nagios." | /bin/mail -s
"Nagios test mail" YOUR_EMAIL_ADDRESS
```

If this does not reach your mail box or the spam folder, you should check your configuration. If you do not have the mail utility installed already, execute the following command:

```
# mail utility on RHEL like OS
$ sudo yum install mailx


# On Ubuntu or Debian derivatives
$ sudo apt-get install mailutils
```

If you are not happy with the mailing option or want to change the mailer to send mail via a specific mail provider such as Gmail, you should dig into the plugins directory or GitHub to find appropriate alternatives.

Nagios provides a pretty intuitive GUI—a web-based console that immediately highlights anything that is wrong with any service or host. Apart from displaying the immediate state, Nagios also stores the history of monitored events. There are many reporting capabilities that provide a complete infrastructure status overview. One can easily generate a histogram that states the performance of a service, as shown in the following screenshot:

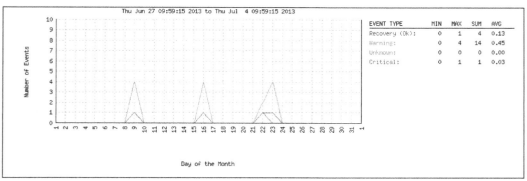

An auto-generated histogram report from Nagios

There are many reporting options, including options to disable alerts during a scheduled infrastructure downtime. It may be worth playing around the Nagios GUI to learn about the various options.

Cassandra log

Last, but not least, Cassandra log is a good tool for monitoring what is going on inside Cassandra. However, monitoring the log file is an extremely non-scalable option. Therefore, if you are starting with fewer than five Cassandra machines, you may consider occasionally looking into their log files. The most common use of the Cassandra log is to perform the postmortem for a failure when you do not have any other monitoring and reporting mechanism in place.

The location of the log4j log can be found from Cassandra's `conf/log4j-server.properties` file:

```
# This has been altered during installation
log4j.appender.R.File=/mnt/cassandra-logs/system.log
```

As long as you view this file filled with lines, starting with INFO, you may think the system has been behaving alright. Lines with WARN may or may not be interesting.

For example, it is ok to have some WARN messages in the system, as follows:

```
INFO [MemoryMeter:1] 2013-05-24 12:31:39,099 Memtable.java
  (line 213) CFS(Keyspace='Keyspace1', ColumnFamily='Standard1')
  liveRatio is 1.0 (just-counted was 1.0).
  calculation took 3ms for 325 columns
WARN [MemoryMeter:1] 2013-05-24 12:31:39,135 Memtable.java
  (line 197) setting live ratio to minimum of 1.0
  instead of 0.8662032831217121
```

However, some warnings, as shown in the following lines, may be a definite sign of danger and should be fixed to avoid a catastrophe (it may not be a big deal if you have RF and CL set properly):

```
# May be a future crash due to lack of disk space
WARN [CompactionExecutor:45] 2013-05-24 17:34:03,709
  CompactionTask.java (line 82) insufficient space to compact all
  requested files SSTableReader(path='/mnt/cassandra-
  data/data/Keyspace1/Standard1/Keyspace1-Standard1-hf-34-
  Data.db'), SSTableReader(path='/mnt/cassandra-
  data/data/Keyspace1/Standard1/Keyspace1-Standard1-hf-35-
  Data.db'), SSTableReader(path='/mnt/cassandra-
  data/data/Keyspace1/Standard1/Keyspace1-Standard1-hf-28-
  Data.db')
```

An ERROR message as shown in the following lines should always be attended to. It usually answers the buts and whys of Cassandra behavior, points out an incorrect configuration, and tells you about what to do next and what to change in the read/write pattern:

```
# oh snap! Dave was right about horizontal scaling.
ERROR [FlushWriter:7] 2013-05-24 17:35:21,617 AbstractCassandraDaemon.
java (line 132) Exception in thread Thread[FlushWriter:7,5,main]
java.lang.RuntimeException: Insufficient disk space to flush 71502048
bytes
[-- snip --]
```

```
WARN [CompactionExecutor:46] 2013-05-24 17:35:26,871 FileUtils.java
(line 116) Failed closing IndexWriter(/mnt/cassandra-data/data/Keyspace1/
Standard1/Keyspace1-Standard1-tmp-hf-42)
```

java.io.IOException: No space left on device

Cassandra logs are great. If you find yourself looking too frequently into them, you probably need a better monitoring mechanism. Also, if you feel like getting blinded by an over-abundance of information, you may change the log a level up from INFO to WARN in the log4j-server.properties file. It is suggested you should not turn on the DEBUG mode, unless you are editing the Cassandra code base and debugging the changes. It may lead to lots of I/O activity and affect the performance.

Enabling Java options for GC logging

JVM options provide a nice way to monitor Java applications. It is not specific to Cassandra. One may set various -XX options as part of arguments when starting the Java application. In Cassandra, these options can be enabled by uncommenting the lines with –XX. The following is a list of the options:

```
# GC logging options -- uncomment to enable
# JVM_OPTS="$JVM_OPTS -XX:+PrintGCDetails"
# JVM_OPTS="$JVM_OPTS -XX:+PrintGCDateStamps"
# JVM_OPTS="$JVM_OPTS -XX:+PrintHeapAtGC"
# JVM_OPTS="$JVM_OPTS -XX:+PrintTenuringDistribution"
# JVM_OPTS="$JVM_OPTS -XX:+PrintGCApplicationStoppedTime"
# JVM_OPTS="$JVM_OPTS -XX:+PrintPromotionFailure"
# JVM_OPTS="$JVM_OPTS -XX:PrintFLSStatistics=1"
# JVM_OPTS="$JVM_OPTS -Xloggc:/var/log/cassandra/gc-`date +%s`.log"


# If you are using JDK 6u34 7u2 or later you can enable GC log
rotation
# don't stick the date in the log name if rotation is on.
# JVM_OPTS="$JVM_OPTS -Xloggc:/var/log/cassandra/gc.log"
# JVM_OPTS="$JVM_OPTS -XX:+UseGCLogFileRotation"
# JVM_OPTS="$JVM_OPTS -XX:NumberOfGCLogFiles=10"
# JVM_OPTS="$JVM_OPTS -XX:GCLogFileSize=10M"
```

It is pretty obvious what these options do. In case you want to enable some of these options, the following table shows what they mean:

Option	Description
`-XX:+PrintGCDetails`	Prints more details at garbage collection
`-XX:+PrintGCDateStamps`	Prints GC events with the date and time rather than with a timestamp that we get using `-XX:+PrintGCTimeStamps`
`-XX:+PrintHeapAtGC`	Prints detailed GC information, including heap occupancy before and after GC
`-XX:+PrintTenuringDistribution`	Prints tenuring age information
`-XX:+PrintGCApplicationStoppedTime`	Prints the net time of every stop-the-world event
`-XX:+PrintPromotionFailure`	Prints the size of the objects that fail promotion
`-XX:PrintFLSStatistics=1`	Prints **free list statistics** (**FLS**) for each young or old collection

The rest of the options are for obtaining log location, log size, and rolling log counts.

Troubleshooting

We have learned cluster configuration, repairing and scaling, and, finally, monitoring. The purpose of all this learning is for you to keep production environments up-and-running smoothly. You may choose the right ingredients to set up a cluster that fits your need, but there may be node failures, high CPU usage, high memory usage, disk space issues, network failures, and, probably, performance issues with time. You will get most of this information from the monitoring tool that you have configured. You will need to take the necessary action, depending on the problems that you are facing.

Usually, one goes about finding these issues via various tools that we've discussed in the past. You may want to extend the list of tools for investigation to include Linux tooling. These include `netstat` and `tcpdump` for network debugging; `vmstat`, `free`, `top`, and `dstat` for memory statistics; `perf`, `top`, `dstat`, and `uptime` for CPU statistics; and `iostat`, `iotop`, and `df` for disk usage.

How do you actually know there is a problem? With a decent monitoring setup and a vigilant system admin, problems usually come to one's knowledge via alerts sent by the monitoring system. It may be a mail from OpsCenter, a critical message from Nagios, or a message from your home-grown JMX-based monitoring system. Another way to see the issues is as performance degradation at a certain load. You may find that your application is acting weird or abnormally slow. You dig into the error and find out that the Cassandra calls are taking a really long time, more than expected. The other, and scarier, way the problems come to one's notice is on production. Things have been working decently in the test environment and you suddenly start seeing frequent garbage collection calls or the production servers start to scream, "Too many open files."

In many of the error scenarios, the solution is a simple one. For cases such as where AWS notifies an instance shutdown due to underlying hardware degradation, the fix is to replace the node with a new one. For a disk full issue, you may add either a new node or just more hard disks and add the location to the data directory setting in Cassandra—yaml. The following are a few troubleshooting tips. Most of these things you might have known from previous chapters.

High CPU usage

High CPU usage can be associated with frequent **Garbage Collections** (GC). If you see a lot of GC call information in Cassandra logs and if they take longer than one second to finish, it means the system has loaded the JVM with the garbage collector.

The easiest fix is to add more nodes. Another option can be to increase the JVM heap size (adding more RAM, if required) and to tweak the garbage collector setting for Cassandra.

Compaction is a CPU-intensive process. You may expect a spike during compaction. You should plan to perform a `nodetool` compaction during relatively silent hours. The same goes for repair. Execute `nodetool repair` during low load.

High memory usage

Before we dive into memory usage, it is nice to point out that providing a lot of RAM to the Java heap may not always help. We have learned in a previous chapter that Cassandra automatically sets the heap memory, which is good in most cases. If you are planning to override it, note that garbage collection does not do well beyond a 16 GB heap.

There are a couple of things you should check when debugging for high memory usage. The bloom filter's false positive ratio can lead to large memory usage. For smaller error rates in the bloom filter, we need a larger memory. If you find the bloom filter to be the culprit and decide to increase the false positive ratio, remember that the recommended maximum value for the false positive value is 0.1. Performance starts to degrade after this. This may not be applicable to Cassandra 1.2 and onward where the bloom filter is managed off-heap.

Continuing the subject of off-heap, another thing that one might want to look into is row caches. Row caches are stored off-heap, if you have the JNA installed. If there is no JNA, the row cache falls back onto the on-heap memory—adding to the used heap memory. It may lead to frequent GC calls.

High memory usage can be a result of pulling lots of rows in one go. Look into such queries. Cassandra 1.2 onward has a trace feature that can help you find such queries.

Hotspots

A hotspot in a cluster is a node or a small set of nodes that show abnormally high resource usage. In the context of Cassandra, it will be the nodes in the cluster that get abnormally high hits or show high resource usage compared to other nodes.

A poorly balanced cluster can cause some nodes to own a high number of keys. If the request for each key has equal probability, the nodes with the higher numbers of ownership will have to serve a high number of requests. Rebalancing the cluster may fix this issue.

Ordered partitioners, such as `ByteOrderedPartitioner`, usually have a hard time making sure that each key range has an equal amount of data, unless the data coming for each key range has the same probability. It is suggested that you rework the application to avoid dependency on key ordering and use `Murmur3Partitioner` or `RandomOrderPartitioner`, unless you have a very strong reason to depend on byte-order partitioning. Refer to the *Partitioners* section in *Chapter 4, Deploying a Cluster*.

High throughput-wide columns may cause a hotspot. We know that a row resides on one server (actually, on all the replicas). If we have a row that gets written to and/or read from at a really high rate, the node gets loaded disproportionately (and the other nodes are probably idle). A good idea is to bucket the row key. For example, assume you are a popular website. If you decide to document a live presidential debate by recording everything told by the candidates, host, and audiences and stream this data live, you allow users to scroll back and forth to see the past records. In this case, if you decide to use a single row, you are creating a hotspot. The ideal thing would be to break the row key into buckets such as `<rowKey>:<bucket_id>` and apply round-robin to the buckets to store the data. Keys are being distributed across the nodes. Now you have the load distributed on multiple machines. To fetch the data, you may want to `multiget slice` the buckets and merge them into the application. The merging should be fast because the rows are already sorted. Refer to the *High throughput rows and hotspots* section in *Chapter 3, Effective CQL*.

Another cause of hotspots can be wrong token assignment in a multi data center setup (refer to *Chapter 4, Deploying a Cluster*). If you have two nodes, A and B, in data center 1, and two nodes, C and D, in data center 2, you calculate equidistant tokens and assign them to A, B, C, and D in increasing order. It seems OK, but it actually makes node A and node C hotspots.

Ideally, one should assign alternate tokens in different data centers. Thus, A should get the first token, C the second, B the third, and D the fourth. If there are three data centers, pick one from each and assign increasing tokens, then go for the second, and so on.

Open JDK's erratic behavior

Linux distros ship with Open Java and Open JDK. Cassandra does not officially support any variant of the JVM other than Oracle/Sun Java 1.7. Open Java may cause some weird issues, such as the GC pausing for a very long time and performance degradation. The safest thing to do is to remove Open Java and install the suggested version.

Disk performance

AWS users often find **Elastic Block Storage** (**EBS**) lucrative to use from the performance and reliability points of view. Unfortunately, it is a bad idea to use it.

It slows down the disk I/O speed. It can cause slow reads and writes. If you are using EBS, try comparing it with the instance store (ephemeral storage) with the RAID 0 setup.

If you see `Too many open files` or any other resource-related issue, the first thing to check is `ulimit -a` to see all available system resources. You can edit this setting by editing `/etc/security/limits.conf` and setting it to the following recommended setting:

```
* soft nofile 32768
* hard nofile 32768
root soft nofile 32768
root hard nofile 32768
* soft memlock unlimited
* hard memlock unlimited
root soft memlock unlimited
root hard memlock unlimited
* soft as unlimited
* hard as unlimited
root soft as unlimited
root hard as unlimited
```

Slow snapshots

Creating a snapshot for backup purposes is done by creating a hard link to SSTables. In the absence of JNA, it is done by using `/bin/ln` by `fork` and `exec` to create a hard link. This is observably slow with thousands of SSTables. Thus, if you are seeing an abnormally high snapshot time, check whether you have JNA configured.

Getting help from the mailing list

Cassandra is a robust and fault-tolerant software. It is possible that your production is running as expected while something is broken within. Replication and eventual consistency can help you to build a robust application on top of Cassandra, but it is important to keep an eye on monitoring statistics.

The tools that have been discussed in this and previous chapters should help you get enough information about what went wrong. You should be able to fix common problems using these tools. But sometimes it is a good idea to ask about a stubborn issue on the friendly Cassandra mailing list: `user@cassandra.apache.org`.

When asking a question on the mailing list, provide as many statistics as you can gather around the problem. Nodetool's `cfstats`, `tpstats`, and `ring` commands are common ways to get Cassandra-specific statistics. You may want to check the Cassandra logs, enable `JVM_OPTS` for GC-related statistics, and profile using Java jhat or JConsole. Apart from this, server specifications such as memory, CPU, network, and disk stats provide crucial insights. Among other things, the following also repay consideration (as required) the replication factor, compaction strategy, consistency level, and table specifications.

Summary

Setting up proper monitoring of your infrastructure is the most recommended and the most disregarded suggestion to a development team, especially in startups where teams are small, resources are limited, and fast development is the only priority. It usually goes hand-in-hand with a reluctance to go through a painfully long mechanical process to set up a system. The importance of monitoring is best understood when a failure that could have been avoided occurs at a critical hour. Monitoring is an important tool for showing the reliability of a system.

With multiple tools in hand, you are knowledgeable enough to take your weapon of choice. Choose a tool or a set of tools that fits your environment. In many cases, having Nagios to monitor Cassandra, CPU, memory, ping, and disk statistics is good enough. Others may want a dedicated monitoring and management tool such as OpsCenter. There are still others who just write code that utilizes the JMX interface to monitor particular statistics. It is really up to you.

Cassandra is a big data store. What is the use of a big data store if you can't analyze it to extract interesting statistics? Fortunately, Cassandra provides hooks to smoothly integrate it with various Apache Hadoop projects such as Hadoop MapReduce, Pig, and Hive. It can be used as a corpus store for Solr. Cassandra plays well with low-latency stream processing tools such as Twitter Storm and can be seamlessly integrated with the Spark project (`http://spark-project.org`). The next chapter is all about using analytical tools with Cassandra.

8
Integration with Hadoop

Big data is the latest trend in the technical community and industry in general. Cassandra and many other NoSQL solutions solve a major part of the problem: storing a large amount of datasets in a scalable manner while keeping the mutations and retrieval queries fast. However, this is just half the picture. A major part is processing. A database that provides better integration with analytical tools such as Apache Hadoop, Twitter Storm, Pig, Spark, and other platforms will be a preferable choice.

Cassandra provides native support to Hadoop MapReduce, Pig, Hive, and Oozie. It is a matter of tiny changes to get the Hadoop family up and working with Cassandra. Third-party support for Hadoop and Solr has taken Cassandra to the next level in terms of integration. Third-party proprietary tooling, such as DataStax Enterprise Edition for Cassandra, makes it easy to work with Hadoop and actually helps text search Cassandra using Solr. Enterprise Edition also provides support for the Spark project.

Cassandra is a very powerful database engine. We have seen its salient features as a single software entity. In this chapter, we will see how Cassandra can be used as a data store for third-party software such as Hadoop MapReduce and Pig.

Using Hadoop

Hadoop is for data processing. You may ask "So are MATLAB, R, Octave, Python (NLTK and many other libraries for data analysis), and SAS, then why Hadoop". They are great tools, but they are good for data that can fit in memory. It means that you can churn a couple of GBs to maybe 10s of GBs, and the rate of processing depends on the CPU on that machine, maybe 16 cores. This poses a big restriction. The data is no more in GB limits at the Internet scale. In the age of billions of mobile phones (there were an estimated 7.7 billion mobile users at the end of 2014, source: `http://mobithinking. com/mobile-marketing-tools/latest-mobile-stats/a#subscribers`), we are generating humongous amounts of data every second (Twitter reports 143,199 tweets per second, source: `http://dazeinfo.com/2014/04/29/7-7-billion-mobile-devices-among-7-1-billion-world-population-end-2014/`) by checking in places, tagging photos, uploading videos, commenting, messaging, purchasing, dining, running (fitness apps monitor your activities), and many other activities that we do; we literally record these events somewhere. It does not stop at organic data generation.

A lot of data, a lot more than organic data, is generated by machines (`http:// en.wikipedia.org/wiki/Machine-generated_data`). Web logs, financial market data, data from various sensors (including ones in your cell phone), machine part data, and many more are such examples. Health, genomics, and medical science have some of the most interesting big data corpora ready to be analyzed and inferred. To give you a glimpse of how big genetic data can be, we should check data from the 1,000 genome projects (`http://www.1000genomes.org/`). This data is available for free (there are storage charges) to be used by anyone. The genome data for (only) 1,700 individuals makes a corpus of 200 terabytes. It is doubtful that any conventional in-memory computation tool such as R or MATLAB can do it. Hadoop helps you process the data of that extent.

Hadoop is an example of distributed computing, so you can scale beyond a single computer. Hadoop virtualizes the storage and processors. This means you can roughly treat a 10-machine Hadoop cluster as one machine with 10 times the processing power and 10 times the storage capacity than of a single one. With multiple machines parallely processing the data, Hadoop is best fit for large unstructured datasets. It can help you clean data (data munging) and perform data transformation too. HDFS provides redundant distributed data storage. Effectively, it can work as your **extract, transform, and load** (ETL) platform.

Hadoop and Cassandra

In the age of big data analytics, there are hardly any data-rich companies that do not want their data to be extracted, evaluated, and inferred to provide more business inside. In the past, analyzing large datasets (structured or unstructured) that span terabytes or petabytes used to be expensive and a technically challenging task to a team; distributed computing was harder to keep track of, and hardware to support this kind of infrastructure was not financially feasible to everyone.

This chapter does not cover Cassandra integration with Hive and Oozie. To learn about Cassandra integration with Oozie, visit `http://wiki.apache.org/cassandra/HadoopSupport#Oozie`.

There are ongoing efforts to bring Hive integration to Cassandra as its native part. If you are planning to use Cassandra with Hive, visit `https://issues.apache.org/jira/browse/CASSANDRA-4131`.

DataStax Enterprise editions have built-in Cassandra-enabled Hive MapReduce clients. Check them out at `http://www.datastax.com/documentation/datastax_enterprise/4.6/datastax_enterprise/ana/anaHiv.html`.

A couple of things changed the demography completely in favor of medium and small companies. Hardware prices dropped down. The memory and processing powers of computing units increased dramatically at the same time. Hardware on-demand came into the picture. You can spend about 20 dollars to rent about a 100 virtual machines with quad-core (virtual) processors, 7.5 GB RAM, and 840 GB of ephemeral storage (you can plug in gigantic network attached storage that is permanent) from AWS for an hour. There are multiple vendors that provide this sort of cloud infrastructure. However, the biggest leap in making big data analysis commonplace is the availability of extremely high, quality free, and open source solutions that abstract the developers from managing distributed systems. This software made it possible to plug in various algorithms and use the system as a black box to take care of getting data, applying routines, and returning results. Hadoop is the most prominent name in this field. Currently, it is the de facto standard of big data processing.

At the time of writing this book, this was the specification of an AWS m3.large machine. The pricing estimate is based on the hourly price of on-demand instances at USD 0.14 per hour.

Hadoop deserves a book of its own. If you wanted to learn about Hadoop, you may want to refer to Yahoo!'s excellent tutorial on this subject (`http://developer.yahoo.com/hadoop/tutorial/index.html`). This section will give a simplistic introduction to Hadoop, which is by no means complete. If you are already familiar with Hadoop, you may skip this section.

Introduction to Hadoop

Apache Hadoop is an open source implementation of two famous white papers from Google: **Google File System (GFS)** (`http://research.google.com/archive/gfs.html`) and Google MapReduce (`http://research.google.com/archive/mapreduce.html`). Vanilla Hadoop consists of two modules, **Hadoop Distributed File System (HDFS)** and MapReduce. HDFS and MR are implementations of GFS and Google MapReduce, respectively. One may consider HDFS as a storage module and MapReduce as a processing module.

HDFS

Let's start with an example. Assume you have 1 TB of data to read from a single machine with a single hard disk. Assuming the disk read rate is 100 MBps, it will take about 2 hours and 45 minutes to read the file. If you could split this data over 10 hard disks and read them all in parallel, it would have decreased the read time by 10 — more or less. From a layman's perspective, this is what HDFS does; it breaks the data into fixed-sized blocks (default is 64 MB) and distributes them over a number of slave machines.

HDFS is a filesystem that runs on top of a regular filesystem. Production installations generally have ext3 filesystems running beneath HDFS. By distributing data across several nodes, the storage layer can scale to very large virtual storage that scales linearly. To provide reliability to store data, the data is stored with redundancy. Each block is replicated three times by default. HDFS is architected in such a way that each data block gets replicated to different servers and, if possible, on different racks. This saves data from disk, server, or complete rack failure. In the event of a disk or a server failure, data is replicated to a new location to meet the replication factor. If this reminds you of Cassandra, or any other distributed system, you are on the right track. As we will see very soon, unlike Cassandra, HDFS has single point of failure due to its master-slave design.

Despite all these good features, HDFS has a couple of shortcomings too. They are as follows:

- HDFS is optimized for streaming. This means that there is no random access to a file. It may not utilize the maximum data transfer rate.
- NameNode (discussed later) is a single point of unavailability for HDFS.
- HDFS is better suited for large files.
- The append method is not supported by default. However, one can change the configuration to allow the append method.

Data management

HDFS uses the master-slave mechanism to distribute data across multiple servers. The master node is usually backed by a powerful machine so that it does not fail. The slave machines are data nodes, these are commodity hardware. The reason behind having a powerful master node is we do not want it to go down as it's a single point failure. If the master node (that is, NameNode) goes down, the storage is down—unlike the Cassandra model. To load the data to HDFS, the client connects to the master node and sends an upload request. The master node tells the client to send parts of the data to various data nodes. Note that data does not stream through the master node. It just directs the client to appropriate data nodes and maintains the metadata about the location of various parts of a file. The following diagram shows how the client makes a request to NameNode to write a block. NameNode returns the nodes where the block is to be written. The client picks one DataNode from the node's list in the previous step and forwards it to other nodes:

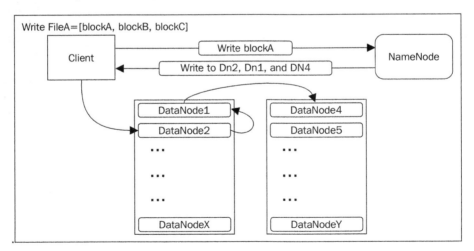

There are two processes one needs to know about to understand how the data is distributed and managed by HDFS.

NameNode

The NameNode process is the one that runs on a master server. Its job is to keep metadata about the files that are stored in the data nodes. If NameNode is down, the slaves have no idea how to make a sense of the block stored. Therefore, it is crucial to have NameNode on redundant hardware. In general, in a Hadoop cluster, there is just one master NameNode.

DataNodes

DataNodes are the slaves. They are the machines that actually contain the data. The DataNode process manages the data blocks on the local machine. DataNode keeps communication with the master node using some sort of heartbeat mechanism. This enables the master node to replicate the data if one of the slaves dies.

Data never goes via NameNode. DataNodes are the ones responsible for streaming the data out. NameNode and DataNodes work in harmony to provide a scalable and giant virtual filesystem that is oblivious to the underlying hardware or the operating system. The way data read or write takes place is as follows:

- The client makes a write request for a block of a file to the master, the NameNode server.
- NameNode returns a list of servers that the block is copied to (in a replicated manner, a block is copied at many places as replication is configured).
- The client makes a ready request to one of the to-be-written-on DataNodes. This node forwards the request to the next node, which will forward it to the next, until all the nodes to write the data on acknowledge the client with an OK message.
- On receipt of the OK message, the client starts to stream the data to one of the data nodes that internally streams the data to the next replica node and so on.
- Once the block gets written successfully, slaves notify the master. The slave connected to the client returns a success.

The preceding figure shows the data flow when a Hadoop client (CLI or Java) makes a request to write a block to HDFS.

Hadoop MapReduce

MapReduce (MR) is a very simple concept once you know it. It is algorithm 101: divide and conquer. The job is broken into small independent tasks and distributed across multiple machines. The result gets sorted and merged together to generate the final result. The ability to distribute a large computational burden over multiple servers into a small computational load provides a Hadoop programmer an effectively limitless computation capability. MR is the processing part of Hadoop; it virtualizes the CPU. The following figure depicts this process.

As an end user, you need to write a Mapper and a Reducer for the tasks you need to get done. The Hadoop framework performs the heavy lifting of getting data from a source and splitting it into maps of keys and values based on what the data source is. It may be a line from a text file, a row from a relational database, or a key-value from Cassandra's column family. These maps of key-value pairs (indicated as **Input key-val** pairs in the following figure) are forwarded to the Mapper that you have provided to Hadoop. Mapper performs unit tasks of the key-value pair; for example, for a word count task, you may want to remove punctuation, split the words by a white space, iterate in this split array of words, forward key as an individual word, and set the value as one. These make the intermediate key-value pair, as indicated in the following figure:

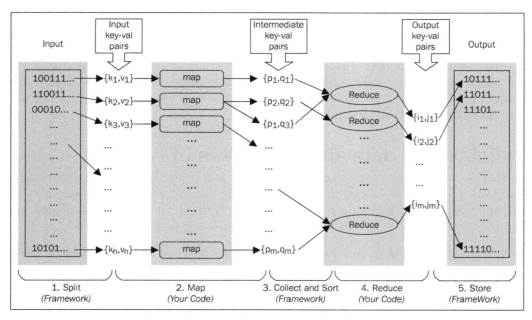

Hadoop MapReduce framework in action (simplified)

These results are sorted by the key and forwarded to the Reducer interface that you provided. Incoming tuples have the same key, and reducers can use this property in their logic. Understanding this sentence is important to a beginner. What it means is that you can just iterate in the incoming iterator and do things such as group or count—basically reduce or fold the map by a key.

The reduced values are then stored in a place of your choice, which can be HDFS, RDBMS, Cassandra, or one of the many other storage options.

There are two main processes that you should know about in context of Hadoop MapReduce, which we will talk about in a bit.

JobTracker

Similar to NameNode, JobTracker is a master process that governs the execution of worker threads such as TaskTracker. Like any master-slave architecture, JobTracker is a single point of failure. Therefore, it is advisable to have robust hardware and redundancy built into the machine that has JobTracker running.

JobTracker's responsibility includes estimating the number of Mapper tasks from the input split, for example, file splits from HDFS via `InputFormat`. It uses already configured values as numbers of Reducer tasks. A client application can use JobClient to submit jobs to JobTracker and inquire the status of a job.

TaskTracker

Like the DataNode in case of HDFS, the TaskTracker is the actual execution unit of Hadoop. It creates a child JVM for Mapper and Reducer tasks. The maximum number of tasks (Mapper and Reducer tasks) can be set independently. TaskTracker may reuse the child JVMs to improve efficiency.

Reliability of data and processes in Hadoop

Hadoop is a very robust and reliable architecture. It is meant to be run on commodity hardware and hence takes care of failure automatically. It detects the failure of a task and retries the failed tasks. It is fault tolerant. A down DataNode is replicated (redundant) and a system heals by itself, if a DataNode is unavailable.

Hadoop allows servers to join the cluster or leave it without any repercussion. Rack-aware storage of data saves the cluster against disk failures, rack/machine power failure, and even a complete rack going down.

The following figure shows the famous schema of the reliable Hadoop infrastructure using commodity hardware for slaves and heavy-duty servers (top of the rack) for the masters. Please note that these are physical servers, as they are in the data centers. Later, when we will discuss using Cassandra as a data store for Hadoop, we will use a ring representation. Even in that case, the physical configuration may be the same as the one represented in the following figure, but the logical configuration, as we have seen throughout this book, will be a ring-like structure to emphasize the token distribution.

Setting up local Hadoop

This section will discuss how to set up Hadoop 2.6.0 (should be valid for all 2.x versions) on your local machine. At the time of writing this, Hadoop has transitioned from version 1 to version 2. Version 2.x is mature now and has disruptive changes. It is presumably better than version 1. HDFS is federated in the new version. The Apache documentation says that this version scales NameNode service horizontally using multiple independent NameNodes. This should ideally avoid the single point of failure that NameNodes faced in the previous version. The other major improvement is in the new MapReduce frameworks, for example, MRNextGen, MRv2, and **Yet Another Resource Negotiator** (**YARN**). More about the new version can be learned on the Apache website (`http://hadoop.apache.org/docs/current/hadoop-yarn/hadoop-yarn-site/YARN.html`). Here are the steps to get Hadoop Version 2.x to work on a Linux machine. To keep things generic, I have used the dowloaded zipped file to install the Hadoop. One can use a binary package for a specific platform without much of a change in the instructions. The following figure shows Hadoop infrastructure. Heavy-duty master nodes are at the top of the rack servers. Each rack has a rack switch. Slaves run DataNode and TaskTracker services. Racks are connected through 10GE switches. Note that not all racks will have a master server:

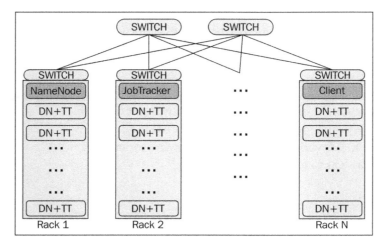

Make sure you can add SSH to your local host using a key-based password-less login. If you can't do this, generate and set a key pair as described in the following commands:

```
# Generate key pair
$ ssh-keygen -t dsa -P '' -f ~/.ssh/id_dsa
Generating public/private dsa key pair.
Your identification has been saved in /home/ec2-user/.ssh/id_dsa.
Your public key has been saved in /home/ec2-user/.ssh/id_dsa.pub.
The key fingerprint is:
6a:dc:53:04:8a:52:50:9f:dd:2a:2e:99:04:86:41:f4 ec2-user@ip-10-147-171-159
The key's randomart image is:
+--[ DSA 1024]----+
|+o.oo    .       |
|  o.. o + o      |
|.  +E. + .o      |
|  . o     o      |
|     . . S .     |
|    . = + .      |
|    + = o        |
|     o   .       |
|                 |
+-----------------+
# Add public key to authorized_keys
$ cat ~/.ssh/id_dsa.pub>> ~/.ssh/authorized_keys
```

At this point, you should be able to add SSH to your machine by issuing `ssh localhost`.

> You may need to install the SSH server, if you do not have it installed already. In Ubuntu, execute the following command:
> `sudo apt-get install openssh-server`
> In RHEL variants, execute the following command:
> `yum install openssh-server`

The first step is to download and extract Hadoop 2.x Version to a desired location:

```
# Download Hadoop
$ wget http://www.us.apache.org/dist/hadoop/common/hadoop-2.6.0/hadoop-
2.6.0.tar.gz


# Extract
$ tar xvzf hadoop-2.6.0.tar.gz


# Create a soft link for easy access and updates without disrupting PATH
$ ln -s hadoop-2.6.0 hadoop
$ cd hadoop
```

Let's assume the directory where the Hadoop tarball is extracted is $HADOOP_HOME. You need to configure Hadoop to get it working. We will perform the minimalistic configuration that gets Hadoop working in a pseudo-cluster mode, where your single machine works as master node with JobTracker and NameNode and slave node with TaskTracker and DataNode. Remember, this is not a production-ready configuration.

Edit $HADOOP_HOME/conf/core-site.xml and add the following lines:

```
<configuration>
    <property>
        <name>fs.defaultFS</name>
        <value>hdfs://localhost:9000</value>
    </property>
</configuration>
```

Edit $HADOOP_HOME/conf/hdfs-site.xml and add the replication parameter for the data blocks:

```
<configuration>
    <property>
        <name>dfs.replication</name>
        <value>1</value>
    </property>
</configuration>
```

Now, it is almost done. However, you need to tell Hadoop where Java lives. Edit `$HADOOP_HOME/etc/hadoop/hadoop-env.sh` and add the `export` statement for `JAVA_HOME` like this:

```
# The only required environment variable is JAVA_HOME.  All others are
# optional.  When running a distributed configuration it is best to
# set JAVA_HOME in this file, so that it is correctly defined on
# remote nodes.

# The java implementation to use.
export JAVA_HOME="/usr/lib/jvm/java-7-oracle"
We are done. Next is testing the installation.
```

Testing the installation

Before we start testing the newly installed Hadoop, we need to format the NameNode to prepare HDFS. We haven't provided any directory to HDFS, so it will default to `/tmp`, which may get deleted after the reboot. Here's the list of commands to run to test the installation:

```
$ bin/hdfs namenode -format
15/01/20 23:03:13 INFO namenode.NameNode: STARTUP_MSG:
/************************************************************
STARTUP_MSG: Starting NameNode
STARTUP_MSG:    host = blackwidow/127.0.1.1
STARTUP_MSG:    args = [-format]
STARTUP_MSG:    version = 2.6.0
STARTUP_MSG:    classpath = /home/naishe/apps/hadoop-2.6.0/etc/hadoop:/
home/naishe/apps/hadoop-2.6.0/share/hadoop/common/lib/hadoop-auth-
2.6.0.jar:/home/naishe/apps/hadoop-2.6.0/share/hadoop/common/lib/
apacheds-kerberos-codec-2.0.0-M15.jar:
[ -- SNIP -- ]
:/contrib/capacity-scheduler/*.jar
STARTUP_MSG:    build = https://git-wip-us.apache.org/repos/asf/hadoop.
git -r e3496499ecb8d220fba99dc5ed4c99c8f9e33bb1; compiled by 'jenkins' on
2014-11-13T21:10Z
STARTUP_MSG:    java = 1.7.0_72
************************************************************/
15/01/20 23:03:13 INFO namenode.NameNode: registered UNIX signal handlers
for [TERM, HUP, INT]
15/01/20 23:03:13 INFO namenode.NameNode: createNameNode [-format]
```

```
Formatting using clusterid: CID-3d2c36d0-de9f-4032-914e-3abe1b40b0c3

[ -- snip -- ]

15/01/20 23:03:16 INFO namenode.FSImage: Allocated new BlockPoolId: BP-
324301922-127.0.1.1-1421775196180

15/01/20 23:03:16 INFO common.Storage: Storage directory /tmp/hadoop-
naishe/dfs/name has been successfully formatted.

15/01/20 23:03:16 INFO namenode.NNStorageRetentionManager: Going to
retain 1 images with txid >= 0

15/01/20 23:03:16 INFO util.ExitUtil: Exiting with status 0

15/01/20 23:03:16 INFO namenode.NameNode: SHUTDOWN_MSG:

/************************************************************

SHUTDOWN_MSG: Shutting down NameNode at blackwidow/127.0.1.1

************************************************************/
```

You may observe that the storage directory is set to `/tmp/hadoop-<username>/dfs/`
`name` by default. You may change it to a sensible location by editing configuration
XML. Alternatively, it will serve its purpose to demonstrate capability.

Let's start everything up and see whether we are OK:

```
# Start Hadoop services locally

$ sbin/start-dfs.sh

Starting namenodes on [localhost]

localhost: Warning: Permanently added 'localhost' (ECDSA) to the list of
known hosts.

localhost: starting namenode, logging to /home/naishe/apps/hadoop-2.6.0/
logs/hadoop-naishe-namenode-blackwidow.out

localhost: Warning: Permanently added 'localhost' (ECDSA) to the list of
known hosts.

localhost: starting datanode, logging to /home/naishe/apps/hadoop-2.6.0/
logs/hadoop-naishe-datanode-blackwidow.out

Starting secondary namenodes [0.0.0.0]

0.0.0.0: Warning: Permanently added '0.0.0.0' (ECDSA) to the list of
known hosts.

0.0.0.0: starting secondarynamenode, logging to /home/naishe/apps/
hadoop-2.6.0/logs/hadoop-naishe-secondarynamenode-blackwidow.out


# Test if all services are running

$ jps

22194 NameNode
```

```
22565 SecondaryNameNode
```

```
22314 DataNode
```

```
22754 Jps
```

The `jps` is a built-in tool provided by the Oracle JDK. It lists all the Java processes running on the machine. The previous snippet shows that all the Hadoop processes are up. Let's execute an example and see whether things are actually working:

```
# Upload everything under conf directory to "in" directory in HDFS
$ bin/hdfs dfs -mkdir /user
$ bin/hdfs dfs -mkdir /user/naishe
$ bin/hdfs dfs -put etc/hadoop input
$ bin/hdfs dfs -ls input
Found 29 items
-rw-r--r--   1 naishe supergroup        4436 2015-01-20 23:20 input/
capacity-scheduler.xml
-rw-r--r--   1 naishe supergroup        1335 2015-01-20 23:20 input/
configuration.xsl
-rw-r--r--   1 naishe supergroup         318 2015-01-20 23:20 input/
container-executor.cfg
[ -- snip -- ]
-rw-r--r--   1 naishe supergroup         690 2015-01-20 23:20 input/yarn-
site.xml
```

All set, time to execute an example on it. We will run an example that grabs all the words that match the `dfs[a-z.]+` regular expression across all the files under the `in` folder and returns the counts in a folder called `out`.

```
# Executegrep example
$ bin/hadoop jar hadoop-examples-*.jar grep in out 'dfs[a-z.]+'
15/01/20 23:27:10 INFO Configuration.deprecation: session.id is
deprecated. Instead, use dfs.metrics.session-id
15/01/20 23:27:10 INFO jvm.JvmMetrics: Initializing JVM Metrics with
processName=JobTracker, sessionId=
15/01/20 23:27:10 WARN mapreduce.JobSubmitter: No job jar file set.  User
classes may not be found. See Job or Job#setJar(String).
15/01/20 23:27:11 INFO input.FileInputFormat: Total input paths to
process : 29
15/01/20 23:27:11 INFO mapreduce.JobSubmitter: number of splits:29
15/01/20 23:27:11 INFO mapreduce.JobSubmitter: Submitting tokens for job:
job_local1885642397_0001
```

```
15/01/20 23:27:11 INFO mapreduce.Job: The url to track the job: http://
localhost:8080/

15/01/20 23:27:11 INFO mapreduce.Job: Running job: job_
local1885642397_0001

[-- snip --]

15/01/20 23:27:15 INFO mapred.LocalJobRunner: reduce task executor
complete.

15/01/20 23:27:15 INFO mapreduce.Job:  map 100% reduce 100%

15/01/20 23:27:15 INFO mapreduce.Job: Job job_local1885642397_0001
completed successfully

15/01/20 23:27:15 INFO mapreduce.Job: Counters: 38
    File System Counters
        FILE: Number of bytes read=1243026
        FILE: Number of bytes written=7750172
        FILE: Number of read operations=0
        FILE: Number of large read operations=0
        FILE: Number of write operations=0
        HDFS: Number of bytes read=1764343
        HDFS: Number of bytes written=437
        HDFS: Number of read operations=1051
        HDFS: Number of large read operations=0
        HDFS: Number of write operations=32
    Map-Reduce Framework
[-- snip stats --]
    File Input Format Counters
        Bytes Read=437
    File Output Format Counters
        Bytes Written=197


# Result of the MapReduce execution
$ bin/hdfs dfs -cat output/*
6   dfs.audit.logger
4   dfs.class
3   dfs.server.namenode.
2   dfs.period
2   dfs.audit.log.maxfilesize
```

2   `dfs.audit.log.maxbackupindex`

1   `dfsmetrics.log`

1   `dfsadmin`

1   `dfs.servers`

1   `dfs.replication`

1   `dfs.file`

Congratulations, you have just executed a job using MapReduce. It was a bit of a boring task. You could have executed the `grep` command on your Linux machine that runs much faster than this. However, it gives you a couple of important insights. One, that the configuration works, and the other is, it is not always the best thing to do everything using Hadoop; for some tasks, it is better to use the tools that are best suited to them. We will see more about this when we will discuss the cons of Hadoop later in this chapter.

Cassandra with Hadoop MapReduce

Cassandra provides built-in support for Hadoop. If you have ever written a MapReduce program, you will find out that writing a MapReduce task with Cassandra is quite similar to how one would write a MapReduce task for the data stored in HDFS. Cassandra supports input to Hadoop with `ColumnFamilyInputFormat` and output with the `ColumnFamilyOutputFormat` classes, respectively. Apart from these, you will need to put Cassandra-specific settings for Hadoop via `ConfigHelper`. These three classes are enough to get you started. Another class that might be worth looking at is `BulkOutputFormat`. All these classes are under the `org.apache.cassandra.hadoop.*` package.

To be able to compile the MapReduce code that uses Cassandra as data source or data sink, you must have `cassandra-all.jar` in your classpath. You will also need to make Hadoop to be able to see JARs in the Cassandra library. We will discuss this later in this chapter.

Let's understand the classes that we will be using to get Cassandra working for our MapReduce problem.

Preparing Cassandra for Hadoop

The nodes that have Hadoop on them need to have virtual nodes disabled. So, if you have a Cassandra cluster, you may want to split it into two data centers. You will need to configure a proper endpoint snitch (such as `PropertyFileSnitch`) to separate the two data centers. The data centers need not actually be in different data centers. To disable the virtual node, change the following in `cassandra.yaml`:

1. Uncomment `initial_token`, set to an appropriate value within the data center or leave it to a default value, say, 1.

2. Set `num_tokens` to 1.

If you are trying to divide an existing cluster into two parts, one for data storage (the normal vnode-enabled data center for data storage) and another for analytics (the ones that have vnode disabled and stays along with Hadoop), make sure, in analytics data center, you decommission those nodes then clean data from data directories and restart them after making the previously mentioned changes. This is the same as adding new nodes to the cluster. Disabling vnode in an existing running cluster is not advised.

ColumnFamilyInputFormat

The `ColumnFamilyInputFormat` class is an implementation of `org.apache.hadoop.mapred.InputFormat` (or `mapreduce` in newer the API). So, its implementation is dictated by the `InputFormat` class specifications. Hadoop uses this class to get data for the MapReduce tasks. It describes how to read data from column families into the Mapper instances.

The other job of `ColumnFamilyInputFormat` (or any implementation of `InputFormat`) is to fragment input data into small chunks that get fed to map tasks. Cassandra has `ColumnInputSplit` for this purpose. One can configure the number of rows per `InputSplit` via `ConfigHelper.setInputSplitSize`. However, there is a caveat. It uses multiple `get_slice_range` queries for each `InputSplit` data, so, as Cassandra documentation says, a smaller value will build up call overhead; on the other hand, too large a value may cause out-of-memory issues. Larger values are better for performance, so if you are planning to play with this parameter do some calculation based on median column size to avoid memory overflow. Trial and error can be handy. The default split size is 64 x 1024 rows.

ColumnFamilyOutputFormat

The OutputFormat class is the mechanism of writing the result from MapReduce to a permanent (usually) storage. Cassandra implements Hadoop's OutputFormat, that is, ColumnFamilyOutputFormat. It enables Hadoop to write the result from the reduce task as column family rows. It is implemented such that the results are written, to the column family, in batches. This is a performance improvement, and this mechanism is called lazy write-back caching.

CqlOutputFormat and CqlInputFormat

CqlOutputFormat and CqlInputFormats are Hadoop-specific output and input formats for reducer and mapper tasks, respectively. Functioning similar to ColumnFamilyOutputFormat and ColumnFamilyInputFormat, they provide the ability to access CQL rows and variable binding.

CqlInputFormat requires the keyspace and table name to be specified. You can use ConfigHelper class to set up this and other configurations. A couple of things that you should set are input split size via ConfigHelper.setInputSplitSize, which defaults to 64,000 rows. The number of CQL rows per page via CqlConfigHelper. setInputCqlPageRowSize defaults to 1,000 rows per page. It is a good idea to have CQL rows per page as big as your machine can support without causing memory issues. This will help reducing network overhead. Initial input address and partitioner may be required to mention. To do so, use the ConfigHelper. setInputInitialAddress and ConfigHelper.setInputPartitioner methods.

The CqlOutputFormat allows the reducer task to write keys and values to the specified CQL table. You need to set the output table, output initial address, and output partitioner via ConfigHelper and the CQL that updates the output table via CqlConfigHelper.setOutputCql.

ConfigHelper

The ConfigHelper class is a gateway to configure Cassandra-specific settings for Hadoop. It is a pretty plain utility class that validates the settings passed and sets into Hadoop's org.apache.hadoop.conf.Configuration instance for the job. This configuration is made available to the Mapper and the Reducer.

The `ConfigHelper` class saves developers from inputing the wrong property name because all the properties are set using a method; any typo can appear at compile time. It may be worth looking at JavaDoc for `ConfigHelper`. Here are some of the commonly used methods:

- `setInputInitialAddress`: This can be a hostname or private IP of one of the Cassandra nodes.

- `SetInputRpcPort`: This will set the RPC port address if it has been altered from default. If not set, it uses the default thrift port `9160`.

- `setInputPartitioner`: This will set the appropriate partitioner according to the underlying Cassandra storage setting.

- `SetInputColumnFamily`: This will set the column family details to be able to pull data from.

- `SetInputSlicePredicate`: This will set the columns that are pulled from column family to provide Mapper to work on.

- `SetOutputInitialAddress`: This will set the address of Cassandra cluster (one of the nodes) where the result is being published; it is usually similar to `InputInitialAddress`.

- `SetOutputRpcPort`: This will set the RPC port to cluster where the result is stored.

- `SetOutputPartitioner`: This is the partitioner used in the output cluster.

- `SetOutputColumnFamily`: This will set the column family details to store results in.

Since version 1.1, Cassandra added support to wide row column families, bulk loading, and secondary indexes.

Wide row support

Earlier, having multimillion columns was a problem in Cassandra Hadoop integration. It was pulling a row per call limited by `SlicePredicate`. Version 1.1 onwards, you can pass the wide row Boolean parameter as TRUE, as shown in the following snippet:

```
ConfigHelper.setInputColumnFamily(
conf,
keyspace,
inCF,
true// SET WIDEROW = TRUE
);
```

When wide row is set to `true`, the rows are fed one column at a time to the Mapper.

Bulk loading

The `BulkOutputFormat` class is another utility that Cassandra provides to improve the write performance of jobs that result in large data. It streams the data in a binary format, which is much quicker than inserting data one by one. It uses `SSTableLoader` to do this. Refer to `SSTableLoader` in *Chapter 6, Managing a Cluster – Scaling, Node Repair, and Backup*. Here's how to set it up:

```
Job job = new Job(conf);
job.setOutputFormatClass(BulkOutputFormat.class);
```

Secondary index support

One can use a secondary index when pulling data from Cassandra to pass it on to the job. This is another improvement. It makes Cassandra shift the data and pass only the relevant data to Hadoop instead of Hadoop burning the CPU cycles to weed out the data that is not going to be used in the computation. It lowers the overhead of passing extra data to Hadoop. Here is an example:

```
IndexExpressionelectronicItems =
    newIndexExpression(
    ByteBufferUtil.bytes("item_category"),
    IndexOperator.EQ,
    ByteBufferUtil.bytes("electronics")
      );

IndexExpressionsoldAfter2012 =
    newIndexExpression(
    ByteBufferUtil.bytes("sell_year"),
            IndexOperator.GT,
    ByteBufferUtil.bytes(2012)
  );

ConfigHelper.setInputRange(conf, Arrays.asList(electronicItems,
soldAfter2012));
```

The previous code snippet returns the rows that fall in the electronics category and were sold after the year 2012.

Cassandra and Hadoop in action

Now, with more than enough (rather boring) theory, we are ready to do something exciting. In this section, we will do a word count of a book. It will be more interesting than the `grep` example.

In this example, we load Lewis Carroll's novel *Alice in Wonderland* (http://en.wikipedia.org/wiki/Alice%27s_Adventures_in_Wonderland) in Cassandra. To prepare this data, we read the text file line by line and store 500 lines in one row. The row names are formatted as row_1, row_2, and so on, and the columns in each row have names such as col_1, col_2, and so on. Each row has almost 500 columns, and each column has one line from the file. To avoid noise, we have removed the punctuation from the lines during the load. We could certainly work on the noise reduction in the MapReduce code, but we wanted to keep it simple. What follows is the code and its explanation. It is recommended to download the code either from my GitHub account or from the book's website. Keep it handy while reading this chapter. The code is eventually compiled and submitted to Hadoop MapReduce to execute the compiled JAR file. We use the mvn clean install Maven command to compile and create a JAR file. If you are unaware of Maven or new to Java, you can compile the files using appropriate dependencies or JAR files in the classpath. Refer to the pom.xml file in the project to know the JAR files you need to compile for the example in Java.

Assuming that we have data ready in Cassandra to run MapReduce on it, we will write Mapper, Reducer, and a main method. Here is the Mapper:

```
public static class WordMapper extends Mapper<ByteBuffer,
SortedMap<ByteBuffer, IColumn>, Text, IntWritable>{
private static final IntWritable ONE = new IntWritable(1);
private Text word = new Text();

@Override
protected void map(ByteBuffer key, SortedMap<ByteBuffer, IColumn>
cols, Context context)
throwsIOException, InterruptedException {

//Iterate through the column values
for(IColumn col: cols.values()){
        String val = ByteBufferUtil.string(col.value());
StringTokenizertokenizer = new StringTokenizer(val);

while (tokenizer.hasMoreTokens()) {
word.set(tokenizer.nextToken());
context.write(word, ONE);
            }
        }
    }
}
```

This is what our Mapper looks like. To a person who has some experience in writing MapReduce programs, this does not have much deviation from a regular Mapper. Here are a couple of things to note:

- Cassandra feeds sorted map to Mapper. This is sorted by column name and it is basically column-name, column-value pair.

- The key is of the ByteBuffer type and it is the row key.

- Use org.apache.cassandra.utils.ByteBufferUtil to convert ByteBuffer to meaningful types.

- If you want to process column by column, loop through the column's sorted map.

- Write out the output that you want this Mapper to forward to the Reducer. The values that you write to context is sorted and grouped by the framework and forwarded to the Reducer.

Now that we have done the basic task of splitting the text in each column and forwarding it with key as word and value as ONE, in order to count each word, we need to get all the words that were forwarded by Mapper at one place so that we can just iterate in the grouped key-value pairs of word and ONE and update a counter until all the occurrences of that word is taken care of. Here is how our Mapper looks:

```
public static class WordReducer extends Reducer<Text, IntWritable,
ByteBuffer, List<Mutation>>{

    @Override
    protected void reduce(Text key, Iterable<IntWritable> values,
Context context)
    throwsIOException, InterruptedException {
        int sum = 0;
        for(IntWritable value: values){
          sum = sum + value.get();
        }

    Column col = new Column();
    col.setName(ByteBufferUtil.bytes("count"));
    col.setValue(ByteBufferUtil.bytes(sum));
    col.setTimestamp(System.currentTimeMillis());

    Mutation mutation = new Mutation();
    mutation.setColumn_or_supercolumn(new ColumnOrSuperColumn());
    mutation.getColumn_or_supercolumn().setColumn(col);
    context.write(
```

```
ByteBufferUtil.bytes(key.toString()),
Collections.singletonList(mutation)
                    );
    }
}
```

Reducer is a little more interesting than Mapper. This is because we are doing two things. Firstly, we are counting the number of grouped elements that come to Reducer from our Mapper. We know that it is grouped by word. So, at the end of looping through the values, we will get the number of instances of that word. The second thing that we are doing here is storing this value in Cassandra. Instead of outputting the result to HDFS, we store it in Cassandra with the row key as word, and we add a column named count that will hold the value that we just obtained in the previous step. You can see that there is no environment-specific configuration done here. We instruct what to store in Cassandra and how, and we are done. So, the question arises, where do we set all the environment-specific and Cassandra-specific things? The answer is in the main method. Here is how the main method for this particular example looks. Alternatively, in any Cassandra-based Hadoop project, it will not vary much:

```
public class CassandraWordCount extends Configured implements Tool {

    [-- snip --]

public int run(String[] args) throws Exception {
    Job job = new Job(getConf(), "cassandrawordcount");
job.setJarByClass(getClass());

//  Anything you set in conf will be available to Mapper and Reducer
    Configuration conf = job.getConfiguration();

//  set mapper and reducer
job.setMapperClass(WordMapper.class);
job.setReducerClass(WordReducer.class);

//  Cassandra Specific settings for ingesting CF
ConfigHelper.setInputInitialAddress(conf, Setup.CASSANDRA_HOST_ADDR);
ConfigHelper.setInputRpcPort(conf, String.valueOf(Setup.CASSANDRA_RPC_
PORT));
ConfigHelper.setInputPartitioner(conf, Murmur3Partitioner.class.
getName());
ConfigHelper.setInputColumnFamily(conf, Setup.KEYSPACE, Setup.INPUT_
CF);
```

```
SliceRangesliceRange = new SliceRange(
ByteBufferUtil.bytes(""),
ByteBufferUtil.bytes(""),
false,
Integer.MAX_VALUE);
SlicePredicate predicate = new SlicePredicate()
                .setSlice_range(sliceRange);
ConfigHelper.setInputSlicePredicate(conf, predicate);

job.setInputFormatClass(ColumnFamilyInputFormat.class);


// Cassandra specific output setting
ConfigHelper.setOutputInitialAddress(conf, Setup.CASSANDRA_HOST_ADDR);
ConfigHelper.setOutputRpcPort(conf, String.valueOf(Setup.CASSANDRA_
RPC_PORT));
ConfigHelper.setOutputPartitioner(conf, Murmur3Partitioner.class.
getName());
ConfigHelper.setOutputColumnFamily(conf, Setup.KEYSPACE, Setup.OUTPUT_
CF);

// set output class types
job.setOutputKeyClass(ByteBuffer.class);
job.setOutputValueClass(List.class);
job.setOutputFormatClass(ColumnFamilyOutputFormat.class);

job.setMapOutputKeyClass(Text.class);
job.setMapOutputValueClass(IntWritable.class);

// verbose
job.waitForCompletion(true);
return 0;
   }

public static void main(String[] args) throws Exception{
ToolRunner.run(new Configuration(), new CassandraWordCount(), args);
System.exit(0);
   }

}
```

All right, we went through lots of things, but nothing that we do not know about. Starting from the `main` method, we provide an instance of our main class and any parameter that is passed from the CLI. We kick off `ToolRunner`. The `ToolRunner` class executes the `run` method, where all the settings for environment and Cassandra are. We also can tell where our Mapper and producer for this job are.

We tell Hadoop how to pull data from Cassandra by providing `SlicePredicate` where we pull a complete row by not setting the start column name, the end column name, and setting the count to 2 billion. One may want to modify and just set wide row to `true` and achieve the same without worrying about `SlicePredicate`.

If you are planning to use CQL input and output with Hadoop, the configuration looks like this:

```
// Cassandra configuration
ConfigHelper.setInputInitialAddress(job.getConfiguration(), Setup.
END_POINT);
ConfigHelper.setInputColumnFamily(job.getConfiguration(), Setup.KEY_
SPACE, Setup.SRC_TABLE);
ConfigHelper.setInputPartitioner(job.getConfiguration(),
"Murmur3Partitioner");

// Mapper config
job.setMapperClass(StringTokenizerMapper.class);
job.setInputFormatClass(CqlInputFormat.class);
CqlConfigHelper.setInputCql(job.getConfiguration(),
    "select * from " + Setup.KEY_SPACE + "." + Setup.SRC_TABLE +
    " where token(id) > ? and token(id) <= ? allow filtering");
CqlConfigHelper.setInputCQLPageRowSize(job.getConfiguration(), "100");

// Reducer config
job.setCombinerClass(CassandraReducer.class);
job.setReducerClass(CassandraReducer.class);
job.setMapOutputKeyClass(Text.class);
job.setMapOutputValueClass(IntWritable.class);
job.setOutputKeyClass(Map.class);
job.setOutputValueClass(List.class);
job.setOutputFormatClass(CqlOutputFormat.class);

ConfigHelper.setOutputColumnFamily(job.getConfiguration(), Setup.KEY_
SPACE, Setup.OUT_TABLE);
//job.getConfiguration().set("row_key", Setup.OUT_ROWKEY);
String cql = "update " + Setup.KEY_SPACE + "." + Setup.OUT_TABLE + " "
    + "set word_count = ? ";
```

```
CqlConfigHelper.setOutputCql(job.getConfiguration(), cql);
ConfigHelper.setOutputInitialAddress(job.getConfiguration(), Setup.
END_POINT);
ConfigHelper.setOutputPartitioner(job.getConfiguration(),
"Murmur3Partitioner");
```

Executing, debugging, monitoring, and looking at results

To execute this example, compile the code and create a JAR file. Add any required external libraries or dependency to the classpath or edit conf/hadoop-env.sh and add the location of the JARs. One of the hard requirements to get all this Cassandra-related stuff running is to have the Cassandra's lib directory in Hadoop's classpath. To do that, edit $HADOOP_HOME/conf/hadoop-env.sh and update the classpath like this:

```
$ conf/hadoop-env.sh
```

```
# Extra Java CLASSPATH elements.Optional.
```

```
# export HADOOP_CLASSPATH=
```

```
export HADOOP_CLASSPATH=/home/nishant/apps/cassandra11/lib/*:$HADOOP_
CLASSPATH
```

Make sure Hadoop and Cassandra are completely up and running. To execute your MapReduce program, submit the JAR file to Hadoop with an appropriate classpath, if needed, and a fully qualified class name of the main class, as follows:

```
$ bin/hadoop jar masteringcassandra-0.0.1-SNAPSHOT.jar \
```

The following screenshot shows Hadoop JobTracker GUI. It enables users to watch running jobs and completed jobs; most importantly, you can see logs, system outs, and system error streams by drilling into the job IDs:

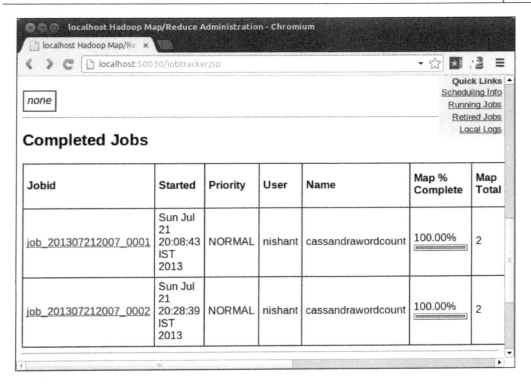

Hadoop provides a pretty simple web-based GUI to monitor and view debug logs, system out stream messages, and system error stream messages. One can monitor the status of a running, failed, or previously run job in detail. By default, this portal is available at `http://JOBTRACKER_ADDRESS:50030`. However, if you are running everything locally, the address will be `http://localhost:50030`. You can click on a job link and view its details. On the job detail page, you can see logs for Mapper or Reducer processes.

As per our Reducer configuration, the results can be accessed by Cassandra from the appropriate column family. You may observe the result there. As expected, you will find `the` in highest use, and there are decent number of references to `Alice`, `Hatter`, and `Cat`:

```
cqlsh:testks> select * from resultCF where key = 'the';
 KEY | count
-----+-------
 the |  1664

cqlsh:testks> select * from resultCF where key = 'Alice';
 KEY   | count
```

```
-------+-------
  Alice |    377

cqlsh:testks> select * from resultCF where key = 'Hatter';
  KEY   | count
-------+-------
  Hatter |    54

cqlsh:testks> select * from resultCF where key = 'Cat';
  KEY | count
-----+-------
  Cat |    23
```

The following figure shows a typical setup for analytics with Cassandra and Hadoop:

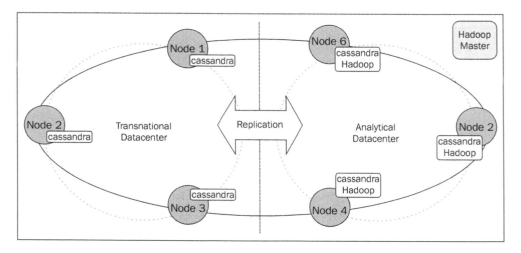

Hadoop in a Cassandra cluster

The production version of the Hadoop and Cassandra combination needs to go into a separate cluster. The first obvious issue is you probably wouldn't want Hadoop to keep polling Cassandra nodes, hampering Cassandra's performance to end users. The general pattern to avoid this is to split the ring into two data centers. Since Cassandra automatically and immediately replicates the changes between data centers, they will always be in sync. What's more, you can assign one of the data centers as transactional with a higher replication factor and the other as an analytical data center with a replication factor 1. The analytical data center is the one used by Hadoop without affecting the transactional data center.

Now, you do not really need to have two physically separated data centers to make this configuration work. Remember `NetworkTopologyStrategy`? (Refer to *Chapter 3, Effective CQL*.) You can tweak Cassandra thinking there are two data centers by just assigning the nodes that you wanted to use for analytics in a different data center. You may need to use `PropertyFileSnitch` and specify the details about data centers in a `cassandra-toplogy.properties` file. So, your keyspace creation looks something like this:

```
createkeyspacemyKeyspace
withplacement_strategy = 'NetworkTopologyStrategy'
andstrategy_options = {TX_DC : 2, HDP_DC: 1};
```

The previous statement defines two data centers, `TX_DC` for transactional purposes and `HDP_DC` for analytics in Hadoop. A node in a transactional data center has a snitch configured like this:

```
# Transaction Data Center
192.168.1.1=TX_DC:RAC1
192.168.1.2=TX_DC:RAC1

192.168.2.1=TX_DC:RAC2

# Analytics Data Center
192.168.1.3=HDP_DC:RAC1

192.168.2.2=HDP_DC:RAC2
192.168.2.3=HDP_DC:RAC2

# For new/unknown/unassigned nodes
default=TX_DC:RAC1
```

We are mostly done setting up machines. Here are a couple of things to remember:

- Install TaskTracker and DataNode processes on each node in the analytical data center.

- Do not have a node that has Cassandra running on it and has running services for TaskTracker and DataNode. Use a separate robust machine to install the master services such as JobTracker and NameNode.

- Make sure `conf/hadoop-env.sh` has all the JAR files that need to execute the MapReduce program as a part of the `HADOOP_CLASSPATH` variable.

With all these configurations, your Cassandra cluster should be ready to serve analytical results to all the concerned people.

Cassandra filesystem

Configuring Hadoop backed by Cassandra may give an illusion that we are replacing HDFS because we take data from Cassandra and dump the results into it. It is not true. Hadoop still needs NameNode and DataNodes for various activities such as storing intermediate results, JAR files, and static data. Therefore, essentially, you are backed by no **single point of failure** (SPOF) database, but you are still bounded by SPOFs such as NameNode and JobTracker.

DataStax, a leading company in professional support for Cassandra, provides a solution to this. Their enterprise offering of the Cassandra DataStax Enterprise product has a built-in **Cassandra File System** (CFS), which is HDFS-compatible. CFS smartly uses Cassandra as underlying storage. What this gives to an end user is simplicity in configuration and no need to have DataNode, NameNode, and secondary NameNode running.

More about CFS is out of the scope of this book. You may read more about CFS on the DataStax blog, CFS Design, at `http://www.datastax.com/dev/blog/cassandra-file-system-design`.

Integration with Pig

Configuring Hadoop with Cassandra in itself is quite some work. Writing verbose and long Java code to do something as simple as a word count is a turnoff to a high-level user like a data analyst. Wouldn't it be nice if we have a SQL-like interpreter that converts commands to MapReduce programs for us? Pig is exactly that tool.

Hadoop does not only support Java but MapReduce programs can also be written more concisely in multiple languages such as Scala, Python, C++ (Pipes), R, and many adapter languages.

Pig provides a SQL-like language called **Pig Latin**. One can write complex MapReduce programs using Pig Latin. You can create a set of intermediate variables that are the result of an operation and it can be used in subsequent operations, in the same way as a stored procedure in the RDBMS world. Finally, the output of an operation can be displayed on a screen or can be stored in a permanent storage such as HDFS or Cassandra.

Installing Pig

Installing Pig is very simple, what is hard is getting it to work with Hadoop and Cassandra nicely. To install Pig, just download the latest version of Pig and untar it as follows:

```
$ wget http://www.eng.lsu.edu/mirrors/apache/pig/pig-0.11.1/pig-
0.11.1.tar.gz
$ tar xvzf pig-0.11.1.tar.gz
$ ln -s pig-0.11.1 pig
```

Let's call this directory `$PIG_HOME`. Ideally, you should just execute `$PIG_HOME/bin/pig`, and the Pig console should start to work given that your Cassandra and Hadoop are up and working. Unfortunately, it does not. Documentation, at the time of writing this, is not adequate to configure Pig. To get Pig started, you need to do the following:

1. Set Hadoop's installation directory as a `HADOOP_PREFIX` variable.

2. Add all the JAR files in Cassandra's `lib` directory to `PIG_CLASSPATH`.

3. Add `udf.import.list` to the `PIG_OPTS` Pig options variable, as follows:

    ```
    export PIG_OPTS="$PIG_OPTS -Dudf.import.list=org.apache.cassandra.
    hadoop.pig";
    ```

4. Set one of the Cassandra nodes' address, Cassandra RPC port, and Cassandra partitioner to `PIG_INITIAL_ADDRESS`, `PIG_RPC_PORT`, and `PIG_PARTITIONER`, respectively.

You may write a simple shell script that does this for you. Here is a shell script that accommodates the four steps (assuming, `$CASSANDRA_HOME` points to the Cassandra installation directory).

> Pig 0.14, Cassandra 2.1.2, and Hadoop 2.6.0 have some classpath conflicts among each other. Some JAR has been added and deleted to make the integration work. You may specifically want to replace all Guava libraries with Guava version 16.0. Cassandra does not like the older version, and Hadoop fails if we have the newer version (17 onwards, https://issues.apache.org/jira/browse/HADOOP-11032).
>
> Also, keep an eye out for the bugs yet to be fixed in version 2.1.2 (https://issues.apache.org/jira/browse/CASSANDRA-8541 and https://issues.apache.org/jira/browse/CASSANDRA-8599).

```
export PIG_HOME=/home/naishe/apps/pig-0.14.0

export HADOOP_PREFIX=/home/naishe/apps/hadoop-2.6.0

export CASSANDRA_HOME=/home/naishe/apps/apache-cassandra-2.1.2

CLASSPATH=""

for cassandra_jar in $CASSANDRA_HOME/lib/*.jar; do

  CLASSPATH=$CLASSPATH:$cassandra_jar

done


PIG_JAR=""

for jar in $PIG_HOME/*.jar $PIG_HOME/lib/*.jar; do

   PIG_JAR=$PIG_JAR:$jar

done


export PIG_CLASSPATH=""

export PIG_CLASSPATH=$PIG_CLASSPATH:$CLASSPATH:$PIG_JAR;

export PIG_CLASSPATH=$PIG_CLASSPATH:/home/naishe/.m2/repository/com/
datastax/cassandra/cassandra-driver-core/2.1.2/cassandra-driver-core-
2.1.2.jar

export PIG_CLASSPATH=$PIG_CLASSPATH:/home/naishe/.m2/repository/org/
apache/cassandra/cassandra-all/2.1.2/cassandra-all-2.1.2.jar


# Hack to avoid ClassNotFound exception

export PIG_CLASSPATH=$PIG_CLASSPATH:/home/naishe/apps/downloads/metrics-
core-3.0.2.jar


export PIG_OPTS="$PIG_OPTS -Dudf.import.list=org.apache.cassandra.hadoop.
pig";

export PIG_INITIAL_ADDRESS=localhost

export PIG_RPC_PORT=9160

export PIG_PARTITIONER=org.apache.cassandra.dht.Murmur3Partitioner
```

If everything works OK and Cassandra and Hadoop are up, you may access the Pig console to execute queries in an interactive mode as follows:

```
pig$ bin/pig

2013-07-22 13:32:22,709 [main] INFO  org.apache.pig.Main - Apache Pig
version 0.11.1 (r1459641) compiled Mar 22 2013, 02:13:53

2013-07-22 13:32:22,710 [main] INFO  org.apache.pig.Main - Logging error
messages to: /home/nishant/apps/pig-0.11.1/pig_1374480142703.log
```

```
2013-07-22 13:32:22,757 [main] INFO  org.apache.pig.impl.util.Utils -
Default bootup file /home/nishant/.pigbootup not found

2013-07-22 13:32:23,080 [main] INFO  org.apache.pig.backend.hadoop.
executionengine.HExecutionEngine - Connecting to hadoop file system at:
hdfs://localhost:9000

2013-07-22 13:32:24,133 [main] INFO  org.apache.pig.backend.hadoop.
executionengine.HExecutionEngine - Connecting to map-reduce job tracker
at: localhost:9001

grunt>
```

Let's copy some Hadoop XML files into HDFS and run a word count on it as follows:

```
# Load all the files in $HADOOP_HOME/conf to pigdata in HDFS
$ bin/hadoopfs -put confpigdata


# --- in pig console ---
# load all the files from HDFS
grunt> A = load './pigdata';


# loop line by line in all the input files from A split them into words
grunt> B = foreach A generate flatten(TOKENIZE((chararray)$0)) as word;


# Group the tokenized words into variable C, groub by attribute "word"
grunt> C = group B by word;


# Generare a map of number of terms in each group and group name
grunt> D = foreach C generate COUNT(B), group;


# print this map to console
grunt> dump D;
```

If it works, you will see this output:

```
...
(31,for)
(2,get)
(4,jks)
(12,job)
(1,log)
(1,map)
```

```
(2,max)
(1,pid)
(8,set)
(1,sig)
(1,ssh)
(83,the)
(1,two)
(6,use)
(3,via)
(3,who)
...
```

Integrating Pig and Cassandra

By getting Hadoop working with Cassandra, we are almost done and ready to use the Pig console to get data from Cassandra and store results back into Cassandra. One thing that you need to know is what storage method is used to store and retrieve data from Cassandra. It is `CassandraStorage()` that you will be using in your Pig Latin to transfer data to and from Cassandra. The usage is exactly the same as you would use in `PigStorage()`.

In Pig, the data structure that is used to store/get data to/from Cassandra is a tuple of row keys and a bag of tuples, where each tuple is a column-name and column-value pair, such as this:

```
(ROW_KEY, { (COL1, VAL1), (COL2, VAL2), (COL3, VAL3), ...})
```

Here is an example of the word count from the Cassandra table. This example uses the same data (from Alice in Wonderland) as we did when we showed the MapReduce example with Cassandra. The book is split into lines, and each row contains 500 lines in 500 columns. There are a total of 6 rows:

```
# Pull Data from dataCF column family under testksKeyspace
grunt> rows = LOAD 'cassandra://testks/dataCF' USING
CassandraStorage();
grunt> cols = FOREACH rows GENERATE flatten(columns);
grunt>vals = FOREACH cols GENERATE flatten(TOKENIZE((chararray)$1)) as
word;
grunt>grps = group vals by word;
grunt>cnt = foreachgrps generate group, COUNT(vals), 'count' as ccnt;
grunt>grp_by_word = group cnt by $0;
```

```
grunt>cagg = foreachgrp_by_word generate group, cnt.(ccnt, $1);

# Put Data into result1CF column family under testksKeyspace
grunt> STORE cagg into 'cassandra://testks/result1CF' USING
CassandraStorage();

2013-07-22 14:12:45,144 [main] INFO  org.apache.pig.tools.pigstats.
ScriptState - Pig features used in the script: GROUP_BY
[-- snip --]
2013-07-22 14:12:50,464 [main] INFO  org.apache.pig.backend.hadoop.
executionengine.mapReduceLayer.MapReduceLauncher - Processing aliases
cnt,cols,grps,rows,vals
2013-07-22 14:12:50,464 [main] INFO  org.apache.pig.backend.
hadoop.executionengine.mapReduceLayer.MapReduceLauncher - detailed
locations: M: rows[6,7],cols[7,7],vals[8,7],cnt[10,6],grps[9,7] C:
cnt[10,6],grps[9,7] R: cnt[10,6]
[--  snip --]
2013-07-22 14:13:45,626 [main] INFO  org.apache.pig.backend.hadoop.
executionengine.mapReduceLayer.MapReduceLauncher - 97% complete
2013-07-22 14:13:49,669 [main] INFO  org.apache.pig.backend.hadoop.
executionengine.mapReduceLayer.MapReduceLauncher - 100% complete
[-- snip --]

Input(s):
Successfully read 6 records (360 bytes) from: "cassandra://testks/
dataCF"

Output(s):
Successfully stored 4440 records in: "cassandra://testks/result1CF"
[-- snip --]
2013-07-22 14:13:49,693 [main] INFO  org.apache.pig.backend.hadoop.
executionengine.mapReduceLayer.MapReduceLauncher - Success!
```

Let's look at the result that is stored in result1CF and compare it with the previous result.

```
cqlsh> use testks;
cqlsh:testks> select * from result1CF where key = 'the';
 KEY | count
-----+-------
 the | 1666

cqlsh:testks> select * from resultCF where key = 'Alice';
 KEY   | count
-------+-------
 Alice |   377
```

```
cqlsh:testks> select * from resultCF where key = 'Hatter';
 KEY    | count
--------+-------
 Hatter |    54

cqlsh:testks> select * from resultCF where key = 'Cat';
 KEY | count
-----+-------
 Cat |    23
```

There is a small difference in counting of the words, but that's likely due to the split that I use and the split function that Pig uses.

Note that the Pig Latin that we have used here may be very inefficient. The purpose of this example is to show the Cassandra and Pig integration. To learn about Pig Latin, look at the Pig documentation. Reading Apache Pig's official tutorial (http://pig.apache.org/docs/r0.11.1/start.html#tutorial) is recommended to know more about it.

You may also want to use CQL with Pig. You will have to use CqlStorage (with some versions, CqlStorage may not work so try using CqlNativeStorage), a word count example looks as follows:

```
grunt> alice = LOAD 'cql://hadoop_test/lines' USING CqlStorage();
grunt> B = foreach alice generate flatten(TOKENIZE((chararray)$0)) as
word;
grunt> C = group B by word;
grunt> D = foreach C generate COUNT(B) as word_count, group as word;
grunt> E = FOREACH D GENERATE TOTUPLE(TOTUPLE('word',word)),TOTUPLE('w
ord_count', word_count);

grunt> STORE E INTO 'cql://hadoop_test/output?output_query=UPDATE%20
hadoop_test.output%20SET%20word_count%20%3D%20%3F' USING CqlStorage();
```

The only noticeable change is the way you load data from and store data in Cassandra. You need to use CqlStorage (or CqlNativeStorage) and pass CQL as the parameter to store. The query format is as follows:

```
cql://[username:password@]<keyspace>/<columnfamily>[?[pa
ge_size=<size>][&columns=<col1,col2>][&output_query=<prepared_
statement>][&where_clause=<clause>][&split_size=<size>][&use_
secondary=true|false][&partitioner=<partitioner>]]
```

Integration with other analytical tools

Although Hadoop and its companion projects are the most widely used tools for the analysis of large datasets, in the recent demand for real-time analytics and machine learning there are very successful tools that have been developed. Some of these tools store their own data like MongoDB, which is basically a database but also provides decent built-in analytics toolings as part of it, and Druid (https://github. com/metamx/druid), which claims to be a column store (like Cassandra) with fast analytical tooling. Software such as Twitter Storm (https://storm.apache.org/) that provide real-time stream analysis and Spark or Shark (https://spark.apache. org/) that do not have their own data store but databases can be plugged into their respective frameworks to get them working. The scope of this chapter does not allow us to discuss the how-to for all this software; however, it is not extremely painful to get them working with Cassandra.

Storm can easily be integrated with Cassandra by actually writing read or write code using the Cassandra driver in its Spout and/or Bolt definitions. This is probably the easiest approach. One may also look into a somewhat older Cassandra–Storm integration project at https://github.com/ptgoetz/storm-cassandra.

DataStax provides integration for Spark with Cassandra. If you need to integrate with Cassandra, it may be worth having a look at the documentation of DataStax's Spark–Cassandra-connector project at https://github.com/datastax/spark-cassandra-connector.

One may want to look into DataStax Enterprise Edition for the built-in integration of some of the popular analytical engines with Cassandra.

Summary

We can store a lot of data and run MapReduce on them to analyze the data. We can also set up Hadoop in such a manner that it does not impact the transactional part of Cassandra in a negative way. We know how to set up Pig for those who want to quickly assemble an analysis instead of writing lengthy Java code. We can also power Solr searches by Cassandra, making Solr more scalable than it already is.

With a plethora of analytical tooling available in the market, you may or may not choose Cassandra. Maybe you could perform stream analysis, which does not require data to be stored and analyzed later; for example, if you decide to apply multiple operations on live streaming tweets and show the result immediately, you would like to use a tool such as Twitter Storm. Although there is no specific project that could guide you on how to do this, it is pretty simple to configure Twitter as Storm Spout. This will emit the tweet stream to the next Bolt and get it processed and forwarded to the next Bolt so that you can use the Cassandra Java driver to simply store the result. It is as simple as that. You may want to put a queue between Bolt and Cassandra as a buffer if you find Tweets are too fast for Cassandra. But normally, you wouldn't need that.

Cassandra is a rapidly developing project. The changes and feature additions in this open source project take place once in six months and don't happen in many big label proprietary applications. You get faster, stronger, and better Cassandra for free (obviously, there are technical debts) every half year. While this is a great thing, it comes with a pain point—new learning. To be able to upgrade, you will need to know new ways to do things. There may be changes that require you to change things at the code level to keep up with Cassandra. Most times, you could just upgrade Cassandra and things will work as expected.

Index

A

ack 47
administration, managing with nodetool
  about 236
  decommission command 237
  move command 238
  removenode command 238
  repair command 238
  snapshot command 240
  upgradesstable command 240
Amazon Machine Image 202
Amazon Web Services (AWS) 138
analytical tools
  Hadoop, integrating with 309
anti-entropy 65
Apache Cassandra. *See* Cassandra
Apache httpd
  configuring 252
application, writing
  about 21
  connection, obtaining 22
  object mapping 23-25
  queries, executing 22
AP system 33
architecture, Cassandra
  about 35, 36
  components 46
  ring representation 36
  working 39, 40
ASFRepository
  Cassandra, installing from 148
ASSUME command 133
authentication 178
authorization 178
availability, CAP theorem 31

B

AWS EBS
  URL 138

backup 214
BATCH statement
  executing 128, 129
BigTable
  URL 28
binary file, Oracle website
  URL 145
blogs table 9
bloom filter
  about 58
  working 59, 60
B+ tree implementation
  URL 54
Byte-ordered partitioner 158, 159

C

caching-specific settings, cassandra.yaml
  key_cache_keys_to_save 190
  key_cache_save_period 190
  key_cache_size_in_mb 190
  memory_allocator 190
  row_cache_keys_to_save 190
  row_cache_save_period 190
  row_cache_size_in_mdb 190
CAP theorem
  about 29
  availability 31
  consistency system 30
  partition-tolerance 31, 32
  significance 32

high memory usage 267
hotspots 268
slow snapshot 270
TRUNCATE command 130
Twitter Storm
URL 309

U

Ubuntu system
Oracle Java 7, installing for 146
upgradesstable command 240
usage share, of operating systems
reference link 140
USE command 129
user
altering 112
creating 111
dropping 112
User Defined Type (UDT) 106

V

virtual nodes (vnodes) 37-39
VisualVM
URL 227

W

wide row column family 79
write pattern, stress testing
about 183
batchtype 183
partitions 183
perbatch 183
pervisit 183
write performance 186

X

XFS filesystem
URL 138

Y

YAML
URL, for example 183
Yet Another Resource Negotiator (YARN)
about 281
URL 281

Thank you for buying
Mastering Apache Cassandra
Second Edition

About Packt Publishing

Packt, pronounced 'packed', published its first book, *Mastering phpMyAdmin for Effective MySQL Management*, in April 2004, and subsequently continued to specialize in publishing highly focused books on specific technologies and solutions.

Our books and publications share the experiences of your fellow IT professionals in adapting and customizing today's systems, applications, and frameworks. Our solution-based books give you the knowledge and power to customize the software and technologies you're using to get the job done. Packt books are more specific and less general than the IT books you have seen in the past. Our unique business model allows us to bring you more focused information, giving you more of what you need to know, and less of what you don't.

Packt is a modern yet unique publishing company that focuses on producing quality, cutting-edge books for communities of developers, administrators, and newbies alike. For more information, please visit our website at www.packtpub.com.

About Packt Open Source

In 2010, Packt launched two new brands, Packt Open Source and Packt Enterprise, in order to continue its focus on specialization. This book is part of the Packt Open Source brand, home to books published on software built around open source licenses, and offering information to anybody from advanced developers to budding web designers. The Open Source brand also runs Packt's Open Source Royalty Scheme, by which Packt gives a royalty to each open source project about whose software a book is sold.

Writing for Packt

We welcome all inquiries from people who are interested in authoring. Book proposals should be sent to author@packtpub.com. If your book idea is still at an early stage and you would like to discuss it first before writing a formal book proposal, then please contact us; one of our commissioning editors will get in touch with you.

We're not just looking for published authors; if you have strong technical skills but no writing experience, our experienced editors can help you develop a writing career, or simply get some additional reward for your expertise.

Rapid Cassandra [Video]

ISBN: 978-1-78355-305-1   Duration: 01:07 Hours

Learn how to design a NoSQL database using Cassandra and implement a real-life application written in Java

1. An in-depth look at the query language and unique data modeling techniques.

2. Discover how to set up a development environment to write Cassandra applications in Java.

3. Learn how to design, develop, and implement a production-grade Java-Cassandra application, in a step-by-step manner.

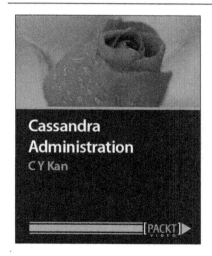

Cassandra Administration [Video]

ISBN: 978-1-78216-420-3   Duration: 02:51 Hours

Configure and administer Cassandra for optimum database performance and a completely operational cluster

1. Quickly grasp the concepts behind Cassandra and understand its internal working mechanism.

2. Build a single node cluster into a running multi-node cluster from scratch.

3. Learn through clearly demonstrated steps how to administrate and manage day-to-day operations with Cassandra, including data migration, backup, restore, monitoring, and performance tuning.

Please check **www.PacktPub.com** for information on our titles